CAMBRIDGE LIBRARY C

Books of enduring scholarly

Women's Writing

The later twentieth century saw a huge wave of academic interest in women's writing, which led to the rediscovery of neglected works from a wide range of genres, periods and languages. Many books that were immensely popular and influential in their own day are now studied again, both for their own sake and for what they reveal about the social, political and cultural conditions of their time. A pioneering resource in this area is Orlando: Women's Writing in the British Isles from the Beginnings to the Present (http://orlando.cambridge.org), which provides entries on authors' lives and writing careers, contextual material, timelines, sets of internal links, and bibliographies. Its editors have made a major contribution to the selection of the works reissued in this series within the Cambridge Library Collection, which focuses on non-fiction publications by women on a wide range of subjects from astronomy to biography, music to political economy, and education to prison reform.

Elizabeth Montagu, the Queen of the Bluestockings

Bluestocking, author and hostess, Elizabeth Montagu (1718–1800) exercised an influence far beyond literary scholarship. Compiled by a relative, Emily Climenson, and published in 1906, this collection of her correspondence provides an excellent introduction to the culture and politics of eighteenth-century polite society. In chapters enriched by portraits of both Elizabeth and her correspondents, readers are invited to witness the public and personal interactions and entertainments of Montagu and her circle. The text contains accounts of operas, masquerades, concerts and marriages, and serious philosophical conjectures are mingled with witty and sometimes acerbic notes on 'gowns and fans', 'the northern gentry' and women suffering from the vapours. Volume 2 covers arguably the most prolific period in Montagu's life, from 1751 to 1761, and reveals her personal views on such diverse subjects as the price of food, David Garrick's playhouse on Drury Lane and the work of Laurence Sterne.

Cambridge University Press has long been a pioneer in the reissuing of out-of-print titles from its own backlist, producing digital reprints of books that are still sought after by scholars and students but could not be reprinted economically using traditional technology. The Cambridge Library Collection extends this activity to a wider range of books which are still of importance to researchers and professionals, either for the source material they contain, or as landmarks in the history of their academic discipline.

Drawing from the world-renowned collections in the Cambridge University Library, and guided by the advice of experts in each subject area, Cambridge University Press is using state-of-the-art scanning machines in its own Printing House to capture the content of each book selected for inclusion. The files are processed to give a consistently clear, crisp image, and the books finished to the high quality standard for which the Press is recognised around the world. The latest print-on-demand technology ensures that the books will remain available indefinitely, and that orders for single or multiple copies can quickly be supplied.

The Cambridge Library Collection will bring back to life books of enduring scholarly value (including out-of-copyright works originally issued by other publishers) across a wide range of disciplines in the humanities and social sciences and in science and technology.

Elizabeth Montagu, the Queen of the Bluestockings

Her Correspondence from 1720 to 1761

VOLUME 2

ELIZABETH MONTAGU
EDITED BY EMILY J. CLIMENSON

CAMBRIDGE UNIVERSITY PRESS

Cambridge, New York, Melbourne, Madrid, Cape Town,
Singapore, São Paolo, Delhi, Tokyo, Mexico City

Published in the United States of America by Cambridge University Press, New York

www.cambridge.org
Information on this title: www.cambridge.org/9781108029537

This edition first published 1906
This digitally printed version 2011

ISBN 978-1-108-02953-7 Paperback

ELIZABETH MONTAGU

THE QUEEN OF THE BLUE-STOCKINGS

HER CORRESPONDENCE FROM

1720 TO 1761

Mrs. Montagu

Emery Walker Ph. Sc.

ELIZABETH MONTAGU

THE QUEEN OF THE BLUE-STOCKINGS

HER CORRESPONDENCE FROM 1720 TO 1761

BY HER GREAT-GREAT-NIECE

EMILY J. CLIMENSON

AUTHORESS OF "HISTORY OF SHIPLAKE," "HISTORICAL GUIDE TO HENLEY-ON-THAMES,"
"PASSAGES FROM THE DIARIES OF MRS. P. LYBBE POWYS," ETC., ETC.

WITH ILLUSTRATIONS

IN TWO VOLUMES—VOL. II

LONDON
JOHN MURRAY, ALBEMARLE STREET
1906

PRINTED BY
WILLIAM CLOWES AND SONS, LIMITED
LONDON AND BECCLES

CONTENTS TO VOL. II

CHAPTER III.

CHAPTER IV.

CHAPTER V.

APPENDICES.

LIST OF ILLUSTRATIONS.

VOL. II.

ELIZABETH MONTAGU

THE QUEEN OF THE BLUE-STOCKINGS

CHAPTER I.

1752–1754—CHIEFLY AT TUNBRIDGE WELLS, SANDLEFORD, AND HAYES—BEGINNING OF FRIENDSHIP WITH PITT—CORRESPONDENCE WITH GILBERT WEST.

**January* 1, 1752, an interchange of letters and compliments from the Wests and Mrs. Montagu take place. Mrs. West sends a huge turkey and ham pie, half for Mrs. Montagu, half for Temple West, Gilbert's brother. Mr. Pitt, Lady Cobham, and Berenger were expected. In a letter to her sister, Sarah Scott, Mrs. Montagu mentions—

"My Father is going to purchase a fine living for Willy, indeed he will not enjoy it till after the death of the present incumbent, but it brings in £470 a year, a fine reversion for a younger brother, and what, joined to another moderate living, will be a comfortable subsistence."

This was the living of Burghfield in Berkshire,

* In 1752 the New Style began. I adhere to the dates as placed on the letters, as I have all through this book.

purchased from the Shrewsbury family, for two lives, of which in after years William Robinson became rector, his son Matthew succeeding him. Further in this letter it says—

"I recommend to your perusal 'The Adventures of Peregrine Pickle.'* Lady Vane's† story is well told. Mr. W. Robinson and the Doctor called on me this morning. The Doctor talks of Bath for his health, but he is the best-looking invalid I ever saw. An Irish Bishopric will cure him entirely. Mrs. Delany is not in England. Poor Mrs. Donnellan has lost her brother, Dr. Donnellan,‡ and is in great affliction."

Mr. W. Robinson, afterwards Sir William Robinson, and Dr. Robinson, were her cousins, brothers of "Long" Sir Thomas Robinson and Sir Septimus, and sons of William Robinson of Rokeby. Dr. Richard Robinson § was chaplain to the Duke of Dorset, then Lord Lieutenant of Ireland, and had just been made Bishop of Killala. They were immense men, with fine features and rosy cheeks. Mr. Richard Cumberland ‖ calls Dr. Richard Robinson "a colossal man." So attached was Sir William to his brother Richard that Cumberland says he imitated the Archbishop in everything, even to the size of his shoes, diet, and physic!

On February 10, Mr. West applied to the Bishop of London ¶ for further preferment for Mr. Botham, and writes to Mrs. Montagu—

* Published in 1751, by T. Smollett.

† *Née* Anne Hawes, of Purley Hall, Berks. Married, first, Lord William Hamilton; secondly, Lord Vane.

‡ The Rev. Christopher Donnellan, a friend of Swift's.

§ The Rev. Dr. Richard Robinson, born 1709, died 1794; afterwards Archbishop of Armagh, and 1st Baron Rokeby.

‖ Richard Cumberland, dramatist, born 1732, died 1811.

¶ Rev. Thomas Sherlock, born 1678, died 1761.

"Wickham, February 10, 1752.

"DEAR COUSIN,

"Inclosed is my letter to the Bishop of London, which I send open for your perusal; if you approve of it, be pleased to seal it and convey it to his Lordship in what manner you think proper. I most sincerely wish it may have any good effect for my cousin Botham's sake, but we must not flatter ourselves too much. Great men often think their smiles sufficient Favors, and you know there is a Beauty in that of my Lord of London that must enhance its value. . . .

"Dear cousin,
"Your most affectionate and
obliged humble serv[t],
"G. W."

The letter was sent to the Bishop. Here is his reply to Mr. West—

"London, ye 18th February, 1752.

"SIR,

"I had the honour of yours of the 10 inst., and tho' I am disabled from writing myself with the Gout in my Hands, yet I will not omit to assure you that there are very few whom I should be better pleased to oblige than yourself, and the Lady at whose instance you write.

"I feel very sensibly the distress of Mr. Botham and his wife, and judge as you do that it is a case that calls for, and deserves assistance. But in considering where my Patronages lye, I cannot find that I have any living within distance of Albury, unless it be in the City of London, where probably Mr. Botham would not choose to live. When I have the Happiness to see you, you shall be more fully acquainted how far I am able to assist you.

"I am, Sir,
"Your very obedient, humble Serv[t],
(Signed by himself) "THO. LONDON.

"Mrs. Sherlock desires to join me in respects to you and Mrs. West."

In March, Mr. Pitt obtained for Mr. Gilbert West the clerkship of the Privy Council, a lucrative office.

On March 25, from Hayes to Wickham, Mrs. Montagu writes—

"DEAR COUSIN,

"I thank you most heartily for immediately giving me the sincerest joy I have felt for this long time. May you long enjoy what you have so late attained. . . . You cannot imagine the pleasure I propose in hearing your friends congratulate you on Fortune's first courtesy. Base Jade! to be so tedious and so sparing in her favours."

With many congratulations to Mrs. West, etc., to which Lydia Botham, then at Hayes, added a few lines, Mrs. Montagu announces she will convey him and Mrs. West to London the next morning in her post-chaise, and they shall stay in Hill Street, where Mr. Montagu was attending to his parliamentary business; and, she adds, to fix an hour "so as to be with the President of the Council at 12 o'clock."

From London, on April 17, Mr. Montagu writes an account of the celebrated surgeon, Dr. William Chesilden's death—

"The papers, I suppose, have informed you of the death of poor Chesilden. I had an account of the manner of his death from one Mr. Vourse, an eminent man in his own profession. He told me the poor man was with Jerry Pierce and others, telling them how soon after his being seized with the Palsy he had been making a bargain with an undertaker to bury him, with this he was entertaining them with his usual humour, and in the midst of his story was seiz'd with an apoplectic fit which finish'd him in half an hour. . . . I forgot to add that Mr. Chesilden had eat a great deal of Bread and drank a good quantity of ale; being asthmatic, this was reckoned to be the cause of his death."

It will be remembered that Mrs. Montagu was always opposed to her sister Sarah's marriage to George Lewis Scott. Unfortunately, her fears as to their felicity were prophetic, for in April, 1752, after only a year's matrimony, they separated; incompatibility of temper was alleged, but from the letters there was evidently much more below the surface. Mrs. Delany, writing in April to her sister, Mrs. D'Ewes, says—

"What a foolish match Mrs. Scott has made for herself. Mrs. Montagu wrote Mrs. Donnellan word that she and the rest of her friends had rescued her out of the hands of a very bad man: but for reasons of interest, they should conceal his misbehaviour as much as possible, but entreated Mrs. Donnellan would vindicate her sister's character whenever she heard it attacked, for she was very innocent."

Sarah was only twenty-nine. Her father and brothers separated her from Mr. Scott, as is shown in his own letters to Mr. Montagu, who had been his original friend. He acknowledged "that Mrs. Montagu knew nothing of the separation till it was communicated to her;" in truth she was at Hayes at the time. Her letters indicate the enmity and rancour of a great lady whose name was kept behind the scenes. Mr. Scott wrote two letters to Mr. Montagu, dated April 29 and May 1, but both are so involved and mysterious as to shed no real light on his misdemeanours.

Meanwhile, Mrs. Montagu received Mrs. Scott at Hayes, and in a letter to her husband, whom she was preparing to join in London, says Morris was urging Mrs. Scott to go to Albury. She says—

"I could leave her at Hayes when I go to town, but her spirits are so bad and she is so ill she cannot be alone. . . . Indeed, poor creature, her situation is miserable, allied to the faults and the infamy of a bad man, subject to his aspersions, and liable to the censures of his friends (for the worst have some), as in all disagreements in wedlock, blame falls ever on the innocent where there is no harmony. 'How happy to behold in wedded pair!' each has the credit of the other's virtues; they have double honour, united interests and all that can make people strong in society. This, my Dearest, is my happier lot, inriched by your fortune, ennobled by your virtues, graced by your character, and supported by your interest."

Mrs. Montagu accompanied Mrs. Scott to Albury. She writes—

"We had a very pleasant journey here, and our horses performed well. We found Lydia and Johnny in health and happiness, surrounded by five of the finest children I ever saw; the youngest boy is a little cherubim and has the finest white hair imaginable."

Mrs. Donnellan, in May, writes from Delville, where she still was, to Mrs. Montagu, to say that Lord Holderness was to give up her house in Hanover Square about August, and as it was too large for her fortune, and the lease was near its end,* she wishes Mrs. Montagu to look out for a house for her "not farther than Windsor from London. Soon after our return, the Dean and Mrs. Delany go to Down, and I fear his affairs will not permit him to go to England this year." She adds—

"I have writ to Mrs. Shuttleworth to bespeak me a chair of Vaughan.† I would have it plain and light, lined with white cloath and green curtains, as white and

* Mr. Macartney took it on.

† Means a sedan chair.

green is my livery. If you should go to town, I should be obliged to you if you would send to Vaughan about it. . . .

"I now come to the interesting part of your letter, the unhappy affair of poor Mrs. Scott. I had heard before I received yours that she and Mr. Scott were parted, but could hardly believe it, a match so much of mutual inclination seemed to promise mutual happiness, and the shortness of the time of their union hardly allowed them to find out they were not happy, so that you are unwilling to hurt the gentleman in his character. I must conclude he is very bad, since in so short a time he could force Mrs. Scott and all her family to come to such an *éclat*. I am extremely concerned for all the uneasiness you have had on the occasion, but you have had the consolation of showing yourself a most generous and kind sister in supporting her in her misfortunes, and especially as it was a match made against your better judgment. I beg my compliments to Mrs. Scott, and I heartily wish her health and spirits to support her situation; 'tis said here she is returning to Bath to live with Lady Montagu. On these occasions people love to seem to know more than perhaps they do; all I say is that you entirely justify Mrs. Scott, and I am sure you must know the truth. I hear, too, he has given her back half her fortune, and has settled a 150 pounds a year on her; this, I think, is a justification to her."

Mrs. Montagu had indeed a great deal of trouble at this time, for besides sheltering and endeavouring to cheer Mrs. Scott's failing spirits, she had, to say nothing of her own constant ill-health, the additional trouble of her favourite brother Jack's illness, now continuing some months, of a nervous disorder, which he never recovered from.

On May 26, from Sandleford, Mrs. Montagu writes to Mr. West, who is at her house in Hill Street, attending as clerk to the Privy Council—

"DEAR COUSIN,

"I was informed by Mrs. Isted* that you intended to return to town in the middle of this week, so I imagine that by this time you are in the Empire of China.† The leafless trees and barren soil of my landscape will very ill bear comparison with the shady oaks and beautiful verdure of South Lodge, and the grinning Mandarins still worse supply the place of a British Statesman: but as you can improve every society and place into which you enter, I expect such hints from you as will set off the figures, and enliven the landscape with rural beauty. I grieved at the rain from an apprehension that it might interfere with your pleasure at South Lodge. I hope it did not, but that you saw the place with the leisure and attention it deserves; if you give me an account of the parts of it which charmed you most, or of the whole, you will lead my imagination to a very fine place in very good company, and I shall walk over it with great pleasure. I imagine you would feel some poetic enthusiasm in the Temple of Pan, and hope it produced a hymn or ode in which we shall see him knit with the Graces and the Hours to dance, lead on to the Eternal Spring, through groves of your unfading bays."

South Lodge, Enfield, was then the residence of Mr. Pitt, the grounds of which he laid out with great taste, and designed the Temple of Pan. Mrs. Montagu had recently been on a visit to him here, as will be seen in West's answer. At the end of a long letter, which contains directions as to the ornaments of her room, comments on her bad health, in which she quotes Pope's saying, "ill-health is an early old age," she winds up with regretting that Sir George Lyttelton and Miss West were going to Tunbridge so soon, for "I fear

* Mrs. Isted, Mrs. Montagu's lady housekeeper.

† She was fitting up her big room in Chinese style, and West was assisting her with hints.

they will leave the place the earlier, as they go at the beginning of the season." She finishes by commending her brother William, who was to spend a day or two in Hill Street, to West, saying—

"I wrote my advice to him to take this opportunity to pay his respects to you, but possibly a little College awkwardness, added to natural timidity, may prevent his doing it. I assure you he is a very good young man, more I will not say, for having for some years had a mother's care of him, I have also a mother's partiality: perhaps you may like him the better for his resemblance to your son."

From Albury she had brought Lydia's second daughter, Bessie—

"Not so handsome as her sister whom you have seen, but she is fair and well shaped, very sensible and of a sweet disposition, and though but ten years of age, reads and writes well, and has made a great progress in arithmetic."

To this letter Gilbert West answers on May 30—

"Mr. Pitt, as you will easily imagine from your own experience, received and entertained us with great politeness, and something still more pleasing and solid, with every mark of friendship and esteem. He had provided for me a wheeling chair, by the help of which I was enabled to visit every sequestered nook, dingle and bosky bower from side to side in that little paradise opened in the wild, and by the help of my imagination doubled the pleasure I received from the various Beauties of Art and Nature, by recalling and participating the past pleasure of a certain person,* some of whose remarks and sayings Mr. Pitt repeated with a secret pride,

* Mrs. Montagu, who had been on a visit to Mr. Pitt.

and I heard with equal admiration and delight. The weather indeed was not so favourable to us as we could have wished. . . . Molly * indeed, who has an insatiable ardour in viewing a fine place, and an almost implicit faith in Mr. Pitt's taste and judgment, stole out often by herself, and in defiance of wind or rain walked many times over the enchanting round. . . . Kitty † has seemed to be inspired with an unusual flow of spirits, which not only emboldened her to undertake, but enabled her also to complete the tour, which I was forced to make in my chair, attended by her, Molly, and Mr. Pitt."

In the reply occurs the following passage:—

"I am very glad you and Mrs. West went over every part of South Lodge, as you see with more judgment you must see with more pleasure than I did, and I think there can hardly be a finer entertainment not only to the eyes but to the mind, than so sweet and peaceful a scene. I was surprised to hear Mr. Pitt say he had never spent an entire week there, this shows one that a person who has an active mind and is qualified for the busy scene of life, need not fear any excess in the love of retirement."

Captain Robinson returned from his Chinese expedition in the *Saint George* the middle of June, and Mrs. Montagu and Mrs. Scott met him from Sandleford at her villa at Hayes. "He has brought me two beautiful gowns and a fine Chinese lanthorn. We are to go on board the *St. George* to-morrow," she writes to her husband. He also brought a gown apiece for Lady Sandwich and her sister, Miss Fane. The greater part of the Robinson family went to dine on the *Saint George*, but on a stormy day, and Mrs. Montagu was very terrified at the tossing of the small boat they went in. Soon

* Miss West, his sister. † Mrs. West.

after this, in the beginning of July, Mrs. Montagu left for her annual visit to Tunbridge Wells, where she had taken the "White Stone House" on Mount Ephraim. Sarah Scott returned to Sandleford to Mr. Montagu, *en route* for Bath, where she was about to take up residence with her friend, Lady Bab Montagu. At Tunbridge were Sir George and Lady Lyttelton, Mr. West, Miss Charlotte Fane, Mr. Garrick, Mr. Bower, the Dean of Exeter, General Pulteney,* etc. At a big ball Mrs. Montagu says—

"I shone forth in full Chinese pomp at the ball, my gown was much liked, the pattern of the embroidery admired extremely. . . . Garrick had an incomparable letter from Beranger which he read with proper humour one day he dined here. . . . I go every day to Mr. King's lectures."

On July 22 Mrs. Montagu writes to her husband—

"Sir George and Lady Lyttelton † went away this morning, as to the lady, she is so unsociable and retired, her departure makes no difference in the Society, in all her manners she signified a dislike and contempt of the company, and in this, the world is always just, and pays in kind to the full measure, and even with more than legal interest at 4 per cent!"

Mr. West from Tunbridge visited his cousins, the Bothams, at Albury, and found Lydia in a terrible state of health, and worried with the preparation of her five children to be inoculated. He persuaded her to go to Tunbridge to consult Dr. Shaw, and writes from Stoke to Mrs. Montagu to suggest that Mrs. Botham should stay with her at Sandleford whilst the children are

* Brother of Lord Bath. † The second Lady Lyttelton, *née* Rich.

inoculated, and left in their father's care. He mentions Mr. Hooke being in a cottage near Stoke, very busy writing. Lydia Botham, despite of all entreaties, returned to Albury to remain with her children. Mrs. Montagu contemplated a visit to Horton, *alias* Mount Morris, with her husband, to stay with her brother Matthew, but violent rheumatism attacked her in the shoulders. She was reluctantly obliged to let Mr. Montagu visit "the brethren," as they termed them, alone. Meanwhile, West, not being satisfied with the tutor with whom his son was residing, hastened to Hill Street to remove him to Oxford. Mrs. Medows* writes from Chute on October 3 to say she had taken her nieces, the Miss Pulses, to see Sandleford, where they ate "a cold loaf,"† and "I was not a little exalted as a planter when I saw chestnuts I had set nuts, five and forty feet high." She mentions that Mrs. Isted gave them a great many good things, "and showed several pretty pieces of her painting, and one of your curtains finished and a handkerchief the little girl you are so good as to take care of is making for you, that will look very like point."

Mr. Montagu set out on October 2 to Horton, and arrived at Canterbury, where he ascended the Cathedral tower for the view, his first sight of that place. His first letter crossed one of his wife's, in which she laments her inability to accompany him, and says—

"I suppose you will see the place with great veneration, where your consort's virtues, charms and accomplishments were ripened to their present perfection, besides the pleasure of seeing my brothers, which would have been great. I should have reviewed the place where I spent the careless days of infancy and the more gay ones of early youth with satisfaction. To the

* Mr. Montagu's sister. † The usual expression for a picnic then.

Fair, the years from 15 to 20 are very agreeable." She continues, "When do my brethren come to town? I hear my brother Robinson stays to cultivate the maternal acres. As to the Paternal they will not come yet. I think he will think of the Père Eternel when he does not say the Lord's Prayer. I design to go to Mrs. Donnellan to-morrow, she is at North End, where she designs to remain till her house is ready for her reception."

These letters are addressed thus:—

"To
"Edward Montagu Esqr. & Mem$^{r.}$ of Parl$^{t.}$
at Matthew Robinson Morris Esqr.,
at Horton,
"Near Hythe,
"Kent."

Morris Robinson, when not in town on business, lived with his brother, and it was a home to all the brothers as they required one, their gay old father, Mr. Robinson, preferring lodgings in London, where he was the life and soul of the fashionable coffee-houses.

Mr. Montagu having complained of his horse not liking stony roads, his wife writes—

"I am sorry your horse does not like hard roads, for the ways about Horton are very stony; a dull horse is like a dull friend, one is safe but not much delighted in their company." She adds, "I hope the sight of so many merry bachelors does not revive in you the love of a single state. Theirs is the joy of the wicked, not the pure comforts of a holy state like matrimony. . . . Poor Mr. Brockman is the only man truly sensible of the evils of celibacy, and he weeps and will not be comforted, as all unmarried men should do, were they truly sensible of their misfortune."

This is playfully malicious, as Mr. Brockman had been one of her earliest admirers.

Her husband, on October 12, answers a long letter of hers about the monuments in Canterbury Cathedral, and says—

"Since I came here I have passed my time much to my satisfaction, the entire freedom and liberty that reigns here, the love and harmony that dwells amongst the brethren, as it is very uncommon, so is the more agreeable to me, as I cannot but take a part and be affected with pleasure and pain in everything that relates to you. If you had been here you would have much added to our happiness, and I believe this not only to be my sentiments but that of all the rest of the company. I have never before now had an opportunity of sufficiently observing this house, which is very large and perfectly regular, though it is not placed just where one could wish it, 'tis easy to see is capable of great improvement by openings and cuttings in a good deal of that fine prospect which is now shut out by the walls and trees; and by grubbing up the bushes and hedges and making a kind of Paddock on the South side of the house. A bason of water like that at Newbold might also be easily made. . . . Some of these things the worthy owner is not without having some thoughts of doing, as well as cutting some walks and vistas through his wood."

There is a picture of Mount Morris in Harris' 'History of Kent,' 1719, a large square house with a cupola surmounted by a big ball and weathercock. In front of the house and round it are the small walled gardens, formally planted, the fashion of the period. These were eventually pulled down by Matthew Robinson, the hedges grubbed and all thrown into one large park,* in which his numerous horses and cattle roamed

* A picture of Mount Morris as altered by Matthew is in the Kent volume of "Beauties of England and Wales.

at large. Mr. Montagu seemed to have enjoyed some fine partridge shooting whilst at Horton. He also frequented "'Old Father Ocean' at Hythe, with whose solemn majestic look I am always delighted."

Visits to the Scotts of Scotts Hall, the Brockmans of Beachborough, etc., are spoken of. In a letter of the same date, October 12, to her husband, Mrs. Montagu first mentions Archibald Bower * and his wife.

To give the whole biography of Archibald Bower would take too much space in this book. An account of him can be found in the "National Biography," vol. vi. p. 48. He was a Scotsman, was sent to Douai, and entered the Jesuit Society in 1706. In 1717 he studied Divinity at Rome; became Reader of Philosophy and Adviser to the College of Arezzo. Horrified at the "hellish proceedings" of the Court of Inquisition, where he witnessed the torture of two innocent gentlemen, he fled to England, and while there made the acquaintance of Dean Berkeley, the old admirer and friend of Mrs. Donnellan, who was afterwards Bishop of Cloyne. He entered, as tutor, the family of Mr. Thompson, Coley Park, Berks, and afterwards that of Lord Aylmer. He revised the "Universal History." In 1748 he was made keeper of the Queen's Library, and in 1749 he married a widow with one child, a niece of Bishop Nicholson. His first volume of his "History of the Popes" was published in 1748, the second in 1751, the third in 1753. Though renouncing the Jesuit order, he seems to have had business dealings with the Society, some of which brought him into considerable obloquy, but they are too lengthy to be detailed here.

Mrs. Montagu, returning to Hayes, says—

"Mr. Bower and his wife are to come to me on

* Archibald Bower, born 1686, died 1766; wrote "The History of the Popes," etc., etc.

Friday, and stay till Saturday or Monday, he is a very merry entertaining companion. He left all gloominess in that seat of horrors—the Inquisition. I breakfasted with him on Tuesday, he is but between two or three miles from Hayes. His wife is civil and silent, so I asked her to come over with him. I never saw any country more beautiful than about Chislehurst, where he lives. I cannot say much in praise of his habitation, which he terms his Paradise, but indeed to a mind so gay and cheerful as his, all places are a Paradise. He is much engaged with those old ladies, the Popes, but says he will leave the Santi Padri for his Madonna. He will teach me the pronunciation of Italian, which he has reduced to a Method, so it may easily be acquired. He taught it to Mr. Garrick at Tunbridge."

Apparently Bower was introduced to Mrs. Montagu by Gilbert West. He was an intimate friend of Sir George Lyttelton. Both he and Sir George gave Mrs. Montagu the sobriquet of "Madonna," but as Bower's first letter of 1753 addresses her as "Madonna," with him probably the nickname originated. They corresponded for some years in Italian.

In the next letter of October 14, she says—

"The Bowers came here yesterday. Mr. and Mrs. West met them here at dinner, and to-morrow we are all to dine at Wickham. This morning I shall carry Mrs. Bower to see Cæsar's Camp, the prospect from which is now in high beauty."

The five Botham children had been inoculated! Their mother had been persuaded in her bad health to leave them in their father's care. Lydia, writing to Mrs. Montagu to thank her for a present of Madeira, says—

"You will desire to hear something of my Babes.

My letter from their good Father to-day says they were well when he wrote, but that my kind and humane friends, Dr. Shaw and Winchester, who had both been with them in the morning, said their eyes were so heavy and their pulses so loaded that they would not hold up long."

A postscript to this letter gives the next day's account in Mr. Botham's words—

"My dear Babes are all drooping round me, and wonder not if I tell you I am glad they are so, since from the gentlest symptoms of the distemper I have a good foundation to hope they will do well. They are sometimes up and sometimes down, and sicken so gradually that Winchester doubts not that they will have a favourable sort of the smallpox. I expect they will be in their beds to-morrow."

By November 16 the five children were well, and Mrs. Montagu writes to Mr. West from Sandleford—

"Mrs. Botham returns to her little family to-morrow, they are all quite recovered, and I hope this lucky event will hasten the recovery of my Lydia. I should indeed be glad to behold the happy smile that will illuminate her countenance at her return to her babes. Mr. Rogers * is recovering from another mortification. . . . I really believe he will live to the age of Methuselah, for he recovers of those illnesses which destroy the strongest.

"I find the Princess of Wales will have a drawing-room as soon as the King returns, and I hope you will consult with your friends, whether it will not be proper you should appear there. . . . Mr. Linnell † brought me

* John Rogers, of Denton Hall, to whom Mr. Montagu, his cousin, was trustee, as he was a lunatic.

† Linnell had been decorating rooms in her house at Hill Street, and Mr. West was also employing him at Wickham.

his bill the morning I left town, and I think I will send a copy of it as a proper warning to your Mrs. West, and if you will still proceed in spite of my sad and woeful example, I cannot help it. I shall repent my misdeeds as the daughters of Israel did theirs in sackcloth and ashes. Adieu Brocade, Embroidery, and lace, and even the cheaper vanities of lutestring and blonde."

Mr. West took Mrs. Montagu's advice as to going to Court and "kissing hands, a ceremony which upon more deliberation I think it most advisable to go through, however glad I should have been to avoid it."

In a letter to Miss Anstey from Mrs. Montagu, of November 23, we gain a glimpse of the books being read then—

"Mr. Hooke has published a second edition of his 'Roman History,' which is much admired. Mr. Brown's * essays on the 'Characteristics of Lord Shaftesbury' † are well spoken of; Lord Orrery ‡ has just published his Observations on the 'Life and Writings of Dr. Swift.' . . . The 'Biographia Brittanica' will entertain you with the Lives of many great men, some of them are very well written. Mr. Warburton's § Edition of Mr. Pope's Works contains some new pieces, and some alterations of old ones. 'The Memoires du Duc de Sully' ‖ are very entertaining. . . . The Duke of Cumberland has been dangerously ill, is now something better. Lord Coventry ¶ they say is to marry Miss.Gunning. Some actors have appeared

* John Brown, D.D., born 1715, died 1766. Eminent divine, indefatigable writer.

† 3rd Earl of Shaftesbury, born 1671, died 1713; wrote "Characteristics of Men, Manners, Opinions, and Times."

‡ Charles Boyle, 4th Earl of Orrery.

§ William Warburton, born 1698, died 1779. Divine and writer; Bishop of Gloucester.

‖ Duc de Sully, favourite minister of Henry IV. of France.

¶ Lord Coventry, married March 5, 1782, to Maria Gunning.

at the Theatre, and their characters are not of the first rank. One of them imitates Mr. Garrick." This must have been Foote.

Gilbert West was busied at this time planting his garden at Wickham with firs and laurels, and Mrs. Montagu teased him by letter about his "evergreen-nevergreen garden," as she called it. She says—

"Remember that while you avoid winter, you exclude Spring, and forbid the glad return of the vernal season, as well as the sad approach of autumn. In your garden and in your life, may all that is necessary for shade, for shelter and for comfort be permanent and unchanged. May the pleasures and aromatics be various, successive, sweet and new! . . . I shall be much obliged to you if when you see the incomparable Mr. Bower you will get of him the second volume of the 'History of the Popes.' I have almost finished Mr. Hooke's history. I do not care to quit the city of Rome till I have seen the establishment of its spiritual Monarchy. . . . I have just received a collection of letters, wrote by Madame de Maintenon, though Voltaire has diminished my opinion of her in some degree; yet I have an impatience to open the book. . . . I shall like to see what alteration there is in her from the wife and widow of poor Scarron to becoming the consort of Louis le Grand."

On December 2 Lady Courtenay sent feathers and shells to Mrs. Montagu for her work. She was the daughter of Heneage, 2nd Lord Aylesford, and married to Sir William Courtenay, afterwards 1st Viscount Courtenay. She was a sister of Lady Andover's, and a great friend of Lydia Botham's, and in this letter expresses great concern at Lydia's sad state of health.

On December 29 Mrs. Montagu writes to her sister Sarah that she had sustained the great loss of her lady housekeeper, Mrs. Isted, who had died very suddenly whilst Mr. and Mrs. Montagu had been spending a few days with Lydia Botham. The latter was then supposed to be dying.

From the letters it appears Mrs. Isted was a widow lady, who had lost an only child, and had been known to Mrs. Montagu in her more prosperous years. Lydia Botham rallied for a time.

A great dispute was going on at Leicester House at this time on the subject of Prince George's tutors. Amongst the sub-preceptors, it will be remembered, was Mr. George Lewis Scott, Sarah's (*née* Robinson) husband. Soon after this he was dismissed from the list of tutors. One reason alleged was that he was a Jacobite, but there was little ground for this supposition. Though a clever man, he seems to have been quite an unsuitable person to be tutor to the princes, and Mrs. Montagu comforts Sarah by saying his true character will now appear. "You will see shortly that he and you will have justice done you, and with this difference, that to you it will be a guardian angel, to him an avenging minister. In the mean time 'leave him to Heaven, and the thorns that prick his bosom,' as says good Mr. Hamlet."

On December 23 she had an assembly, and writes to Mrs. Boscawen that "the Chinese Room was filled by a succession of people from eleven in the morning till eleven at night."

The year ends with a letter to Gilbert West, who had had a terrible attack of gout, sending him Birch's * "Life of Archbishop Tillotson," † "which Mr. Birch left for you himself."

1753 opens with a letter from Mrs. Donnellan on

* Rev. Thomas Birch, born 1705, died 1766.

† John Tillotson, born 1630, died 1694. Archbishop of Canterbury in 1691.

January 2, to Mrs. Montagu, then at Sandleford. In this she says—

"Two letters from Ireland informed me of a sort of determination both of Dr. Delany's affair and my own. I had a very particular account of both from my Six Clerk and Manager, Mr. Croker, who is Six Clerk to Delany's adversarys, and a short letter from Mrs. Delany. My Lord Chancellor has acquitted Dr. Delany of a hard word in the law, called spoliation, but has ordered an account before two masters in Chancery to be taken of all the late Mrs. Delany's personal estate, and what she was worth when she married the Dean."

This law-suit, which lasted some years, and was a great annoyance and expense to the Delanys, was caused by his having inadvertently burnt a paper of importance belonging to his first wife. Mrs. Donnellan's brother had claimed the lease of the house lately belonging to their mother, in London, owing to a defect in the execution of the will. Mrs. Donnellan got the books, and some few hundred pounds, but, as she had been residuary legatee in the will, suffered severe loss which she bore with exemplary patience.

It is probable that at this period her brother-in-law, Bishop Clayton, being wealthy and generous, gave up his wife's marriage portion to her sister, Anne Donnellan.

Anne now took a house in Bolton Row, London.

On January 3 Mrs. Montagu writes to thank Mrs. West for a portion of Turkey "pye," and some verses of her composing with it. She says—

"January 3.

"Dear Madam,

"For your pye and your verses what strains are sublime enough to return proper thanks! You have held the balance of justice so exactly and directed its sword so well where to fall that Mrs. Temple West and I are determined to divide the pye this evening according to the rules prescribed. Though our pye has not yet been toasted, your verses have been well relish'd by some of the greatest connoisseurs. About an hour after I had your letter Miss West came to call on me; I communicated your poetic strains and we were very merry over them. When Lord Temple and Sir George Lyttelton came in we let them have a share, and they joined in the laugh and commendation. Lord Temple desired his best and kindest compliments to you and my cousin. He is not at all the worse for his late illness. . . . Sir George and he were going to dine with Mr. Pitt, whose health, I believe, is in much the same state as when you saw him."

Mrs. Medows wrote on January 6 from Chute, Wilton, then her brother-in-law's residence, to wish the Montagus a happy new year, and in this letter she says—

"The Duke of C(handos) * our neighbour kept his Son's † birthday with great magnificence. I was invited, and not foreseeing such an occasion for dress, I had neither manto nor sack, and desired leave to come in a white apron in the evening, but the Duchess insisted on my coming with it to dinner. You may imagine how well I dined on two and forty dishes, and a dessert of one and twenty, very well ordered and served; but the Duchess's behaviour was really an entertainment, not in the least embarrassed, she did the honours perfectly well, and seemed conscious she should make a good figure, and pleased with the opportunity. In the evening there was a ball, cards for the grave people. I am pleased to find that I can still see the young people dance and with pleasure; our nieces ‡ Pulses were the best dancers. I

* 2nd Duke of Chandos.

† His only son by first wife, afterwards 3rd Duke.

‡ Mrs. Medows' nieces.

won four rubbers and past for a good player; content with this, I came away before supper. I was charmed with Mrs. Ironmonger * . . . If you would have me think you well get a Vandike Hankerchief. Mrs. Ironmonger had one, and I am sure it will become you."

The duchess here alluded to was the second wife of the duke, Anne Jefferies, *née* Wells. In the "Complete Peerage" we read, "See the story of her being sold with a halter round her neck by her husband, Jefferies, an ostler at the Pelican Inn, Newbury, and purchased by the Duke of Chandos in 'N & Q,' 4th l. vi. p. 179." She was married in 1744 to the duke, and died in 1759 *s.p.*

January 18, Miss Anstey, writing from Trumpington, says—

"Have you heard that Mr. Gray † is going to publish his whole stock of poetry, which, though it will consist of only one volume, and contains but few things which have not been already printed, the price will be half a guinea; but what seems most extraordinary, it is expected there will be a very great demand for them, and I am told there is already a great number bespoke, for they are to be embellished and illustrated in the most curious and ingenious manner with copper plates drawn and imagined by Mr. Bentley.‡ I hear they are all very clever, and was told for a specimen that the little ode on the cat is to have in the frontispiece the Fates cutting her nine threads of her life, and the rats and mice exulting upon the death of their enemy. At the end Puss is represented as just landed from Charon's Boat, and in her approach towards Pluto's Palace, she sets up her back and spits at Cerberus. How do you like the conceit? They are said to be very highly drawn, and Mr.

* Probably Mrs. *Iremonger*, of Wherwell, Hants.

† Thomas Gray, born 1716, died 1771.

‡ Richard Bentley, junior son of the Master of Trinity, Cambridge.

Gray gives his poetry. Mr. Horace Walpole * is at the whole expense of the printing and copper plates for the benefit of Mr. Bentley. . . .

"I hear the scholar † of St. John's who has admitted himself of the play house performs much better in a personated than he did here in his real character. I suppose he does not regret his being expelled the University, as he finds himself well received by the Town, for excommunication would not hurt him there. I hear he is really a good actor, which is a thing, I am afraid, much more rare than a bad clergyman, so I am glad he has taken to the stage instead of the Pulpit. I hear there were fourscore of this University present at his first performance, and that if he has a benefit the whole body will be present at it."

This edition of Gray was published in March, 1753, printed at Mr. Horace Walpole's private press at Strawberry Hill.

Mr. West, attacked by his enemy the gout, was now a prisoner at Wickham. On January 24, in a long letter, these paragraphs are of interest—

"The joyous Berenger passed five days with us last week, read to us a play in Shakespeare and the 'Volpone' of B. Johnson, and repeated innumerable scraps out of a hundred others, laughed a great deal, said many droll and some witty things, and then disappear'd, after promising to come frequently to strut upon the little stage of Wickham, which you may perceive has been lately graced with almost as great a variety of characters as are exhibited at Drury Lane, so that we have little occasion to run to the great city in search of company, much less for the sake of society, which indeed there is almost lost, in the various bustle of Resort,

* Horace Walpole, younger son of Sir Robert Walpole, born 1717, died 1797.

† Is this Churchill?

the busy hum of Men, the embarrassments of Hoops,—Interruptions of Messages and ostentatious dinners and Drums, Trumpets, Politics, etc., etc.,—but besides the pleasures of social converse, we have had amusements of a stiller kind furnished by the obliging civility of some of my brother Authors; among which are two new papers, 'The Adventurer' and 'The World,'* by Adam Fitz-Adam. The writer of the former sent me the first 14 numbers with a very handsome letter. To the other I had indeed a kind of right since I am inform'd that the judicious Tasters of the Town have declared it to be written by Sir G(eorge) L(yttelton), by Mr. Pitt, or your humble servant; with how much sagacity this opinion is form'd I shall leave you to judge, for I doubt not but this character will recommend them to your perusal, as it precludes me saying anything in their favour: of the former I may be so free as to declare I like them very well, but I will be still bolder in recommending to you Dr. Leland's 'Observations of Lord Bolingbroke's letter,' which was sent me by the author yesterday, and which I have read through with great pleasure and edification. I must transcribe a part of my boy's† letter about the death of the Bishop of Cloyne: 'We have had a great loss at Oxford; the poor Bishop of Cloyne died on Sunday about 8 o'clock in the evening. Mrs. Berkeley‡ was sitting by him, and spoke to him several times, and he never answered, so it is supposed he was dead a quarter of an hour before it was discovered, for he died without a groan or any sign of pain.'

"He has received Rollin, for which I thank you in his name."

To this Mrs. Montagu rejoins—

"How happy was the Bishop of Cloyne's exit, or

* Edward Moore published "The World."

† His son Richard, then at Oxford.

‡ George Berkeley, born 1684, died 1753. Celebrated divine and author.

rather entrance, one should call it into another, than departure out of this life, for it had none of the agonising pangs of farewell. I pity poor Mrs. Berkeley, who had so little preparation for so heavy a stroke. I hope the constant conversation and example of a man so eminent in every Christian virtue may have given her an uncommon degree of fortitude and patience. I have heard her temper and understanding highly commended. She had a perfect adoration of the Bishop. . . . Dr. Berkeley had formerly made his addresses to Mrs. Donnellan: what were her reasons for refusing him I know not, friends were consenting, circumstances equal, her opinion captivated, but perhaps aversion to the cares of a married life, and apprehensions from some particularities in his temper hinder'd the match; however their friendship always continued, and I have always heard her give him for virtues and talents the preference to all mankind."

Mrs. Montagu continues that she had neither health nor spirits to read with pleasure. "The misfortunes I have suffered and those I have feared have worn me out; after the various turns of hope and fear on my poor Lydia's account, I am at last in despair about her. Mr. Botham sent to us for a milch ass for her some days ago." After a long lamentation on Lydia's behalf, she ends, "I am that poor little selfish animal, a human creature, made more poor, more little, more selfish by the Vapours; in all Sir Hans' Museum there is not so ugly a monster as a woman in Vapours." Lydia becoming worse, Mrs. Montagu wrote to inform her sister, Mrs. Laurence Sterne, whose curious letter I give in full as a specimen of her style. Both she and her sister Lydia wrote large, legible hands, much alike.

"Sutton,* March ye 9th.

"DEAR MADAM,

"I return you my sincere and hearty thanks for the Favour of your most welcome letter; which had I received in a more happy Hour, wou'd have made me almost Frantick with Joy; for being thus cruelly separated from all my Friends, the least mark of their kindness towards me, or Remembrance of me gives me unspeakable Delight. But the Dismal Account I receiv'd at the same time of my poor Sister, has render'd my Heart Incapable of Joy, nor can I ever know Comfort till I hear of her Recovery.

"Believe me, Dear Madam, you were never more mistaken than when you imagine that Time and Absence remove you from my Remembrance. I do assure you I do not so easily part with what affords me so great Delight, on the Contrary I spare no pains to improve every little accident that recalls you to my Remembrance, as the only amends which can be made me for those Unhappinesses my Situation deprives me of. As a proof of this I must inform you that about three weeks ago I took a long Ride Through very bad weather, and worse Roads, merely for the satisfaction of enjoying a Conversation with a Gentleman who though unknown to you had conceiv'd the highest opinion of you from the perusal of several of your Letters, for which he was indebted to Mrs. Clayton. Had this Gentleman nothing else to recommend him, it certainly would be Sufficient to have made me desirous of his acquaintance; but he is both a Man of Sense and good Breeding, so that I am not a little pleas'd with my new Acquaintance. Your Supposition of my Sister's having Boasted to me of her Children is doubtless extremely Natural, I wish it had been as Just: But I can in three words inform you of all I know about 'em,—to wit their number and their Names, for which I am indebted to Johnny. Had my Lydia been so obliging as to have made them the

* The Rev. Laurence Sterne was Vicar of Sutton-in-the-Forest, Yorkshire.

Subject of her Letters, I shou'd by this time have had a tolerable Idea of them, by considering what she said with some abatement: but as it is I no more know whether they are Black, Brown or Fair, Wise, or other wise, Gentle, or Froward than the Man in the Moon. Pray is this strange Silence on so Interesting a Subject owing to her profound Wisdom or her abundant Politeness? But be it to which it will, as soon as she recovers her Health I shall insist on all the satisfaction she can give on this head. In the meantime I rejoice to find they have your approbation and am truly thankful that Nature has done her part, which indeed is the most Material, though I frankly own I shall not be the first to Forgive any slights that Dame Fortune may be dispos'd to shew them.

"Your god-Daughter, as in Duty bound, sends her best Respects to you. I will hope that she may enjoy what her poor Mother in vain Laments, the want of a more intimate acquaintance with her Kindred.

"Be so good as to make Mr. Sterne's and my compliments to Mr. Montagu, and Believe me, Dear Madam,

"Your most affectionate Cousin,
and oblig'd Humble Servant,
"E. STERNE."

The godchild was Lydia Sterne, born December 1, 1747, then in her sixth year. The Sternes had lost their first child, also a *Lydia*, born in October, 1745.

Lydia Botham did not long survive; I do not know the exact day of her death, but West, writing on April 2, to Mrs. Montagu, says—

"I cannot conclude without thanking you, my dearest Cousin, for informing me of your health, about which I should have been under great alarms upon hearing of Lydia's Death, of which your letter brought me the first intelligence. This kind attention to my happiness at a time when your heart was overflowing with sorrow is such a proof of your regard for me I shall always remember with gratitude."

Though deeply lamented, Lydia's sufferings, latterly from asthma, dropsy, and a complication of disorders, made her death more or less a release. Mr. Botham was now left a widower with five children.

Writing from London, the end of April, to Sarah Scott in John Street, Bath, where she and Lady Bab were living, Mrs. Montagu says—

"I have been at Oratorios so crowded and plays so hot I have almost fainted, but first of all crowds and greatest of all mobs, I must in justice name Lady Bath's * assembly, from whence at hazard of life and limb I broke away a little after one on Tuesday last. Her ladyship had happily gathered together eight hundred Christian souls, many of which had like to have perished by famine and other accidents. I suffered the most from the first of these; being ill, I had not eat a morsel of dinner, and there was not a biscuit nor a bit of bread to be got, and half the company got out through the stables and garden. The house was not empty till near 3 in the morning."

Mrs. Montagu had for some time been expecting Miss Carter, the young daughter of Mr. Montagu's faithful agent, to stay with her. She says—

"My little disciple † is very good, and takes to me wondrous well. I expect the eldest Miss Botham next week, you may suppose it was some denial not to choose the second, but I thought the other my duty rather, and the eldest would have been much grieved to be passed over."

* *Née* Anna Maria Gumley, wife of Pulteney, Earl of Bath. She is said to have been a great "screw."

† Miss Carter.

Writing to Mr. Montagu (who had gone to Sandleford on business, and to cure a bad cold) on May 3, his wife describes a Rout she had given. "I had rather more than an hundred visitants last night, but the apartment held them with ease, and the highest compliments were paid to the house and elegance of the apartments."

Gilbert West from Wickham, on May 23, gives the following account of Mr. Pitt, whose health had been causing much anxiety to his friends—

"Had I answered your letter last night I should have given you a good account of Mr. Pitt, who was yesterday in better spirits than I have seen him in since he came hither, but I find by inquiring after him this morning that he has had a bad, that is, a sleepless night, which has such effect on his spirits that I am afraid we shall see him in a very different condition to-day. This has happened to him every other night since Friday last, so I am persuaded there is something intermitting in his case, of which neither the Physicians nor himself seem to be aware. I think he ought to go to town to consult with them, but to this he has so great an aversion that I question if he will comply with our request. Sir George Lyttelton, who saw him on one of his bad days, Saturday last, promised to come hither to-day, and his voice added to ours may possibly prevail. . . .

"Mr. Pitt express'd a due sense of your goodness in inquiring so particularly after him, and that you may know how high you stand in his opinion, I must inform you that in a conversation with Molly he pronounced you the most *perfect woman* he ever met with."

Mr. Pitt was recommended by his doctors to go to Tunbridge Wells to drink the waters. Accompanied by Mr. West, Mrs. West, and Miss West, he set off on May 26. West, writing to Mrs. Montagu, says—

"Tunbridge Wells, May 27, 1753.

"MY DEAREST COUSIN! MY BEST AND MOST VALUABLE FRIEND!

"Your kind letter which I received on coming from Chapel is the most agreeable thing I have met with at Tunbridge, where we arrived last night about 7, after only stopping at Sen'nocks, and dining at Tunbridge Town. It came very seasonably to relieve my spirits which were much sunk by the extreme dejection which appears to-day in Mr. Pitt, from a night passed entirely without sleep, notwithstanding all the precautions which were taken within doors to make it still and quiet, and the accidental tranquillity arising from the present emptiness and desolation of this place, to which no other invalids, except ourselves are yet arrived, or even expected to arrive as yet. He began to drink the waters to-day, but as they are sometimes very slow in their operations, I much fear both he and those friends who cannot help sympathizing with him, will suffer a great deal before the wished-for effect will take place, for this *Insomnium* his Physicians have prescribed Opiates, a medicine which, in this case, though they may procure a temporary ease, yet often after recoil upon the spirits. He seems inclined to take Musk, and intends to talk with Molly about it. I think his Physicians have been to blame in giving all their attention to the disorder in his bowels, and not sufficiently regarding the Distemperature of his spirits, a Disease much more to be apprehended than the other; while he continues under this Oppression, I am afraid it will be impossible for me to leave him, as he fancies me of the greatest use to him as a friend, and a comforter, but I hope in God he will soon find some alteration for the better, of which I shall be glad to give you the earliest information. In the meantime I beg you will take care of your health, and as the most effectual means of establishing it, I most earnestly desire you will follow Mr. Montagu's exhortations to repair forthwith to Tunbridge, as by so doing you will not only contribute to the regaining your own health, but to the comfort and felicity of some here who love you. . . . Kitty, Molly and Mr. Pitt desire their affectionate compliments. Molly begs you will communicate this account of Mr. Pitt to Sir G(eorge) L(yttelton)."

In West's next letter, of May 30, he says—

"I think Mr. Pitt is somewhat better, tho' his spirits are too low to allow him to think so, and his nights are still sleepless without the aid of Opiates. I write this from the 'Stone House' to which we were driven by the noisy situation of our house at the foot of Mount Sion. How many pleasing ideas our present habitation recalls I leave you to judge, though there needs no such artificial helps to make you ever present to my memory. . . . Mr. Pitt is lodged in your room, and I in that which was Mr. Montagu's dressing-room on the ground floor."

The Montagus and Wests together had rented the "Stone House" the year before this. On May 31 West writes to say he is leaving Mr. William Lyttelton with Mr. Pitt, and will return to Wickham on Saturday, and dine with Mrs. Montagu at Hayes *en route*. He adds, "Mr. Pitt feels a little gout in his foot, which we hope will increase so as to be an effectual Remedy for all his disorders."

On June 6, West, who had been commissioned to find a house for Mrs. Montagu, looks at the last two left on Mount Ephraim, a Mr. Spooner's and a Mr. Sele's; he decided on the latter, orders the chimney to be made higher, and a *hovel* put on it to stop smoking, and to order the owners to lie in the beds to air them!

"The price he told me was 4 guineas a week, or thirty-five guineas for the whole season, that is till Michaelmas, or a week or two over; for this price you are to have stabling for eight horses, and a coach house for two carriages. . . . Mrs. West will be obliged to you if you will bring her jewels with you."

Mrs. Montagu arrived at Tunbridge on June 11, and on the 13th writes to her husband, then in London, to say

"my cough is much abated, and my appetite increased: the asses' milk sits well on my stomach. . . . I have a constant invitation to dinner at the 'White House'; Mr. Pitt is too ill to dine abroad, and the Wests cannot leave him, so as often as I am disposed for company, I dine there; the rest of my time passes in taking air and exercise, and now and then the relief of a book."

On account of the Jew Bill and other unpopular measures coming before Parliament, a General Election was anticipated, and Lord Sandwich was already arranging for it by canvassing his constituents, and those at Huntingdon, and summoned Mr. Montagu to meet him at Hinchinbrooke the second week in August. Previous to this he spent a few days with his wife at Tunbridge hence proceeding to Yorkshire for his annual estate business. Old Mr. Robinson accompanied his friend, Sir Edward Dering, to canvass for him in Kent, and his daughter says, "My Father would have made a good counterpart to Sir Edward Dering; if *bon mots* could carry a county, I know few that would care to contend with them."

Previous to going to Tunbridge, Mrs. Montagu placed her two young charges, Miss Carter and Miss Botham, in a boarding-school. She writes to her sister Sarah—

"Mr. Montagu thought Miss Carter's dancing would

be better improved if she went to School, and he is as desirous she should be a fine dancer as if she was to be a Maid of Honour. I was the more willing in regard to Miss Botham going, for my cousin is of such a 'diversian' temper, as Cotes used to express it, that I feared she would not be easily restrained in a place of this sort; she is a fine girl, but so lively and so idle, she requires infinite care. With great capacity of learning she has prodigious desire to be idle, and thinks it quite hard not to take her share of all the diversions she hears of. On being asked how she liked London she said very well, but should do so much better if she was to go to Ranelagh every night! I have left them at a very good school, but an expensive one; however, they are only to stay there till the 15th of August, for then the school breaks up, and if I do not leave this place sooner, they must come. I believe no gouvernante ever took half the pains I have done with these children, explaining to them everything they read, and talking to them on all points of behaviour."

On July 4, in a letter to Mr. Montagu, who was at Theakstone, his wife writes—

"All the family at the 'Stone House' and myself in their train went yesterday to Penshurst; we spent a good deal of time in viewing the pictures. I was most pleased with the portraits, as I know not any family that for Arts and Arms, greatness of courage and nobility of mind have excelled the Sydney Race. Beauty too, has been remarkable in it."

And on July 8—

"It has been much the turn of the Society I am in to go out in parties to see places, and last post day we settled upon an expedition of this sort with such precipitation, I had not opportunity to write without keeping the company waiting. We went to see an old seat of a Mr. Brown's; it is well situated, was built by Inigo Jones, has some fine portraits. . . . We went from this venerable seat to a place called New Vauxhall, where Mr. Pitt had provided us a good dinner; the view from it is romantic; we staid there till the cool of the evening, and then returned home. We drank tea yesterday in the most beautiful rural scene that can be imagined, which Mr. Pitt had discovered in his morning's ride about half a mile from hence; he ordered a tent to be pitched, tea to be prepared, and his French horn to breathe music like the unseen genius of the wood: the company dined with me, and we set out, number 8. . . . Sir George Lyttelton and Mr. Bower are come to spend a few days with Mr. Pitt."

To this her husband replies, "I very much approve of the excursions you make, and think the more the better, as they both entertain the mind and give exercise to the body." He adds, the epidemic then raging amongst cattle in England had not been so severe on his northern property as in other parts of the country.

Mr. Pitt went to Hastings for two days, and on his return, Mr. West made a tour to Canterbury, Dover, etc., which lasted five days. Dr. Smith,* Mr. Montagu's old friend, was then at Tunbridge, and Mrs. Montagu says—

"We fell into discourse upon some embellishments and ornaments to be added to the fine Library at Trinity College. There are to be 26 Bustos put up, 13 in memory of the ancients, 13 of modern, these are to be cast in plaister of Paris: but Mrs. Middleton talks of a fine Marble Busto of Dr. Middleton to be done by Roubilliac,† which I think very proper, as he was so

* Dr. Robert Smith, then Master of Trinity College, Cambridge. Founded "Smith's Prizes."

† Louis François Roubilliac, born 1695, died 1762. Eminent sculptor.

eminent, there should be a public memorial of him, and as he was long Librarian it is proper it should be in that place: there are likewise to be 48 portraits of considerable persons that have been of the College."

To this Mr. Montagu replies—

"I am very well pleased with what Dr. Smith is doing at Trinity College. I hope he has not lay'd aside the noble design he had form'd of having a Statue * of the great Newton. Such men as he and Dr. Middleton should be represented in something more durable than plaister of Paris, and I honour Mrs. Middleton for her intention."

After seeing to the business consequent on his trusteeship to his cousin, Mr. Rogers, of Newcastle, Mr. Montagu had returned to Theakstone on July 29. He describes Gibside, the seat of Mr. Bowes †—

"I dined this day sennight at Gibside; it was one of the finest summer days I ever saw. It set off to great advantage the whole vale through which the river Tyne runs, which consists of a great deal of good rich land. The Moors, tho' not so pleasing to the eye, make abundant amends by the riches of the mines. All the gentlemen are planting and adorning their Seats, but nothing comes up to the grandeur and magnificence of what Mr. Bowes has done, and is a (*sic*), doing, I mean without doors, for his house is but an indifferent one. It stands in the midst of a great wood of about 400 acres, through which there are a great many noble walks and rides interspers'd with fine lawns, with a rough river running thro' it, on each side of which are very high rocks, which gives it a very romantick look. Mr. Bowes is at present

* In 1755 Dr. Smith gave the statue of Sir T. Newton, sculptured by Roubilliac.

† George Bowes, of Streatlam Castle, and Gibside, Durham.

upon a work of great magnificence, which is the erecting a column of above 140 feet high. This, as far as I know, may be the largest that ever was erected by a subject in this Island, and may yield to nothing but the Monument at London. I ought not to omit telling you that he has already erected upon a rising ground a gothick building which he calls a Banquetting room, in which the night before there was a concert of Musick (*sic*), at which Jordain and an Italian woman performed, whom Mrs. Lane * brought with her from Bramham Moor, from which she came in a day. . . . On Monday I dined with Sir Thomas Clavering.† This gentleman's house is very old and bad, but the situation good and prospect pleasant. He has made a long road leading to his house and improved his park, and made a serpentine river. . . . He has also, as well as all the other gentlemen in that county, made a kitchen garden with very high walls, planted with the finest fruit trees. I question not peaches and nectarines may succeed very well, but for grapes they must be beholden to fire."

From this it would appear that walled kitchen gardens were new things in the North then; probably "Kail yards" reigned supreme. Miss Carter and Miss Botham now joined Mrs. Montagu at Tunbridge from their school. Another excursion to Stonelands ‡ with Mr. Pitt took place, and in a letter to Mr. Montagu on August 3 we learn—

"This dry Summer has been so favourable to the Waters that they have made several surprising cures. I think Mr. Pitt may be numbered amongst them. The first time I saw the Duke of Bolton,§ I could hardly

* Mrs. Lane, of Bramham Park, Yorkshire.

† 7th Baronet, related to the Roger family, Oxwell Park.

‡ A seat of the Duke of Dorset's, now called Buckhurst, in Surrey.

§ 3rd Duke; he died August 26, 1754. Married as second wife Lavinia Fenton, *alias* "Polly Peacham."

imagine he would last a month, but seeing him again yesterday I was amazed at the amendment."

In the afternoons Mrs. Montagu and Mr. Pitt were attending Mr. King's lectures on philosophy, etc., and "Mr. Pitt, who is desirous of attaining some knowledge in this way, makes him explain things very precisely." In another letter she says—

"Miss Carter will excell in dancing. I did not think it right she should dance Minouets at the ball till she was quite perfect in it, but Mr. West, Mr. Pitt and all their family and some other company were here the other day, and I made her dance a Minouet with Master West by way of using her to do it in company; she acquitted herself so well as to get great commendation."

As usual, the husband and wife exchanged loving letters on the anniversary of their wedding-day, August 5. Mrs. Montagu mentions—

"There is a report that Lord Coke is dying; his wife, Lady Mary, is here; she is extremely pretty, her air and figure the most pleasing I ever saw. She is not properly a beauty, but she has more *agrémens* than one shall often see. With so many advantages of birth, person and fortune, I do not wonder at her resentment being lively, and that she could ill brook the neglects and insults of her husband."

Lady Mary was the daughter of the 2nd Duke of Argyll and Duke of Greenwich. She is often mentioned by Horace Walpole. Her husband treated her with great brutality, and she gained a separation from him. He died August 31, 1753; she survived him till 1811.

Mr. Herbert is mentioned as being very ill at Tunbridge; this was the uncle of the 6th Earl of Carnarvon,

John Nixon, pxt.]

TEA AND COFFEE IN THE BATH-ROOM.

[*To face p.* 38, *vol. ii.*

of Highclere Castle, Hants. Mr. Montagu says, "He has done a great deal to adorn and beautify Highclere; he had designed to do much more, if he dies it will want his finishing hand." On August 13 Mrs. Montagu writes to her husband—

"Mr. Nash * had a fit yesterday, by which it is imagined this Monarch will soon resign that Empire over Mankind, which in so extraordinary a manner he gained and has preserved. The Young Pretender is now known to be at Passi, near Paris, where he keeps himself so concealed that he may on any project be able to leave it without exciting the attention of the people. It is said in case of a Minority he will make us a visit. Lord Rochford intercepted a letter from a Cardinal in France to his brother in Italy, in which he said he had supped with Prince Charles the night before. I hear this young adventurer is much a favorite with the French officers and soldiers, whose romantic visions of honour may excite them to do more than even the policy of their Monarque requires."

On August 20 Mr. Montagu arrived at Hinchinbroke to stay with Lord Sandwich, in order to beat up votes for the next election for Huntingdon and the county. A Mr. Jones, an eminent merchant, was to be his fellow-candidate.

"On Tuesday we are to go about the town and canvass, where an entertainment will be prepared for the Burgesses, who will to-morrow night be treated with their wives, with a ball for them only, a thing intirely new and which must produce something new and out of the common. On Friday we shall be at liberty to move off, but on Monday night we are to meet and entertain the Londoners at the King's Head, Holbourn."

* Richard Nash, "Beau Nash," Leader of Fashion at Bath and Tunbridge, born 1674, died 1761.

Writing on August 21 to Mrs. Boscawen, Mrs. Montagu mentions—

"I am living in the very house my dear Mrs. Boscawen inhabited three years ago. At the Stone Castle reside Mr. Pitt, Mr. and Mrs. West and Miss West. Instead of making parties at Whist or Cribbage, and living with and like the *beau monde*, we have been wandering about like a company of gipsies, visiting all the fine parks and seats in the neighbourhood."

These excursions were much encouraged by Mr. Pitt, who considered them "as good for the mind as the body," and that an occasional day without drinking the waters gave them a greater effect.

Mention of a ventriloquist now occurs as something new—

"I have been this morning to hear the man who has a surprising manner of throwing his voice into the Drawer, a bottle, your pocket, up the chimney, or where he pleases within a certain distance. . . . I was last night at Mr. King's, we had the Orrery and an astronomical lecture."

Mr. Montagu joined his wife for a week at Tunbridge, when he had to return to London. On September 16 she writes to him—

"I intend to be with you on Thursday. . . . I find Mr. Pitt has some intentions, as *I told you when you was here, of going to Heys*, in case he should not be well enough to take the long journey he intends, and he seems much pleased that I will lend him that little tenement; but as I apprehend a feather bed more will be wanted than used to be, I propose to send one from Hill Street. . . . Mr. Pitt leaves this place to-morrow, he is now going to Dr. Ascough's, and from thence to

Thos. Malton, pxt.]

THE CIRCUS, AT BATH.

[*To face p.* 40, *vol. ii.*

Stowe * and Hagley.† Mr. West goes to Stowe with him."

Probably it was from this time that Pitt took such a fancy to Hayes, which endured all his lifetime.

The next letter to Gilbert West I transcribe in portions—

"Sandleford, September 27, 1753.

"MY MOST HONOURED COUSIN,

"Your kind and agreeable letter restored me in some measure to the temper I lost at going out of town the very day you came to it. I know not what poets may find in the country, when they have filled the woods with sylvan Deities, and the rivers with Naides; but to me groves and streams and plains make poor amends for the loss of a friend's conversation. You have better supplied Mr. Pitt's absence by reading the Orations of his predecessor, Demosthenes, and I can easily imagine you would rather have passed the evening with the British than the Grecian Demosthenes, whom in talents perhaps he equals, and in grace of manners and the sweet civilities of life, I dare say he excels. But when you seem to say you would even have preferred the simple small talk of your poor cousin to the Athenian Orator, I cry out,—Oh wondrous power of friendship, which like the sun gives glorious colours to a vapour, and brightens the pebble to a gem, till what would have been neglected by the common herd is accepted by the most distinguished. . . . On Tuesday morning about eight o'clock I called upon Mr. Hooke at his hermitage. I found him like a true Savant surrounded by all the elements of Science, but though I roamed round the room, I could not perceive any signs of the Author, no papers, pen, ink, or sheets just come from the press. I fear the fine ladies and fine prospects of Cookham divert his attention from the Roman History. . . . I

* Lady Cobham's.

† Sir George Lyttelton's seat.

desired him to carry me to Mrs. Edwin's, which I heard was a pretty place.* There is an old ferry woman who crosses the Thames very often before Mrs. Edwin's terrace. . . . While we were in Mrs. Edwin's garden he betrayed my name to her . . . she came down, showed me her house and the pictures, which are very fine, but the views from her windows gave one no leisure to consider the works of art. . . . Cliefden Hill rises majestically in view, and the only flat shore you see from this place lies straight before it, and is a large plain of the finest verdure and full of cattle."

To this letter Gilbert West replies—

"I am glad your journey to Sandleford was relieved by the agreeable digression you made to Cookham, where I hope to find, at least in the memory of Mr. Hooke, the vestiges of your having been there, which will be an additional motive to me to make him a visit from Stoke, for I am going once more from Wickham, notwithstanding the neighbourhood of Sir Thomas Robinson,† the Archbishop,‡ and Bower, and the arrival of my Urn, which is to come this very day, and which Mr. Cheer hath taught me to consider as an emblem and monument of the polished, elegant and accomplished Mrs. Montagu, by assuring me 'that it is indebted for all the extraordinary and highly finished ornaments he hath bestowed upon it, to the great regard and veneration he hath for her, and that he will not either for love or money make such another.' . . . I was paying a visit at Fulham, where I enjoyed the smiles of my beloved Bishop,§ the presence of Mrs. Sherlock, and the agreeable conversation of Mrs. Chester, with the more substantial delicacies of an excellent English Venison Pasty."

* Could this be Hedsor?

† "Long" Sir Thomas, Mrs. Montagu's cousin.

‡ Archbishop Secker.

§ Thomas Sherlock, born 1678, died 1761. Bishop of London.

Further on he says he is going to Lillingston Dayrell to see his mother, Lady Langham.

In the next letter (Oct. 3) from Sandleford to Mr. West occurs this sentence, "Mr. Montagu returned hither on Monday with the new four-wheeled post-chaise; it is the pleasantest machine imaginable in rough roads, but I think it too easy on even roads." The coachmen had nothing intermediate between the two-wheeled vehicles and the ponderously long six- or four-horsed coach, which required elaborate skill in turning.

Staying again at Fulham, Mr. West mentions that he has been urging Bishop Sherlock to publish some of his sermons, which he promised to do. West had a fresh attack of the gout, which made him return home. Mr. Pitt had left Hayes suddenly for Bath, Tunbridge waters not having been of sufficient use to him; and in a letter of October 13, to West, in capital letters, her inquiries not being answered, Mrs. Montagu asks, "I desire TO KNOW WHAT YOU HAVE HEARD CONCERNING MR. PITT'S HEALTH?" Describing her daily life, she says she keeps up the Tunbridge habit of driving an hour or so after dinner (which, it must be remembered, was then early) over the adjacent common; after these airings she drank tea, and retired to her dressing-room for two or three hours of reading.

On October 14 West writes—

"The Duke and Duchess of Portland, with two of their daughters, dined here last Thursday, and we are to make them a morning's visit to-morrow at Bullstrode. Her Grace was extremely courteous and obliging to me, but never made any inquiry after you, which piqued me so much, that I put her against her upon talking about Mr. Botham, and from what she said about the distrest situation of his family, took occasion to extol you as the most generous and sincere friend, and indeed the only one the poor man could depend on."

The reader will have doubtless missed the frequent mention of the duchess and her letters. There is no doubt that the coolness between the quondam intimate friends was on account of the Scott separation. It will be remembered the duchess sided with Mrs. Scott's engagement against Mrs. Montagu's opinion. After the Scott separation, probably influenced by her intimate friend, Lady Bute, who with the Princess of Wales seems to have defended him,* the duchess appears to have taken his part; but his true character is shown by the fact that the Prince of Wales (George III.), on being given a Household in 1756, begged that Scott† should not be continued about him, and to make up for this dismissal he was given a commissionership in the Excise. Later on the duchess and Mrs. Montagu had a *rapprochement*, but the letters were never as cordial as in previous times.

Writing from Lillingston on October 27, West describes his visit to Bullstrode—

"I was very kindly received both at Bullstrode and Cookham; at the former we were shown a great many fine and great many curious things, both in doors and without; the day proved too cold, and I was not enough recovered to see all the rarities of the animal as well as the vegetable kind, which were dispersed over the Park and gardens. Those that might be seen from the windows, as some spotted Sheep and a little Bull from Fort St. David's, whose resemblance I have often seen in China ware, I beheld with admiration and applause, and

* *Vide* Walpole's "Memoirs of the Reign of George III.," vol. ii. p. 259.

† Scott is said to have been a Jacobite secretly. That he was double-faced is evident from letters.

ventured two steps into the garden to take a view of the orange trees against the wall. . . . Her Grace promised to make me a present of some trained up for that purpose. In her closet we were shown some curious works in Shells, performed by Mrs. Delany, whom her Grace expected at Bullstrode in a short time, and expressed great pleasure and not a little impatience in the prospect of seeing so dear and so ingenious a friend. Of you she said nothing, till upon her naming Mrs. Donnellan, I said I could give her some account of her, having been informed by you that she was gone to town; she then asked when I heard from you, and where you was, but carried her enquiry after you no further. At Cookham I spent some hours with Mrs. Stanley, for Mr. Hooke had gone out with Mrs. Edwin to make a visit to Dr. Freind. . . ." He further states that he found his mother well, and "very little alter'd since I last saw her, excepting that she has grown a little fatter, a circumstance to a woman of seventy is greatly preferable to wrinkles. In my way thro' Stowe Park I met Miss Banks riding out with Lord Vere,* of her I enquired much about Mr. Pitt, and received from her the same answer, which I must have made for your enquiries after him, that they had heard nothing of him since he left Stowe. . . . While he staid at Stowe he was in good health and spirits, he went from thence to Hagley, and she believed he intended to go from Hagley to Bath."

On November 10 Mrs. Donnellan, to whom Mrs. Montagu had lent her house in Hill Street, whilst she searched for lodgings in the suburbs, her lungs not permitting her to live in the town during the winter, writes—

"I have taken a little house on tryal at Kensington Gravel Pits . . . both Richardson's house at Northend and Mrs. Granville's at Chelsey I think too low for

* Baron Vere, of Hanworth.

me. . . . I want you to read 'Sir Charles Grandison,' it is not formed on your plan of banishing delicacy. I am afraid it carrys it too far on t'other side, and is too fine spun, but there are fine things and fine characters in it, and I don't know how it is, but his tediousness gives one an eagerness to go on; there is a love-sick madness that I think extremely fine and touching, but if you have not read it I must not forestall. I think I will own to you, the great fault of my friend's writings, there is too much of everything. I really laughed at your nursery of 'Clarissas,' but I hope you did not think of me as the old nurse, there was nobody there while I stayed!"

Mr. Richardson had just completed his novel of Sir Charles Grandison. The Clarissas is an allusion to Miss Botham and Miss Carter, then with Mrs. Montagu.

This same month Mrs. Montagu was again very unwell. West urged her to go to London, but Mr. Montagu, who loved the retirement at Sandleford, was unwilling to leave it, and she says—

"Tho' I am told I may go to town, I know it would not be agreeable where I ought to please, and I can hardly think it right to be in such haste to quit the place where I live most in the manner I ought to do, where only I am useful. I relieve the distresses and animate the industry of a few, and have given all my hours to the two girls under my care, whose welfare, whose eternal welfare perhaps, depends on what they shall now learn."

Mr. Hooke and Mr. Botham were both at Sandleford. In Mr. Hooke's conversation Mrs. Montagu found much enjoyment; as West put it, "He (Hooke) is a very worthy man, and has in him the greatest compass of entertainments of any one I know, from nonsense (as Lord Bath calls it), to sense, and beyond sense to Metaphysics."

On December 20 Mrs. West writes to present her Christmas wishes, and Mr. West's, to the Montagus, as "Tubby" (Mr. West), as was his uneuphonious family nickname, had the gout in both hands. Mrs. Montagu writes to him—

"The 27th of December, 1753.

"And what, my dear Cousin, are both hands prisoners of the gout! such innocent hands too! Hands that never open'd to receive or give a bribe, that never dipped into the guilt of the South Sea fraud, of Charitable Corporations, or pilfer'd lottery tickets, clean even from perquisite in office, and the most modest means by which the Miser's palm wooes and sollicits gain. So far have your hands been from grasping at other's gold, they have not held fast your own with a tenacious grip, but open'd liberally at the petitions of the poor, for the productions of Art, or to feast your friends at the genial board. Most of all do I resent the fate of the writing hand, which was first dedicated to the Muses, then with maturer judgment consecrated to the Nymphs of Solyma, and shall it be led captive by the cruel gout? Why did you sing the triumphs * of the dire goddess? Oh, why could you not describe them unfelt, as Poets often do the softer pains and gentler woes of Venus and her Son?"

The first amusing paper I have of 1754 is a school bill for the two younger Miss Bothams, Molly and Kitty. I am sorry that several of the items are torn away, but it is curious as to things then required, and also for the extraordinarily bad spelling and wording of the preceptor entrusted with their care. It is addressed to—

* West wrote a poem entitled "The Triumphs of the Gout."

"The Revd. Doc^{r} Botham,
"These."

"SIR,

"According to your desire by the honour of your Last, I send you the Bill of the two Miss's Botham, your daughters, to ye first of this month, altho' wee had spoak of it before the Holydays I had quite forgot it, and was very easy on that account. I hope, Sir, that you'r satisfied of us, if so I shall alwise thry, as well as my wife, to do all wee can to improve your daughters in everything, especially in their Morals and manners. I was very sorry of your last indisposition, and hope you'r much better, it is the sincere wish of

"Sir,
"Your most humble
and obedient Servant,
"E. SAGE ROBERTS.

"Kensington, the 20th January, 1754.

"P.S.—My wife with her compliments to you joyns with me in compts. of the Saison, wishing you health, prosperity and all you can wish yourself for many years."

"*The two Miss's Botham's Bill.*

	£	s.	d.
"To Board from the 9th of August, 1753, to the 1st January, 1754, at £25 per year, maketh	19	16	0
To a Seat at Church	0	8	6
To copy Books, pens, pencils, Ink, paper, &c.	0	7	0
To the Dancing Master	4	10	
To sundry things furnished, viz.—			
To a chest of Draws	1	5	0
To silver spoons, knife and Fork	1	1	0
To a tea chest	0	(torn off)	
To a Spelling book, 1 Grammar	0	3	–
To two Hats and two Bonets	0	15	0
To three pair of Shoes	0	(torn)	
To Gloves, 6 pairs	0	(torn)	

	£	s.	d.
To tea and suger	0	(torn)	
To Thread, Tape and pins, needles, worsted, laces, &c.	0	13	–
To Hair cutting, Pomatum Powder		(torn)	
To Pocket Money	0	10	9
To Pots and Mugs, &c.	0	1	6
To a percel recd. by the Coach	0	0	2
To Soap, Oatmeal for to wash, &c.	0	2	6
Total ...	30	15	0"

In the beginning of March in this year Mr. Pelham, the Premier, died suddenly, and there was a General Election. Mr. Pelham's brother, the Duke of Newcastle, was appointed first Lord of the Treasury; Mr. Legge, Mr. Botham's uncle, Chancellor of the Exchequer; Sir George Lyttelton, Cofferer. Mr. Montagu proceeded to Hinchinbrooke early in April to canvass, and his wife writes to him on the 11th—

"I hope you had a pleasant journey, and arrived without fatigue. You are proceeding quietly and well at Huntingdon, while many are hustling with infinite animosity in other Boroughs. The votes are eleven hundred paid a piece at Bury as I am informed. . . . Morris is very busy with the Canterbury Voters, he does not like them so well as law Clients."

Morris was canvassing for his elder brother Matthew, of Horton.

Mr. Montagu writes on April 16 to say, "Yesterday our Election came on, and was, I believe, one of the most quiet and peaceable that ever was."

In her next letter to her husband she says—

"I have had a letter to-day from my brother Robinson, informing me that he is chosen along with

Creed; Mr. Best declined the Poll. My brother has carried his Election without expence. . . . I cannot take leave of you without expressing my pride and satisfaction in seeing you again enter the House of Commons, where you have behaved with such steadiness and integrity. I have a joy and pride whenever I reflect on any part of your moral character. May your virtues meet with the happiness they deserve!"

Bower writes to Mrs. Montagu on April 16 from Oakhampton, where he had gone with Sir George Lyttelton for his election, in fervid Italian. He was disgusted at the orgy of the election, and says that at the election dinner given by the mayor and magistrates in their robes to Sir George Lyttelton, they sat down at 3 o'clock p.m., and none rose to leave till two in the morning! "e tutti, o quasi tutti partirono cordialmente ubbriachi" ("and all, *nearly* all, parted thoroughly drunk"). He continues, "The cavaliers then went from house to house to kiss the ladies, as was customary, and ask for the votes of their husbands." After fervid speeches made to the "celeste imagine della Madonna del Monte e della Strada del Monte" (the celestial image of the Madonna of the Mount and the Madonna of Hill Street), meaning Mrs. Montagu, his pen is taken up by Lyttelton, who says, "The Italian language affords such lofty expressions, as the poverty of ours will not come up to, and therefore the Madonna must be content with my telling her that the good Father with all his Devotion does not honour her more than I do. . . ." At the end of his letter he says, "I hear from my wife that my Boy has been with you: a thousand thanks for your goodness to him." This is the first mention of Thomas, afterwards 2nd Baron Lyttelton, then only ten years old. Lyttelton had early besought the interest and influence of Mrs. Montagu for his son and daughter by his first marriage. Both became truly attached to her, would that her influence had prevailed on "Tom" later in life.

At this period Mrs. Donnellan was very ill, and Mrs. Montagu did her best to nurse her. Lady Sandwich came to town to inoculate her daughter, Lady Mary. Miss Mary Pitt had been to see Mrs. Montagu, and "she assures me Mr. Pitt is in good health, but has had another attack of gout in his hand, owing, 'tis imagined, to his being blooded for a sore throat."

Mr. Montagu at this period sustained the heavy loss of his faithful agent, the second Mr. Carter, who died at Theakstone, and whose loss necessitated his immediate journey to the north to attend to his own and Mr. Rogers' affairs, all of which had been confided to Mr. Carter's care. Taking Mr. Botham as his temporary secretary and companion, they started off northward by post-chaises, a most expensive process, as Mr. Montagu called it. On June 13 Mrs. Montagu writes—

"I am sorry Mrs. Carter (the grandmother), has set her heart so much on having her granddaughter with her, she is of the proper age to receive instruction and take impressions; a few years passed innocently will not leave her as amiable a subject as she is now, her mind will be less flexible. . . . Mr. Pitt drank tea with me this afternoon; he has recovered his health entirely, if one may judge by his looks. He tells me he has built a very good house at Bath for £1200. He mention'd to me his intention of going on Saturday to Wickham to propose the place at Chelsea to Mr. West, the offer will certainly be an agreeable one."

This place was that of the paymaster to Chelsea College. In the next letter to Mrs. Boscawen, Mrs. Montagu says—

"The place is call'd a thousand pounds a year, it is in the gift of Mr. Pitt, and was given with grace that few know how to put into any action . . . they have excellent lodgings annexed to the place. . . . Mr. Pitt dined with them on Saturday; I imagine he was very happy, but he so well deserved to be so. It is a fine thing to act the part of Providence and bless the good. Miss Carter was sent for by her old grandmother, last week she left me."

Writing to her husband on June 15, Mrs. Montagu states she shall be glad to hear as soon as Mr. Montagu thinks he will return, "that I may disfurnish Hayes, which I shall quit as a man does a homely but a quiet wife, with some little regret, but not much tender sorrow; it is not a beautiful place, but it is quiet, and when one steps out of the bustle of Town, appears on that account amiable." She adds that her sister's health is greatly improved, and her temper less petulant, on account of having taken to a milk and vegetable diet.

On July 9 Mrs. Montagu mentions—

"My brother Robinson came to town last night; he dined here to-day, and we are all going to Vauxhall, where Mr. Tyers has had the ruins of Palmyra painted in the manner of the scenes so as to deceive the eye and appear buildings."

Her sister Sarah and brother Charles were with her. She concludes with an affectionate appeal to her husband not to apply himself too much to business at Newcastle, but to take exercise for his health's sake.

In another letter undated, but about this period, as it mentions West's thanks to Mr. Montagu for his congratulations on his appointment to Chelsea Hospital, allusion is made to Elizabeth Canning, whose curious story of having been kidnapped* and ill-treated had convulsed London opinion.

"The town is in great agitation about Elizabeth Canning; she is condemn'd to Transportation, but her guilt is so far from appearing certain, that the Sheriffs refuse to conduct her among the other felons. All the Aldermen but Sir Crispe Gascoigne† petition in her behalf, all the great officers of the State almost, interpose for her, and the Archbishop of Canterbury also desires that she may have a decent person of her own sex to attend her over, and then to board in a private family. Some fear there will be a rising of the Mob in her favour; in general all seem to agree that the matter is entirely doubtful. As to Sir Crispe Gascoigne he dare not stir without being guarded. . . . I wish the whole affair was brought to light, there is great iniquity somewhere."

On July 19, writing from Hayes, she says—

"Miss Mary Pitt, youngest sister of Mr. Pitt, is come to stay a few days with me, she is a very sensible, modest, pretty sort of young woman, and as Mr. Pitt seem'd to take every civility shown to her as a favour, I thought this mark of respect to her one manner of returning my obligations to him."

Mr. Montagu and Mr. Botham proceeded to Newcastle to regulate Mr. Rogers' affairs, which, as before mentioned, required attention, owing to the death of the head agent, Mr. Carter.

In consequence probably of worry, Mr. Montagu returned from the north at the end of July with a fever, "which," as his wife writes to Sarah, "bleeding and wormwood draughts have taken off," and as soon as he

* *Vide* vol. ix., Smollett, "History of England," p. 231.

† Then Lord Mayor of London.

was fit he was to go with her to Hayes to pack up her books. Miss Anstey was staying with them, and was to accompany them to Sandleford. Mention is made of a portrait of herself which Mrs. Montagu was going to send Mrs. Scott: "Mr. Cambridge call'd on me the other day, he spoke much in your praise. I told him I hoped he would call on you at Bath, he promised he would." This was Richard Owen Cambridge,* a friend of Dr. Johnson, who wrote the "Scribbleriad."

Writing to West from Sandleford of her neighbours at Hayes, she regrets the society of Mrs. Herring and the Archbishop,† and desires her regards to them. He answers—

"I made your compliments to the Archbishop and Mrs. Herring, who dined with us the very day I received your letter. He is very well and as amiable and polite as ever. Dick‡ has been very dilligent and very successful in partridge shooting, and t'other day sent the prime fruits of his labours, a landrail, as a present to his Grace of Canterbury."

At the beginning of September, through the influence of West, the Bishop of London gave the living of Ealing to Mr. Botham. Botham was at Brighthelmstone with his two boys for sea-bathing, as they were not in health. The joy of Mrs. Montagu was great at this preferment, as the bishop permitted Mr. Botham to continue to hold Albury as well, placing a curate in the living he did not occupy.

Writing again to West, Mrs. Montagu says—

"Dr. Mangey kept a curate at Ealing as he did not reside there, but undoubtedly Mr. Botham will discharge

* Mr. Cambridge died in 1802.

† Thomas Herring, born 1671, died 1757. Archbishop of Canterbury.

‡ Young West.

the duties of the living he resides at without assistance; the Bishop of London required Mr. Botham's residence: as the girls and boys are growing up and must soon live with him, they will be better placed at Ealing in a good neighbourhood than at Albury. They will learn nothing there but eating and drinking plentifully of Lord Aylesford, and Mr. Godschall's house is generally full of poetic Misses, who are addressing each other by the names of Parthenia, Araminta, etc., with now and then a little epistle to Strephon or Damon. I was uneasy whenever they were at home, for fear they should enter into the *precieuse* character of Mrs. Godschall."

This style of conversation is taken off in Molière's "Precieuses Ridicules."

West's mother, Lady Langham was now paying her son a visit. Mrs. Montagu writes—

"I think the vast territories of imagination could not afford any view so pleasing as the meeting of such a son and such a mother; the pictures not only pleased my mind, but warm'd my heart . . . that you may at Lady Langham's age be as well able to take a journey, and your son as well deserve, and as joyfully receive such a visit is my sincerest and most earnest wish . . . another pleasure attends you all, and which your benevolence and not your pride will feel, that of setting an example of those various charities, of parent, child, husband and wife, which make the happiness of domestic life; and there is surely more honour in filling well *the circle mark'd of Heaven* in these spheres of relation, than in running the wild career of Ambition in its most shining track. Indeed there is no part of a conduct that so certainly deserves our approbation as an acquittance of family regards. Actions of a public nature often are inspired by vanity, domestic behaviour has not popular applause for its object, tho' with the sober judgment, as Mr. Pope says of silence, '*its very want of voice makes it a kind of fame.*'"

She then proceeds to thank West eloquently for Botham's presentation to *Kingston* (this must be a mistake for Ealing), and ends with desiring some paper hangings "she and Mrs. Isted had laboriously adorned" to be taken down with care at her house at Hayes, but leaves the rest of the hangings to the landlord. "I presume some retail grocer, haberdasher of small wares, or perhaps a tallow chandler, will shortly be in possession of my Castle at Hayes."

At Sandleford were staying young Mr. Hateley, an artist, and Miss Anstey. The latter being in treaty for a house in London, accepted Mr. Montagu's escort thither, and Mr. Hateley wishing to accompany them a portion of the way, mounted a horse, which flung him at the first start off and grievously cut and bruised him. The doctor was summoned after the departure of Mr. Montagu and Miss Anstey, who "blooded him, and he was ordered to take no food but balm tea lest he should have a fever. . . . The Harvest Home Supper last night was very jolly, the guests had as good appetite as those who meet to eat Turtle," writes Mrs. Montagu to her husband on September 23.

Miss Anstey, having lost her parents, and Trumpington having become her brother's property, had determined to live in London. She took Mr. Montagu to help her in choosing a residence in Queen Street, a new-built house for £800. Miss Anstey executed several commissions for Mrs. Montagu, amongst which she mentions, "I have sent several prints of Nun's habits, some one of which I hope may become the beautiful Eloise, and I shall very much rejoice to hear she has taken the Veil."

Mention is made in a previous letter of Mrs. Montagu's of Hateley painting a picture of Eloise, but who sat for it I cannot say. Hateley recovered from his accident. A new post-chaise had been ordered for the Montagus, and Mr. Montagu found it "nothing showy or brilliant," but his wife assures him, "I shall find no fault with the plainness of the post-chaise, neatness being all that is aimed at."

West, writing on October 8 from Wickham, says—

"I have the honour to agree with my dearest and most excellent cousin in looking upon writing letters as one of the evils of Human Life, and for that reason I have always declined engaging in a correspondence of that kind with anybody but her, tho' I was once invited to it by the great Mr. Pope. . . . I am now turning my thoughts towards Chelsea, where I hope to be settled for the whole winter by the beginning of next month. My Mother and Mrs. Ives * go from hence to my brother's † house in the country, where they will remain a week or ten days, and from there return to Lillingston.‡ Mr. and Mrs. Dayrell were prevented by the death of two of his Aunts from making us a visit at Wickham, by which accident and the absence of my sister Molly, my Mother lost the opportunity of exhibiting the pleasing picture of a Hen gathering with a careful and maternal tenderness all her chickens at once under her wings, but she will have them by turns."

From this it would appear that Mrs. Dayrell was a daughter of Lady Langham's. The Dayrells have owned Lillingston Dayrell for some eight hundred years!

Mrs. Medows writes from Chute on October 16 to Mrs. Montagu—

"I am impatient to wait on you; all the horses and all the Maids have been taken up with Wey Hill Fair,§

* Mrs. Ives appears to be Lady Langham's sister.

† Temple West.

‡ Lillingston Dayrell in Bucks.

§ On October 10 and five following days.

now I hope to hire a couple of cart-horses: I dare not venture with a common postboy and horses, because the postboys are not used to a four-wheeled chaise, nor the Road I must go. . . . I wish you joy of a pleasure for life at least, the good you have done to Mr. Botham and his family. . . . I am pleased you have hired the wood, now one may walk in the bowling green without coveting what is your neighbour's. I hope hiring is a step to purchasing; laying field to field is a natural thought and not a blameable one, when no injustice is meant. I have often thought what a pretty place Sandleford would be if it was bounded by the little river, Newbury Wash, and Greenham Heath."

This wood was on the east side of Sandleford, and was eventually purchased, and Sandleford at this moment is bounded exactly as Mrs. Medows wished.

"A Buck, we are told, is come to Grateley, his name is Mitchell, he has laid out a £1000 in furnishing it completely, altho' he could not be sure of having it more than a year. He intends to keep Stags in the paddocks, and turn them out on the Downs, which will give him fine chases. He says the Drawing room is a good drinking room."

Sarah Scott and Lady Bab Montagu had taken a house at Bath Easton for use in the summer, and desiring plants for the garden there, Mrs. Montagu sends on November 6 to them a vast number of pinks, roses and honeysuckles, together with a home-cured ham In the accompanying letter she mentions Ealing being

"two hundred pounds a year, his house a very pretty one, a good garden with a great deal of wall fruit, and there is a neighbourhood of genteel people, who have all shown him great civility. . . . Mr. Hateley is still with us, he has made a very pretty Landskip (*sic*) with Eloisa, and her figure is pretty, her face amiably triste. He has done my portrait so like, and got a good likeness, and with a spirit in the countenance and attitude that is very uncommon."

To this Sarah writes on November 17, to thank her for the plants and to say she and Lady Barbara had returned to Bath for the winter, Bath Easton being too near the water for them. She says—

"Have I sent you word of a subscription making for Nash? I believe it began since I wrote last. It is entitled a subscription for a 'History of Bath and Tunbridge for these last 40 years,' by Richard Nashe, Esqre., with an Apology for the Author's life. The whole money, two guineas, is to be paid down at once, for he does not pretend any book is to come out. Some have subscribed 10 guineas, many five, and a great many hundred pounds are already subscribed. It is to be kept open for life, and people give to him who will not part with a guinea to relieve the greatest real and unmerited distress imaginable. The pretence is that he has but little more than £200 a year, which is not supposed true, but if it was, surely it is full equal to his merits, whether one considers them as moral or entertaining. To such ladies as have secret histories belonging to them, he hints that he knows every one's private life and shall publish it. This place grows so full of subscriptions that no person of moderate fortune will long be able to come to it. The people of the rooms are endeavouring to obtain a subscription of half a guinea each man, and a crown each woman for the season. As yet it has not been complied with, but they require it with such insolence, that I make no doubt it will be complied with. I shall be glad to hear you are safely settled in Hill Street. I assure you the picture * you were so good as to give me is a great ornament to a pretty room, and people are so civil to me as to see the

* A portrait of Mr. Montagu.

likeness, which I take well of them; as it is placed near the fire it may grow warmer, which is all that can improve it."

"Beau" Nash had reigned a despotic Master of the Ceremonies over Bath for fifty years, living in a most expensive style, mainly supported by his success at the gaming tables. The Act of Parliament against gambling put an end to his chief means of obtaining money. The Corporation, however, settled a pension of 120 guineas on him for his services. He was eighty-one years old at this period, having been born in 1673. His rules for general behaviour and manners are most amusing, but are too long to insert.

At this time Mr. Pitt became engaged to Lady Hester Grenville, daughter of Mr. Richard Grenville and his wife, Lady Temple, and sister of Viscount Cobham. She was a cousin of West's and Sir George Lyttelton's.

On November 5 Mrs. Montagu writes to West—

"MY DEAR COUSIN,

"Since the days that Cupid set Hercules to the distaff, he has not had a nobler conquest than over the elevated soul of Mr. Pitt. I congratulate you on the affinity, and I hope he will be happy: his long acquaintance with the lady makes the hazard much less than where people marry without knowing the disposition of the person they choose. I believe Lady Hester Grenville is very good-humoured, which is the principal article in the happiness of the Marriage State. Beauty soon grows familiar to the lover, wit may be pernicious, and many brilliant qualities troublesome; but a companion of gentle disposition softens cares and lightens sorrows. The sober matches made on reflection, are often happier than those made by sudden and violent passion, and I hope this will prove of this kind; and there is an authority in the character of Mr. Pitt, that

T. Rowlandson, pxt.]

THE KING'S BATH, AT BATH.

[*To face p.* 60, *vol. ii.*

will secure him the deference and obedience of his wife; proud of him abroad, she will be humble to him at home; and having said so much, I consign them over to Hymen, who, I hope, will join their hands in the most auspicious hour. I was prevented writing to you by Sunday's post, Dr. Pococke having stayed with us on Saturday night, and the first Sunday of the month I always go to Newbury Church;* the length of the service made me too late to write. I am glad Mr. Cambridge has been with you at Wickham. . . . We were in Wiltshire last week to visit Mrs. Medows."

She ends with expressing a wish to exchange the country for London, but is determined not to say a word to Mr. Montagu, whose health had been recently restored by country air.

In her next letter to West, of November 14, she says—

"As the Virtues and Graces as well as Cupid and Hymen will assist at Mr. Pitt's nuptials, I think he could not choose a better place for their celebration than Wickham, their capital seat. I wish them many happy years together, and God bless them with health and every good. . . . I hope while you are at Croydon the good Archbishop will animate you to defy that foul fiend my Lord Bolingbroke; I believe I shall take some of Ward's sneezing powder to clear my head of the impieties and impurities of his book. I am not satisfied with Mr. Warburton's† answer, the levity shocks me, the indecency displeases me, the *grossièreté* disgusts me. I love to see the doctrine of Christianity defended by the spirit of Christianity. When absurdity is mix'd with impiety, it ceases to be a jest. I can laugh at his Lordship's cavils at Mr. Locke, his envy to Plato and

* St. Nicholas, Newbury. They generally attended Newtown church, as it was nearer.

† Rev. William Warburton, born 1698, died 1779. Chaplain to the King; Bishop of Gloucester; author of various works.

all the old Philosophers, but I could with great seriousness apply to him the words of his friend and Poet to the Dunces—

> "'Tis yours a Bacon and a Locke to blame,
> A Newton's genius or a Milton's flame.
> But oh! with one, immortal one dispense
> The source of Newton's light or Bacon's sense.'

But I must do his Lordship the justice to say that what he wants in faith he makes up in confidence, for after having assured you it is absurd to affirm God is just or good, he declared he is willing to trust the being whose attributes he cannot know, to dispose of him in another world, not at all doubting that the Supreme Being will be good to him, without goodness, and just to him without justice! He laughs at the faith of Abraham, and I should do so too, if Abraham had disputed God's veracity, and then trusted to His promises. I never read such a mass of inconsistencies and contradictions, such a vain ostentation of learning, and if I durst, I would say it, all that can show 'the trifling head, or the corrupted heart.' I think I may venture to say trifling, for whatever does not relate to the argument is so, and to teize the gentle reader with all the miserable sophisms that perplex'd the world 2000 years ago, is barbarous. I wanted to apply to him the Epigram on Hearne* the antiquarian—

> "'Fye on thee! quoth Time to Thomas Hearne,
> Whatever I forget, you learn. . . .'

I thank his Lordship, though, for making me once more look into Mr. Locke and Doctor Clarke,† in the veneration of whom I believe I shall live and dye."

The return letter from West is so interesting that I give it *in extenso*—

* Thomas Hearne, born 1678, died 1735; antiquarian and author.

† Samuel Clarke, D.D., born 1675, died 1729; celebrated theologian and natural philosopher.

"Croydon, November 18, 1754.

"My dear Cousin,

"Your admirable letter found me at the Archiepiscopal Palace at Croydon, where Mrs. West, Dick and I had been ever since Wednesday; and it was lucky that it found me there, as I had by that means an opportunity of showing the Archbishop, whom you very properly style good, your most ingenious and judicious Reflections of Lord Bolingbroke's pompous Rhetorical and inconsistent Declamations with which his Grace (who, by the bye agrees entirely with you in the censure you there pass'd upon Mr. W(arburton)'s way of answering him,) was so pleas'd that he desired me to give him a copy of the whole paragraph, promising that if he show'd it to anybody he would, however, cautiously conceal the name of the author. After this I need not tell you how much we both said in praise of you; I shall only add that I, this morning, received his commands to present his respects to you, and to tell you in his name that if you allow'd yourself the liberty of saying fine things of him, he would be even with you. These are his own words, grounded on a piece of information I had given him of the great honour and esteem you had for him. We quitted Wickham, as I told you, on Wednesday last, that we might throw no obstacle in the way of that amorous impatience which Mr. Pitt had in all his notes express'd of bringing Lady Hester to our sweet and hospitable Habitation, as he call'd it; but to our great surprise, and to the no small mortification of Mrs. West in particular, who was afraid that all the good things, with which she had fill'd her larder, would be spoil'd by their delay—the happy Bridegroom and his Bride did not arrive till Saturday, on which morning they were married * by Dr. Ayscough † with the Archbishop's License. They came down alone, and have continued alone ever since, and, I imagine, will

* Married November 16, 1754, by special license, in Argyll Street.

† Rev. Francis Ayscough, D.D., married Anne Lyttelton, Sir George's sister.

continue during their stay at Wickham, in that Paradisaical Solitude, tho' by the quantity of provisions which Mr. Campion * brought with him, and more which he has since sent for from Croydon, we conclude he expected some visitants from Town, as Lord Temple, etc.,† but having heard of no such visitants being expected, I suppose that all this profusion was owing to Mr. Campion's solicitude to testify in his own way his respects to his new Lady, and make his compliments on this joyous occasion, in the polite, that is, in the French Phraseology: this is all the intelligence I can at present give you of this important affair, for we have had no communication by messages, either to or from Mr. Pitt, whom we were unwilling to disturb, or interrupt the free course of those pleasures, which for a time at least, possess the whole mind, and are most relished when most private; for this reason I cannot yet acquaint you when we shall leave Wickham, but I believe it will be about the middle of this week, and I suppose we shall not be able to go to Chelsea before the latter end of the next, or the beginning of the week after, and by that time I am still in hopes you will come to Hill Street, and by giving me the pleasure of seeing you there in good health, compleat the happy change which you observe is already begun in the once gloomy month of November. I do often, my dear Cousin, look back with pleasure and thankfulness on many incidents of my past Life, and compare them with my present situation, so much changed for the better in a thousand instances, such as Health, fortune and Friendship, among which there is none that has given me more happiness than yours, and which therefore I hope will continue, till it is lost where only it can be lost, in the brighter and warmer radiance of an unchangeable and everlasting Society, where I hope to have it continued to me through all eternity. I am going to take the air with the good and amiable Archbishop, and therefore must conclude.

* The chef. † Richard, Earl Temple, brother of Lady Hester.

W Hoare. R.A. Pinx. Emery Walker Ph. Sc.

Philip, 4th Earl of Chesterfield.

"Adieu, my dear, dear Cousin, and assure yourself that all that period I shall continue

"Ever most affectionately Yours, etc.,

"GIL. WEST.

"Mrs. West and Mrs. Herring desire their compliments to Mrs. Montagu and Miss Anstey."

I give a portion of the reply to the foregoing letter—

"Hill Street, November 23, 1754.

"MY DEAREST COUSIN,

"From country Joan I am, according to my ambitious views, turned into 'Gossip' Joan, and by no supernatural metamorphosing power, but merely by the help of so ordinary a vehicle as a post-chaise, which wrought this happy change between the hours of 7 in the morning and 5 in the afternoon; the subject, no doubt was well prepared that would so easily receive the alteration. In my town character I made 15 visits last night: I should not so suddenly have assumed my great Hoop if I had not desired to pay the earliest respect to Lady Hester Pitt. I came to town on Wednesday night, and was too weary to write to you. I proposed doing it on Thursday evening, but my brother Robinson hinder'd me by making a long visit. Yesterday morning was divided amongst Milliners, Mantua makers, Mercers and such as deal in the small wares of vanity."

The year ends with a letter from Mr. Nathaniel Hooke—

"Cookham, December 22, 1754.

"MADAM,

"If it were not for a certain text of Scripture, I should be very impatient for the time to come when I must be in London for some days. The idea of

Hill Street and what is to be seen and heard there, is very lively and pressing. But alas! What says St. John the Divine? *Little children keep yourselves from Idols.* If you can satisfy my conscience in this point I shall be much obliged to you, and I beg you will study it thoroughly, and let me have your Resolution by a line, directed to be left at Mr. Watson's in Cavendish Street. 'Tis uncertain just now *when* I shall move, but I think it will be some time this week. Till then I am not your religious worshipper, but Madam,

"Your most obliged and most obedient
and most humble Servant,
"N. HOOKE.

"Give me leave to add best compliments to Mr. Montagu."

CHAPTER II.

1755–1757—IN LONDON, AT SANDLEFORD, AT TUNBRIDGE WELLS, AND WITH THE BOSCAWENS AT HATCHLANDS —LETTERS ON EVENTS OF THE WAR.

In January, 1755, but with no date of day, is a letter of Mrs. Montagu's to Sarah Scott on Lord Montfort * committing suicide after gambling heavily.

"I imagine that you will be glad to hear the history of the times, which indeed bring forth daily wonders; nor is it the least that the most profound arithmetician and the greatest calculator, one who carried Demoivre's † 'Probabilités de la Vie Humaine' in his pocket, never foresaw that spending ten times his income would ruin his fortune, and that he found no way to make the book of debtor and creditor even, but paying that debt which dissolves all other obligations. You will guess I mean Lord Montfort and his pistol. He had not discovered any marks of insanity, on the contrary, all was deliberate, calm and cool; having said so much of his indiscretion, I think, with the rest of the world, I may acquit him of the imputation of cunning and sharping, but what can one say in defence of a conduct that had all the appearance of deep knavery and the consequences of inconsiderate rashness and folly. . . . Many reasons have

* Lord Montfort shot himself on January 1, 1755, at White's Coffee House, after playing whisk all night. *Vide* Horace Walpole's "Letters to George Montagu," vol. i. p. 252.

† Abraham Demoivre, born 1677, died 1754. Great mathematician; wrote "The Doctrine of Chances," etc.

been given for his Lordship's violent act, but by what I learn from those best acquainted with his person and fortune, he was not under the pressure of any very heavy debt, but had a true Epicurean character, loved a degree of voluptuousness that his fortune could not afford, and a splendour of life it could not supply, much of his relish for the world was lost, and like one that has no appetite to ordinary fare, chose to rise from table unless fortune would make him a feast. . . . When Lord Montfort's children were paid their demands on his estate, I hear he had only £1200 a year clear, and in table, equipage and retinue he equalled, and in the first article perhaps excell'd, the largest fortunes. To retrench or die was the question, he reasoned like Hamlet, but left out the great argument of a future state."

In the same letter is—

"I have lately been engaged in a melancholy employment, condolence with poor Mr. and Mrs. West on the loss of their son, who died of a bilious fever, occasioned by his want of attendance to the jaundice, which attacked him in the season of plays and Operas, and he preferred them to the care of his health; he died very suddenly, the poor parents bear the blow with surprising patience. Mr. Lyttelton* is going to S. Carolina as Governor, and his sister dreading such a separation desires to accompany him.

"Pray have you read Mr. Hume's History of James I. and Charles I.? I am afraid it will rather promote Jacobitism, but it is entertaining and lively and will amuse you. . . . I suppose you know there are two volumes of Madame de Sevigné's letters come out this winter; they are amusing as the anecdotes of a person one has a great regard for, but they were rejected in former editions as not being so brilliant as those published before. My brother Robinson is emulating the

* This was William Henry, brother of Sir George Lyttelton.

great Diogenes and other budge Drs. of the Stoic fur; he flies the delights of London and leads a life of such privacy and seriousness as looks to the beholder like wisdom, but for my part, I think no life of inaction deserves that name."

This is the first mention of Matthew's increasing love of retirement and the hermit-like habits which he adopted at Horton.

In March occurs a long letter from Mrs. Pococke, of Newtown, the very learned lady mentioned before. She dispensed money for charitable purposes given by Mrs. Montagu. She mentions that her son, Dr. Pococke, is coming for a few days to see her before going abroad, "probably for the last time, unless I live to the age of the late Bishop of Man." She mentions having walked eight miles that day as an excuse for bad writing, which was superfluous, as her handwriting is amazingly good and clear, and she was between eighty and ninety! *Mens sana in corpore sano!*

On June 9, presumably in this year, Mrs. Montagu writes—

"I suppose you know that Lady Sandwich has at last left her kind Lord. To complete the measure of of his good usage, he keeps her daughter to educate with the Miss Courtenays. I hope her Ladyship will be happier than she has been for many years, she has nothing to harass her but the apprehensions for Lady Mary, but God knows that is a dreadful object. She has taken a house at Windsor for the summer." This daughter died June 25, 1761.

And in the same month to Sarah Scott, she says—

Mrs. Boscawen and Miss Pitt came from Hatchlands to London to spend two days with me; we went to

Vauxhall each night, and Mrs. Anstey and I went with them as far as Epsom: we saw Lord Baltimore's house, [*sic*] which speaks bad french, so I will not rehearse what I saw there. Why should I teize your imagination with strawberry colour'd wainscotts, doors of looking-glass, fine landskips on gilt leather, and painted pastorals with huge headed Chloes and gouty legg'd Strephons, with french mottoes to explain those tender glances. We were glad to quit this palace of bad taste for a little arbor in the garden of the inn at Epsom. The Sunday following Mr. Montagu and I went to dine with Mr. Bower at Sidcop, his little habitation has the proper perfections of a cottage, neatness, chearfulness, and an air of tranquillity, a pretty grove with woodbines twining round every Elm, a neat kitchen garden, with an Arbor from whence you look on a fine prospect. Here he may write of heresies and schisms, of spiritual pride and papal usurpations, while peaceful retirement and the amenity of the scene about him, rob controversy of its acrimony, and allay the bitterness of censure by a mixture of gentle pity."

Writing to Mrs. Boscawen from Sandleford, June 19, Mrs. Montagu begins—

"'When the Mower whets his scythe,
And the Milk-maid singeth blythe,
And every Shepherd in the dale
Under the Hawthorn tells his tale,'

there am I, and no longer in the sinfull and smoaking City of London; this happy change was brought about on Tuesday, by very easy and speedy measures. We got into our post-chaise between 10 and 11, arrived at Maidenhead Bridge about one; were refreshed by a good dinner, and amused by good company. Mr. Hooke* meeting us at our inn, we staid with him till after 5, and about ten arrived at Sandleford. . . . I have not for these

* He was then living at Cookham.

ten years been so early in the Season at Sandleford, and it appears therefore with greater charms. It cannot afford to lose any of its natural beauties, as it owns none to Art, it is merely a pretty shepherdess, who has no graces but those of youth and simplicity; but my dear Mrs. Boscawen may turn it into a paradise when she pleases. When may I hope to see her here. . . . I spent two days at Wickham last week; our good friends had left the Archbishop of Canterbury only a few days before I went to them. Mr. West seemed a good deal affected by this return to Wickham, as to Mrs. West I cannot so well judge, the cheerfulness she puts on is *outré*. . . . Mr. West told me he would alter the room where poor Dick dyed, for he did not like to go into it, and then a soft tender shower fell down his cheeks, he added he had lost much of his relish for Wickham; however on the whole I found them better than I could have expected!"

Directly after this, West was ordered to Tunbridge Wells, where he was accompanied by Lady Cobham, Miss Speed, and his wife. He writes to Mrs. Montagu that he hopes she will like a long stay in the country, as its tranquillity will not

"produce the same effect which an Admiral of my acquaintance found from the tranquillity of his friend's house in the country, to which coming directly from his ship, where he had been so long accustomed to noise and bustle as to be grown fond of it, said, after having passed a restless night, 'Pox on this house, 'tis so quiet there is no sleeping in it.'"

To this letter she answers—

"Mr. Montagu has been studiously disposed ever since we came to Sandleford, so that I pass seven or eight hours every day entirely alone. Five months are to pass before I return to the Land of the Living, but

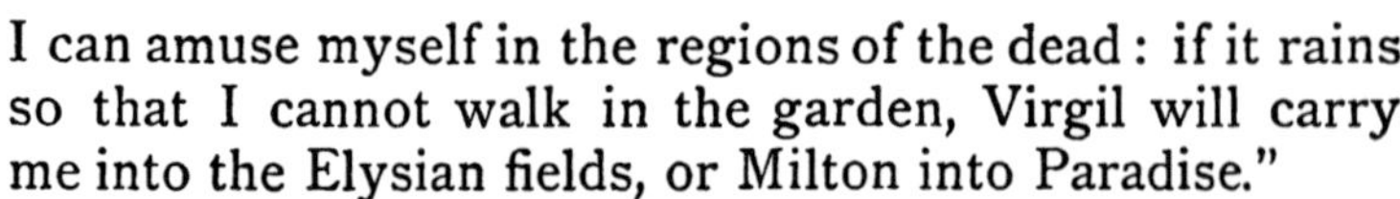

I can amuse myself in the regions of the dead: if it rains so that I cannot walk in the garden, Virgil will carry me into the Elysian fields, or Milton into Paradise."

Mention is also made of Sam Torriano's engagement to Miss Scudamore, "who is said to have been handsome, and it was on both sides a marriage of inclination. He has delicacy enough to make him very happy or very miserable, and restlessness enough to be very uneasy in a state too insipid to allow of neither."

Mrs. Montagu might well make this remark on Torriano's marriage, as her friend Sir George Lyttelton's * second matrimonial contract had by mutual consent ended in a separation. In a former letter it will be remembered that the haughty tone and unpleasant manners of the lady were commented on. It was a case of incompatibility of temper and thought, and a constant imagination of bad health on her part. Lady Lyttelton was a great friend of the Wests, and from a letter of Lyttelton's to West of this year it is evident that a little coldness, which did not endure long, had sprung up between West and his friend.

On July 8 and July 14 Sir George Lyttelton writes to Archibald Bower a complete diary of his tour in North Wales, accompanied by "Parson Durant and Mr. Payne." These letters Bower gave to Mrs. Montagu. They contain many messages to the "Madonna," but are, though interesting, too long to insert here. At this period West was at Tunbridge Wells, seeking health, but depressed at the absence of Pitt, Lyttelton, Torriano, and, above all, Mrs. Montagu; and from this letter it appears that 1750 was the year in which they first made friends at Tunbridge. "Where are the happy seasons of 1750, 1751, 1752, and 1753?" he cries. "In the 'Stone House'

* With Miss Rich, daughter of Field-Marshal Sir Robert Rich.

are Mr. Walpole and Lady Rachel, persons with whom I have no concern." The only people he now consorts with are Mrs. Vesey, to whom he talks of Mrs. Montagu, "we both love and honour you;" and Bishop Gilbert and his daughter.* The Bishop of London was expected. West laments "a difficulty of breathing, accompanied with wheezing," he thought asthma. "The Doctors said Hysterical as only fit for *petticoats!*" They prescribed assafœtida, valerian, and gum ammoniac. He laments that Torriano "has done the irrevocable deed, and is married on £500 per annum."

In Mrs. Montagu's answer to West of July 13 she laments Torriano's marriage not only as

"the world will lose him, but as he is to lose the world, which with all its faults is not to be entirely quitted; man and wife should always have something to charge with their ennui, the impertinence of society bears the blame very well, in solitude they must accuse each other of all they suffer of it. I do not understand why they should live in Herefordshire, unless they are very fond of cyder, for, in my opinion, London is the best place for people of moderate circumstances. In the country people are respected merely according to the acres they possess, an equipage is necessary, and company must be entertained at a great expense. . . . I am afraid his friend Stillingfleet † has left Herefordshire. . . . Last Tuesday Mr. Botham came hither, as did Dr. Gregory,‡ an ingenious agreeable man. Miss Pitt § has arrived here to my great joy, and we are to go to Hatchlands on Thursday."

* Miss Gilbert became Countess of Mount Edgecumbe.

† Dr. Benjamin Stillingfleet, born 1702, died 1771. Author of "Calendar of Flora," etc., and a prominent member of the Bas Bleu circle.

‡ Dr. John Gregory, physician and miscellaneous writer; Professor of Philosophy at Edinburgh.

§ Mary Pitt, sister of Mr. W. Pitt.

Hatchlands, near Guildford, belonged to Admiral Boscawen. Writing thence to her husband Mrs. Montagu says—

"We were received by Mrs. Boscawen with the most joyful welcome, as we found her in great spirits on account of the taking of the two French men of war. Mr. Hoquart had been taken twice by Mr. Boscawen in the last war, but did not surrender himself in this engagement till 44 men were killed on board of his ship. Mr. Boscawen writes that he lived at great expence, having 11 French officers at his table, whom he entertains with magnificence, and there were 8 companies of soldiers on board the *Alcide* and the *Lys.* I hope as Admiral Holborn has joined Mr. Boscawen, we may soon hear of a more considerable victory. . . . The Duke* declares himself well pleased with Mr. Boscawen for his enterprise. . . . Mr. Boscawen was very much concern'd that the *Dauphin*, which had stands of arms and some silver on board, has escaped by means of a fog. . . ."

On July 27, to West, is this—

"Monsieur Mirepoix† threatened us with *la guerre la plus sanglante qui fut jamais*, but by his *dépit* I imagine the French would have been better pleased if we would have let them silently and quietly possess themselves of the West Indies.

"I walked round the park this morning, it does not consist of many acres, but the disposition of the ground, the fine verdure and the plantations make it very pretty: it resembles the mistress of it, having preserv'd its native simplicity, tho' art and care has improv'd and soften'd it, and made it elegant."

She mentions a miserable inn on Bagshot Heath, which they drove over, "situated in the middle of a

* Duke of Cumberland. † The French ambassador.

dreary Heath, which has been famous for robberies and murders. The inn has for its sign the effigies of a man who practised this dreadful trade 40 years."

Whilst at Hatchlands Mrs. Boscawen took her guest to Sheep Leas, belonging to Mr. Weston, also to Sir John Evelyn's and Mr. Hamilton's places. Of Sheep Leas, in a letter to Sarah, who was with Lady Barbara at Badminton, is this description—

"The Sheep Lees consists of a most beautiful down, adorn'd with noblest beeches, commanding a rich gay and extensive prospect, a prodigious flock of sheep enliven the scene; it has a noble simplicity, and one imagines it to be the abode of some Arcadian Prince. . . . Our next visit was to Sir John Evelyn's,* you pass over a high hill, finely planted, at the bottom of which lies the good old seat, which is venerable and respectable, and put me in mind of the song of 'the Queen's old Courtier,' and it has a library of good old books, handsome apartments furnished and fitted up just as left them by their ancestor, the Sylvan Evelyn.† I cannot but own that tired of papier maché ceilings and gilt cornices, I was glad to see an old hall such as ancient hospitality and the plain virtues of our ancestors used to inhabit before country gentlemen used to make fortunes in Parliament or lose them at 'White's,' hunted foxes, instead of Ministers, and employ'd their finesse in setting partridges. The garden at Sir John Evelyn's is adorn'd with *jets d'eaux* in the old style, then you pass on to the woods, which are great and noble, and lye on each side a fine valley."

Mrs. Ann Evelyn is mentioned as deserving this habitation.

"Pray follow me to Mr. Hamilton's:‡ I must tell you

* Leigh Place.

† John Evelyn, born 1620, died 1706. Author of the "Sylva, or Discourse on Forest Trees," etc., etc.

‡ Painshill.

it beggars all description, the art of hiding art is here in such sweet perfection, that Mr. Hamilton cheats himself of praise, you thank Nature for all you see, tho' I am inform'd all has been reformed by Art. In his 300 acres you have the finest lawns, a serpentine river playing in the sweetest valley, hills finely planted, which command charming prospects, winding walks made gay with flowers and flowering Shrubs, part of a rude forest, sombre woods, a river deep and still, gliding round the woods and shaded by trees that hang over the bank, while the serpentine river open and exposed to the sun, adorn'd with little Islands and enlivened by waterfowls, gladdens the vallies."

At the end of this letter mention is made of Travile, a poor lady originally recommended by Lady Sandwich as lady's-maid to Mrs. Montagu. She was dying of consumption. Three doctors had treated her, and now Dr. Gregory put her on a diet of vegetable and asses' milk.

Mr. Botham, writing from Albury, July 23, 1755, says—

"A Captain Cunningham past through Guildford last night express from the Governor of Hallifax in Nova Scotia with advice that Col. Warburton of the land forces had taken a fort at the back of Louisbourg called Bouche, (by the bye the most material Fort belonging to the French settlements), 500 men and 20 cannon; that the Colonel had blocked up Louisbourg by land, and Admiral Boscawen had done the same by sea; that the town was very bare of provisions and must soon surrender, and the sooner as the Colonel has turned in the 500 brethren to help to consume the faster; so that there is great reason to suppose we shall soon be masters of Louisbourg, and the Admiral of the 4 French men of war blocked in the Harbour. We have taken papers of the utmost consequence, which let us into the secret schemes of the French, which were nothing less than a design of taking all our Plantations from us in America, and Hallifax in the first place, was destined for destruction."

West, writing on August 22 from Tunbridge Wells, mentions that Lady Cobham and Harriet had left them for Stoke, Mrs. Vesey was returning to Ireland, and the Bishop of London had just left, "but while he was here put into my hands some sheets of a third Volume of Discourses now printing, which, as I had the chief hand in prevailing upon him to publish, I received as a mark of his regard for me." The bishop was then in very bad health. West was persuaded by the three doctors, Duncan, Burgess, and Morley, to stay on at Tunbridge Wells.

In a letter to Miss Anstey, who was with her friends, Lord and Lady Romney, at Brighthelmstone, Mrs. Montagu says that Miss Pitt had left her to join her brother, Mr. Pitt, and Lady Hester, at Sunninghill.* Mrs. Montagu accompanied her as far as Reading,

"where we dined in the garden of the inn, from whence there is a fine gay prospect, and after dinner we walked to see the ruins of the old Abbey, which was most delightfully situated. The river winds about the richest meadows I ever saw; hills crowned with woods and adorn'd by some gentlemen's houses bound the prospect, and make it the most soft and agreeable landscape imaginable."

She and Mr. Montagu were contemplating visiting Mrs. Scott and Lady Bab Montagu at Bath Easton, "but I do not propose to leave poor Travile as long as she continues in this life; her end draws very near." The invalid seems to have been most religious, and one

* Sunning Hill, at that time rising in repute for its mineral wells.

learns that by her request Mrs. Montagu nightly read her the Service for the Sick.

On September 26, West informs Mrs. Montagu that the Archbishop of Canterbury * had written to tell him of the release of Governor Lyttelton, who, with his sister, had been taken prisoners by the French in the *Blandford*, which was conveying the Governor to his province, South Carolina. This was William Henry, brother of Sir George, and his sister Hester. The *Blandford* was soon after this given up by the French. Mary Pitt, writing to Mrs. Montagu, said that Governor Lyttelton's only loss was his wine and provisions on the *Blandford*, he having sent most of his baggage by another ship.

Mr. Pitt was then at Bath, while Lady Hester awaited her confinement at the Pay Office, of which Pitt was then master. Miss Pitt says, the sudden arrival of Governor Lyttelton "has proved very fortunate for Sir George at Bewdley,† where, by the Election of a Bayliff, the Borough was gone, if his brother had not thus dropt out of the clouds to give his vote and the turn to the scale."

Travile becoming slightly better, Mrs. Montagu went to Bath Easton to visit Mrs. Scott and Lady Bab Montagu. In a letter to Dr. Gilbert West, October 16, after her return to Sandleford, the following account is given of the life led by the two lady friends :—

"My sister rises early, and as soon as she has read prayers to their small family, she sits down to cut out and prepare work for 12 poor girls, whose schooling they pay for; to those whom she finds more than ordinarily capable, she teaches writing and arithmetic herself. The work these children are usually employed in is making child-bed linen and clothes for poor people

* Rev. Dr. Thomas Herring. † Bewdley, Worcestershire.

in the neighbourhood, which Lady Bab Montagu and she, bestow as they see occasion. Very early on Sunday morning these girls, with 12 little boys whom they also send to school, come to my sister and repeat their catechism, read some chapters, have the principal articles of their religion explained to them, and then are sent to the parish church. These good works are often performed by the Methodist ladies in the heat of enthusiasm, but thank God, my sister's is a calm and rational piety. Her conversation is lively and easy, and she enters into all the reasonable pleasures of Society; goes frequently to the plays, and sometimes to balls, etc. They have a very pretty house at Bath for the winter, and one at Bath Easton for the summer; their houses are adorned by the ingenuity of the owners, but as their income is small, they deny themselves unnecessary expenses. My sister* seems very happy; it has pleased God to lead her to truth, by the road of affliction; but what draws the sting of death and triumphs over the grave, cannot fail to heal the wounds of disappointment. Lady Bab Montagu concurs with her in all these things, and their convent, for by its regularity it resembles one, is really a cheerful place."

Writing to Sarah Scott of their safe return from Bath Easton, Mrs. Montagu says—

"You would hardly imagine that the calm, meek Miss Pococke† is as great a heroine as Thalestris, Boadicea, or any of the termagant ladies in history. One Wednesday night, she was awaken'd by a robber, who threw himself across her bed and demanded her money; she started up, seized him with one hand and rang her bell with the other, and held him till the maid came into the room, but at last he broke from her, and by the ill-

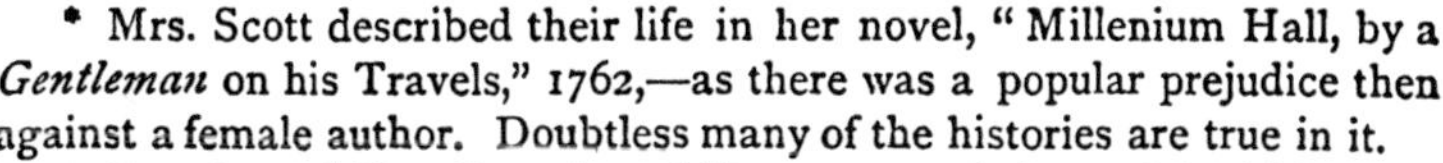

* Mrs. Scott described their life in her novel, "Millenium Hall, by a *Gentleman* on his Travels," 1762,—as there was a popular prejudice then against a female author. Doubtless many of the histories are true in it.

† Daughter of Mrs. Pococke, of Newtown, and sister of the bishop.

management of her assistants made his escape. He is our late Gardener's son, whom you may remember a boy in the gardens, his name Moses. He attempted to break open our house two nights before, opened the parlour sash, but could not force the shutters, which I am glad he did not do, for any alarm to the poor sick woman would have been a grievous thing."

Mrs. Donnellan, in a letter from Fulham, August 28, reproached Mrs. Montagu "for not having visited Mrs. Southwell and me, for actually from Bagshot to her house is not quite 3 miles and a straight road. . . . My very near relation and friend, my Lord Mornington * and his son † and *my godson* young Wesley, are at London and come often to me."

"I shall hope to make you acquainted with them next winter; you have known my regards to them, the son is the best creature I ever knew of his age, his whole attention is to make his Father as happy as he can, who is greatly hurt since the death of his daughter, Mrs. Fortescue.‡ The young man's behaviour to me is like a tender child to a parent, so you may believe he must engage me; he says he shall not think of marrying till he is of age, and assures me I shall have a negative in his choice, you may believe he is not likely to meet one from the ladies as his estate will be a good ten thousand a year all within 25 miles of Dublin. . . . The Duke and Duchess of Portland, and the Marquis, and young ladies have been at D'Ewes § at Wellesbourne in a tour."

Mrs. Donnellan was in very bad health at this time.

Now occurs a joint letter from Mr. Bower and Sir

* Baron Mornington, cousin through the Ushers to Mrs. Donnellan.

† Garrett *Wesley*, or Wellesley, 1st Earl Mornington; famous for his musical talent; father of the Duke of Wellington.

‡ Elizabeth Wesley, married in 1743, Chichester Fortescue, of Dromisken.

§ Mrs. D'Ewes, *née* Granville, sister of Mrs. Delany's.

George Lyttelton on October 6; the first writing in Italian from Hagley. Bower calls Hagley, "questo Paradiso ed O! Madonna che paradiso! Non v'é luogo sulla terra più degno di tal nome." Further on he assures her that the first volume of the "Life of Henry II." which Sir George was engaged upon, should, as soon as printed, be sent to her. Sir George adds—

"Till Bower came we were very uneasy at your not writing a line to Miss West, nor am I yet without great anxiety for fear that your attendance on the Deathbed of your servant should hurt your health. The goodness of your heart, most amiable Madonna, is too much for its strength. I hope by this time your servant is releas'd from her sufferings here, and you from the sight of them; otherwise I am sure this melancholy office of Virtue and Friendship will cost you dear. I do not blame your obeying the impulse of that most sweet Nature which is all tenderness and Benevolence; but remember you have other friends interested in your health, and for whose sake you ought to take care of it. I have a 1000 more things to say to you, but there is a country gentleman just come to visit me whom I must attend, and Bower brought me his letter, so that the post is just going out. I shall be in London at latest by 10th of November. I need not tell you that Mr. Pitt has made Fox, Secretary of State. After a hard struggle, I have secured my Borough of Bewdley. Adieu, this vexatious man will have me come to him, and the post will not wait."

On October 15, Admiral Boscawen writes to inform Mrs. Montagu of the birth of a daughter stillborn, but that Mrs. Boscawen was doing well.

On October 20 West writes to say that Miss Pitt

"is gone this morning to congratulate Lady Hester and

her brother on the birth of a daughter * of which Lady Hester after a hard and long labour was delivered on Saturday. . . . Miss Pitt returns to us after she has paid her compliments to the happy Father and Mother, and taken an exact survey of this future fair and fine lady."

In a letter to Mr. West of November 1, after congratulating him on the birth of Miss Pitt, Mrs. Montagu says—

"I wish her nurse in the first place, and then her governess, would keep a journal of all the instructions the young lady has, and all her employments, and the world might get a better treatise of education than any yet extant. Mr. Pope says of Voiture 'that trifles themselves were elegant in him,' a moderate praise to a man who dealt only in trifles, but Mr. Pitt mixes the elegant with the sublime."

Great fears were entertained at this time of an invasion by the French. Mrs. Medows writes from Chute to say her brother-in-law, Sir Philip Medows

"has with a grave face told me that in troublesome times such places as Conhault Farm often escaped, by being unseen and out of the way, as it possesses both these advantages, I hope we shall have the benefit of them, and seriously offer you our retreat if anything should happen to make you prefer it to being near a town."

At last, Travile having breathed her last, and Parliament being summoned, the Montagus started for London on November 10, dining that night with Miss Anstey at her new house. Mrs. Montagu tells Mrs. Scott that

* This was Hester, who became Lady Mahon, afterwards Stanhope, mother of the celebrated Lady Hester Stanhope.

W. Hogarth. Pinx. Emery Walker Ph. Sc.

Garrick and his wife
from the picture in the possession of H.M. The King.

"I find the town very busy; the men are full of Politicks, the Ladies of the Birthday Cloaths. New Ministers and new fashions are interesting subjects, but I hear Messrs. Legge, Pitt, and Grenville, tho' against the subsidy, are not to be turned out. What gives me most concern is Mr. Boscawen's delay; the Admiralty do not know where he is or what he is doing, he may be gathering laurels, but as they are a deadly plant, I could wish he was at his inglorious fireside. I am very uneasy for the poor woman (Mrs. Boscawen) who is still at Portsmouth, if any accident should happen to him I should go post to her. It is thought that a certain great, very great Dowager * has given some discontent to her Father-in-law.† I shall call on the Marechalle D'Ancre the first time I go out to hear what they say on the present situation of affairs. I think between his mysteriousness and her openness one may find out something. I don't believe Signor Concini advised the Dowager to offend the old gentleman. The bell is very clamorous."

This last sentence I place here, as I do not think I have mentioned that at this period a postman was sent round with a bell to collect all the latest letters.

"There is a great bustle at Mr. Garrick's playhouse ‡  about some dancers, though they are chiefly Germans and Swiss, the mob considers them French, and I imagine they will be driven off the stage, tho' the dancers and scenery have cost Mr. Garrick an immense sum; this evening is to decide their fate, and I imagine that at this time there may be a very bloody engagement. I rejoice with you on the gallant behaviour of Captain Stevens animated by your brother, to whom L'Esperance struck to Admiral West,§ but I met Lord Cadogan last night at

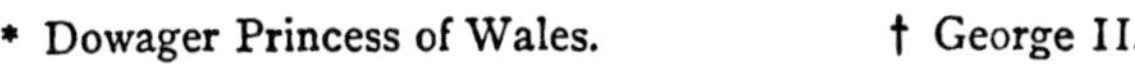

* Dowager Princess of Wales. † George II.

‡ Drury Lane rows every night. On November 15 the Galleries were victorious over the young men of quality, who protected the dancers.

§ Temple West.

Mrs. Southwell's, who said the French did not strike till Mr. West came up to them."

In this letter it is stated that Admiral Boscawen had just returned.

On November 25, in a letter to Sarah Scott, Mrs. Montagu says—

"The House of Commons sat till after 5 o'clock in the morning on the motion for the address, which was carried by 311 against 105, there were many speeches made which were talk'd of in all the drawing rooms in town; with the same cool spirit of criticism you would hear the speeches in a new Play of Mr. Whitehead's,* and Garrick and Mrs. Cibber's manner of speaking them examined. . . . I expected to find the town full of the subsidies,† they are entirely forgot and never did the publick stand by more quiet and contented. Mr. Fox and Mr. Pitt say a great many very lively things to each other, which those who are not personally attach'd to either hear with a great deal of pleasure. Messrs. Legge, Pitt, and Grenville are dismiss'd, but no one positively named to succeed them; Lord Egmont, Lord Dupplin, Mr. Doddington, and Charles Townsend are talk'd of. Sir George Lyttelton is Chancellor of the Exchequer, which place he was sollicited to accept. I wish the fatigue of it may not impair his health, which is very delicate."

Remarking on their friend, Miss Grinfield, being dismissed as Maid of Honour to the Princess of Wales, Mr. Montagu writes—

"I suppose Lord B(ute)'s interest got Mrs. Ditched her place, there is no man has such instinct for the Heir Apparent as his Lordship. I would have him take the 'Ich dien' for his motto, he serves and will serve, the

* Paul Whitehead.

† Aid to be raised in supplying additional troops and seamen.

hour of his ministry will never come. I wish he would leave behind him a treatise on hope, or at least answer Plautus who *grossièrement* decides that hunger, thirst and expectation are the greatest evils of human life. . . . The news will tell you the sad tydings of an earthquake * at Lisbon, some say a 100,000 persons were destroyed by it. The commotion began in the Atlantick Ocean. . . . As to the fuss of an invasion, it chiefly possesses those who have money in the public funds, the state of things consider'd it appears probable. The Boom across the Thames perhaps is to hinder such insults from the French as we once receiv'd from the Dutch; I cannot describe it particularly to you, not having seen it. . . . Lord Temple † very generously wrote a letter to Mr. Pitt in polite and earnest terms to desire his acceptance of a £1000 a year while he continues out of place.

"Voltaire, in compliance with the taste of the age, has written a Chinese tragedy, it is called 'L'orphelin de la Chine.' . . . I have not seen Dr. Delany's remarks on Lord Orrery's ‡ letters, but they certainly deserved the animadversions of Dr. Swift's particular friend."

Through Sir George Lyttelton's influence, Gilbert West was reinstated in his office at Chelsea, which from the change of parties would lapse to the paymaster. The following letter from Sir George hints at the trifling coolness between himself and West:—

"Hill Street, December 13, 1755.

"MY DEAR WEST,

"My endeavours to serve you, which from Lord Dupplin's goodness have proved successful, are indeed marks of affection, but not of *returning* affection. Mine for you has been constant and uniform. What variations may have happened in yours for me I can't tell. Your

* Took place November 1.

† Richard Grenville, Earl Temple, brother-in-law to Mr. Pitt.

‡ Charles Boyle, 4th Earl of Orrery, born 1703, died 1731.

behaviour has certainly indicated some, and I could not but observe it. However, I can most truly assure you that one of my greatest pleasures in my present situation has been it's enabling me to show you that my heart will ever be most eagerly warm in your service. Indeed no Friend you have can more honour your vertue or more affectionately desire your happiness than I," etc.

The last letter of the year, December 31, to West from Mrs. Montagu, contains this mention of Sir George Lyttelton's son, Thomas *—

"Master Lyttelton paid me a visit yesterday morning, it gave me great pleasure to find he had an air of health and strength beyond what I had ever hoped for him; every sentence he utters shows an understanding that is very astonishing. Mr. Torriano and Mr. Stillingfleet came in while he was with me, the share he took in a very grave conversation surprized them very much."

1756 begins with two letters of West's. At the end of January he moved to Chelsea; soon after this a stroke of the palsy brought him to the grave on March 26.

On March 30 Mrs. Montagu writes to her sister—

"Ye 30th March.

"I imagine my dear sister would see a paragraph in the newspaper that would excuse my not having written to her a farther account of my poor friend, Mr. West. On the melancholy event I brought his sister to Hill Street, where she is to stay a few days to recover in some measure the consequences of her fatigue and the shock her spirits have received. Mrs. West is with Lady Cobham. She is sensible of her great loss, but says she will behave under her affliction worthy the

* Afterwards 2nd Lord Lyttelton.

example of her excellent and worthy husband, and his sentiments of resignation to the will of God, this resolution join'd to natural good spirits and vivacity of mind, supports her in a surprizing manner. I wish the good man could have known she would have endured her misfortune so well, apprehensions for her were all that disturbed the peace, I might almost say the joy of his deathbed. Miss West went thro' the sad duties of nursing with great fortitude, but, she is much affected by her loss; the Admiral * his brother is in deep affliction, Lady Langham † finds great resources in a very extraordinary degree of piety. For my part, tho' I went thro' the most melancholy scenes every day between the sick and the afflicted, I have not suffered so much in my health as might have been expected. . . . Lord Chesterfield ‡ has gone to Blackheath in a very bad state of health. The King has had an ague but is well again. . . . Mr. Wortley Montagu § has published a pious pamphlet titled, 'Reflections physical and moral upon the uncommon Phenomena in the air, water or earth which have happened from the Earthquake at Lima, to the present time.' I think you will send to Mr. Lake's for it, it is written on the Hutchinsonian ‖ principles."

Miss West being ordered to Bath, Mrs. Montagu gave her an introduction to Mrs. Scott and Lady Bab Montagu, then residing in Beaufort Square. In this letter mention is made of Miss Anstey's death, and her not having left a will. "Poor Mr. Anstey is not likely to survive his sister, he has a violent fever." We also hear of William Robinson,¶ then recently ordained a curate

* Temple West. † West's mother, then over seventy.

‡ The celebrated statesman, and author of the Chesterfield "Letters" to his son.

§ Old E. Wortley Montagu.

‖ Rev. John Hutchinson, born 1674, died 1734; author of "Moseis Principia."

¶ William was the intimate friend of the poet Gray, who called him the "Rev. Billy."

at Kensington. William seems to have been rather a *souffre douelur* all his life, which annoyed his sister perpetually: his harping on small worries and domestic trifles is constantly alluded to. Mr. Botham bids him "fight a good fight, and by diligence and spirit in his curacy to show himself worthy of a good living."

A heavy affliction now fell on the sisters; early in June came the tidings that their favourite brother Robert, the sea captain, had died at sea. This was acutely felt by Sarah Scott, as he was her favourite brother, probably from being nearest in age to her.

On June 24, in a letter to Mrs. Boscawen, this sad subject is touched on—

"I know not how to reconcile myself to the loss of one of the companions of my youth, the recollections of one's earliest season, the spring of life is usually pleasant and gay, but whenever it offers itself to my mind, I cannot help asking where are those who were my playfellows? Faith should answer, with their Maker, reason, patience, resignation, should take place, but there is a weakness and stubbornness too in the human habit. . . . My poor sister bears her loss patiently, but it touches her heart very sorely."

Mrs. Montagu had been extremely unwell, and had spent some weeks at Ealing Vicarage, lent to her by Mr. Botham. Dr. Shaw ordered her to Tunbridge Wells. Mrs. Boscawen had asked for her letters to Mr. West to be returned; Mrs. West promises to do this. At the end of the letter one reads this—

"Mr. Montagu had just come in from the coffee-house. Mr. Byng's * expedition is unfortunate, not to say disgraceful, instead of throwing succour into Minorca, it

* Admiral John Byng, born 1704, was shot in pursuance of the sentence of a court-martial in 1757.

was agreed in the Council of War that as there were 18,000 Frenchmen there, it would be these men; then it was agitated whether they should engage with the French, that was also carried in the negative; the third question was whether they should go to take care of Gibraltar, which was agreed on. Alas! Alas! the report to-day is that Admiral West's son is dead: one should lament this if we had not greater reason to lament that the English spirit is dead. Arthur was going to make illuminations and bonfires yesterday, and Lord Anson came in and forbade it."

A letter to Sir George Lyttelton to Hagley in return for his condolences runs thus—

"Your publick life will raise a high expectation of your son, it is but just that you should give some of your private hours to qualify him so as to answer it: his happy genius makes him worthy of such a Preceptor. . . . You need but do justice to my affection for him to give me some share of his love."

Sir George had specially commended his son "Tom" to the "Madonna's" care, and they kept up a correspondence. Alas! that in future years, despite his brilliantly intellectual qualities, and his careful bringing up, he should almost break his father's heart by his wild and dissolute life. She continues—

"Most people think that Mr. Byng will have some good excuse, if not justification, for what he has done; but however that may be, Sir Edward Hawke * and Captain Saunders (now made an Admiral) are gone to take command of the fleet."

In a letter of July 28, from Tunbridge to Mr. Montagu, one finds—

* Afterwards Lord Hawke, born 1705, died 1787.

"The people at the Walks were all rejoicing poor Admiral Byng was arrested at Portsmouth. I cannot think of him without some compassion, a criminal is not always an object of mercy, but frail man is ever an object of pity. People here seem to think that a shameful death must end his shameful life. Birth and Station bring a man into an elevated station, but do not give to him the qualities necessary to become it."

Lyttelton, in a letter of August 8, writes to the "Madonna," "the Admiral (Temple West) triumphs and pouts, and is gone to George Grenville's* with Jenny Grenville. He blames Byng, though unwillingly, because he would rather condemn those that sent him"

In another letter is—

"Dr. Shaw tells me that the mob at Portsmouth would not suffer Mr. Byng to be brought away, lest he should escape punishment. It is said that Mr. Boscawen has taken a great number of Martinico ships, and that part of the Brest squadron have got out, and gone to join M. Galissionière.† Mr. Bower's affidavit has had a very good effect. I hope Mr. Millar has got some of them to distribute among his friends in the country. I am sure his good heart will rejoice to see innocence re-instated in reputation."

Bower's enemies had set about many evil reports of him at that period, and Mr. Hooke had specially warned Mrs. Montagu against Bower, but she refused to give up her friendship with one who had been introduced to her by the saintly Gilbert West, and was the intimate friend of Lyttelton. Bower's change in religion from Roman

* George Grenville, born 1712, died 1770; became 1st Lord of the Treasury and Chancellor of the Exchequer, time of George III.

† The French Admiral.

Catholicism to Protestantism exposed him to all the virulence of the priests, who in revenge formulated all sorts of charges against him.

Mrs. Montagu now took a house on Mount Ephraim at Tunbridge Wells, leaving Mr. Montagu in London, from whence he went to Sandleford. She requiring wine, he sends her, from a "new wine merchant," Madeira, port, and claret.

At Tunbridge mention is made of David Hume * and his wife, who were there, the latter in bad health: "I remember her twenty years ago as a fine woman, though swarthy, but she is now a most melancholy object."

Writing to her husband at Sandleford, she says—

"Dr. Smith inquired after you this morning, he is much pleased with your present of Dr. Barrow's † bust to the Library.‡ . . . He is angry with Mrs. Middleton for being so tardy as to Dr. Middleton's bust, at which, I own, I am a little offended. . . . All the people here are impatient for the tryal of Mr. Byng. They say he was surprised at the reception, tho' he had so much reason to expect the treatment he has found. Sir William Milner and his Lady are here, they are people of considerable fortune in Yorkshire, they seem very good-natured and obliging."

Mention is made of Miss Dashwood § being at Tunbridge, much gone off in looks: "Miss Dashwood dined with me yesterday. This place must appear as melancholy to a lady who has formerly been a reigning beauty,

* David Hume, born 1711, died 1776; philosopher and historian.

† The Rev. Dr. Isaac Barrow, born 1630, died 1677; eminent scholar and mathematician; preceptor of Sir Isaac Newton; Master of Trinity College, Cambridge. The bust is by Roubilliac.

‡ The library of Trinity College, Cambridge.

§ The "Delia" of Hammond.

and is on the decline, as the coronation of an usurper to a dethroned Prince!"

During this summer Morris Robinson, Mrs. Montagu's third brother, married Miss Jane Greenland, daughter of John Greenland, of Lovelace, Co. Kent, who was the eldest son of Augustine Greenland, of Belle Vue, Kent. Her mother was Jane Weller, of Kingsgate House, Rolveden, Kent, of a good family. Mrs. Montagu did not like the marriage, though she finally adopted their second son, her nephew,* Matthew Robinson, and made him take the name of Montagu. There never was any cordiality between the sisters-in-law. Mrs. Morris Robinson was a violent-tempered woman, and, despite her good birth, very illiterate, which, to a person like her sister-in-law, was extremely annoying, the more so as Morris was one of her favourite brothers, and extremely clever. As mentioned before, he belonged to the Six Clerks' office, and managed both the legal affairs of the Duke of Montagu and Mr. Montagu.

Writing from Hagley † on August 11, Miss West gives an account of her brave young nephew, who had been wounded, not killed, as at first reported—

"My nephew ‡ is at Portsmouth, not being able to bear travelling. He has been in danger from his wound, it beginning to mortify, but he is now in a fair way of recovery. He has shown a spirit suited to his profession, and to the grandson of Admiral John Balchen,§ for when his Father proposed to send him on board a frigate, with Byng's nephew, who was ordered to leave my brother's ship by his uncle, Admiral Byng, before the engagement began, being, like my nephew, too young to be of use.

* Succeeded his elder brother Morris as 4th Baron Rokeby in 1829.

† Sir George Lyttelton's place in Worcestershire.

‡ Son of Temple West.

§ Admiral Sir John Balchen, born 1669, died 1744.

My nephew remonstrated very strongly, 'that Mr. Byng was only a passenger, but he belonged to the ship he was in, and therefore it would be such a disgrace that he could never show his head again, should he quit it at such a juncture:' this joined to lamentation and importunity prevailed; when he received his wound his Father ran to pick him up and said, 'I hope you are not much hurt?' 'I believe I am killed, but pray don't mind me, Papa,' answered the poor fellow. . . . Hagley is now blessed with its master, who came on Monday last with good health, looks and spirits. I was glad to see him accompanied by Stillingfleet, so worthy a man deserves such a countenance, and he is so unexceptionable that no censure can arise from any favours confer'd on him."

Sarah Scott at this time had a dangerous fever at Clifton, where she and Lady Bab had gone to drink the waters. Writing to her, Mrs. Montagu remarks upon the growing eccentricities of their brother Matthew,* who lived upon almost raw meat, and never touched bread at all, considering corn as exotic, and therefore diminishing British trade, at the same time avoiding sugar for the same reason, substituting honey for it.

He lived in the plainest, simplest manner himself, but was mighty hospitable to all who came to Horton. He gradually pulled down the many walled gardens round the house, as well as hedges, and threw the whole of his grounds into one large park, where his cattle roamed at will. He dressed plainly, and allowed his beard (then an unusual hirsute ornament) to grow; but as Sir Egerton Brydges,† who eventually became his nephew by marriage, remarks, "he carried his hatred of artificialities through everything. . . . He was the reverse of

* Afterwards 2nd Baron Rokeby.

† From Sir Egerton Brydges' "Biography," *vide* vol. ii. p. 2. Sir Egerton married for second wife, Mary Robinson, niece of Matthew, daughter of Rev. William Robinson.

his Father, who was never happy out of the high and polished society and clubs of London, and thought a country life a perfect misery." Matthew was, however, greatly esteemed by his neighbours and constituents, was a great reader, and wrote some clever political pamphlets.

Mr. Pitt had taken such a fancy to Hayes since Mrs. Montagu had lent him her house there, that he bought it soon after her tenancy expired, as will be seen by this passage in a letter of Bower's to Mrs. Montagu—

"Mr. Pitt is doing great things at Hayes, he has bought the house, and the house hard by, and some fields. He has built a wall towards the public road 13 feet high. He intends to pull down the old house, and build another in the middle of the garden. His neighbour Elly asks an exorbitant price for his house, £500."

Mary Pitt, writing from Hayes on September 16, mentions she is leaving to go to Howberry to the Nedhams,* in order to make room for Lady Hester's extra attendants, as Lady Hester was expecting her confinement. Mrs. Montagu went for ten days to Bath Easton to see Mrs. Scott. Lord Lyttelton, writing to Mrs. Montagu on October 23, to enquire as to her health and Mrs. Scott's, says—

"Mr. Fox† has determined to lay down the seals, because he says he has not support or credit sufficient to carry on the King's business in the House of Commons, and Mr. Pitt will not take them under the Duke of New-castle. What will be the consequence of all this I can't tell, my fears are great for the publick, for myself I have none in any event: the worst that can happen to me is

* Mrs. Nedham was her married sister.

† Henry Fox, 1st Lord Holland, born 1705, died 1774.

to remain in the office I am in under the Duke of Newcastle, but I will remain for the same sense of honour and duty upon which I came into it, if the King and his Grace shall determine to stand the attacks made upon them. How happy are Mr. Stillingfleet and Mr. Torriano to enjoy the Madonna's conversation, instead of hearing the nonsensical speculations of the town. . . . Little Tom is quite well and desires his best compliments. I am charmed with his sister upon my acquaintance with her during her week's stay at Hagley. To make her as perfect as I could wish she wants nothing but the society of the Madonna."

This was his little daughter Lucy,* afterwards Lady Valentia. She appears to have been brought up at first by the Fortescues, her mother's family.

On November 4 Mary Pitt writes from Howberry, "I thank you for your congratulations on the birth of my nephew, he seems to give prodigious satisfaction at Hayes." This was John Pitt, afterwards Viscount Pitt; he was born on October 9.

On November 6 Admiral Boscawen wrote from the Admiralty Office to Mrs. Montagu, then at Sandleford—

"Last week the Duke of Newcastle and Mr. Fox resigned, and the following are those that come in:—the Duke of Devonshire, Mr. Legge, Mr. Nugent, Lord Duncannon and Mr. James Grenville for the Treasury; Lord Temple, Mr. Boscawen, Mr. West, Mr. Thomas Pitt, Dr. Hay, Mr. Hunter, Mr. Elliot of Scotland for the Admiralty; Lord Bateman, Treasurer of the household, Mr. Edgecumbe, Comptroller of the Household, Lord Berkeley, the band of pensioners, Mr. George Grenville, Treasurer of the Navy, Sir Richard Lyttelton,† the jewel office: these have all kissed hands. Mr. Pitt having the

* About ten years old then.

† Brother of Sir George, married the Dowager Duchess of Bridgewater.

gout at Wickham is not yet Secretary of State. Mr. Amyand is to be a Commissioner of the Customs, Sir G. Lyttelton and Lord Hillsbury have both kissed hands for peerages."

On November 19 Charles Lyttelton, Dean of Exeter, afterwards Bishop of Carlisle, wrote an almost similar account of the new Ministry, and said—

"Mr. Pitt was in his bed at Hayes with a sharp attack of gout in his feet; as soon as he is able to get abroad he will kiss hands as Secretary of State. . . . Sir George's patent for a peerage is making out, which the King granted him in the most gracious manner, which is a solid consolation to him for loss of so considerable employment."

On November 16 Mrs. Montagu writes to Lord Lyttelton from Sandleford—

"MY LORD,

"I think you should have written me a letter of congratulation on Sir George Lyttelton's being made a peer: who can feel more joy for any honour, virtue, etc., he obtains? We congratulate our friends on the most transient prosperity, but this peerage is a most solid and lasting advantage, happily timed and accompanied with such agreeable circumstances, on which I reflect with so much sincere satisfaction. . . . I imagine when you take your seat in the House of Peers, the ghost of Henry II.* will claim his seat in the Temple of Fame near the Heroes, recorded by Livy and the great Historians of Antiquity, assuring them that your Lordship is making out his Patent for Eternal Fame."

To this Lyttelton replies—

* Alluding to Lord Lyttelton's "History of Henry II."

GEORGE, LORD LYTTELTON.

[*To face p.* 96, *vol. ii.*

"Hill Street, November 18, 1756.

"MADAM,

"Whatever advantages there may be in a peerage, which you set forth with an eloquence peculiar to yourself, mine has given me no greater pleasure than your most obliging congratulations." He then alludes to his principal pleasure being the advantage to his son, whose talents he praises, and continues, "An early acquaintance and intimacy with the Madonna will be a further advantage to him, if she will be so good as to favour him with it, which will form his mind to all that is worthy and noble, and make him amends for the loss of a Mother whose instructions she alone can ever supply."

Sarah Scott's husband, George Lewis Scott, was now made a Commissioner of the Excise. Writing on Christmas Day to Mrs. Montagu, Sarah says about this—

"Lady Car Fox * told Lady Bab that to her certain knowledge the Prince of Wales † had desired he might not be placed about him, but unless he has committed some very heinous offence against Lord B(ute) I make no doubt of the Princess ‡ providing for him, as the contrary would be unparalleled, and not to her honour."

The letters for the year wind up with one from Sam Torriano, of November 13. It begins—

"MADAM,

"If the brave and victorious Admiral Byng should be so lucky as to meet with so tender an advocate for him as you have been for me, he stands a good chance of an easy death,§ and so the mob will be disappointed, who now wish that everybody may be hanged but himself. . . ."

* Daughter of Charles, 2nd Duke of Richmond.

† Afterwards George III.

‡ Widow of Frederick, Prince of Wales.

§ Admiral Byng was shot on his own ship, March 14, 1757.

Further he alludes to Pitt being laid up with gout at Hayes, "a legacy you left him," alluding to her formerly owning Pitt's residence at that place. Then he mentions Stillingfleet having been staying at Sandleford, and says, "Monsey swears he will make out some story of you and him before you are much older; you shall not keep blew stockings at Sandleford for nothing." This is the first allusion to blue stockings, but that Stillingfleet's wearing blue stockings gave the name to the coterie entirely, must be false. He was, however, a very learned man, especially upon botany. In later letters allusion is made to his having left off wearing blue stockings! The coterie of friends probably was named thus after the famous *bas bleu* assemblies of Paris, held in the *salons* of Madame de Polignac in the Rue St. Honoré, where the wearing of blue stockings was the rage: but Dr. Monsey is mentioned for the first time here. Dr. Messenger Monsey was the son of a clergyman; he was born in 1698, so was fifty-eight years old at this date. He was a doctor and surgeon, and became private physician to the Earl of Godolphin, and afterwards physician to Chelsea Hospital. He was most eccentric, and, if his portrait at the Soane Museum was like him, hideous in appearance; but he had a coarse rough-and-tumble wit, and evidently was so droll in manner, that he became a sort of pet buffoon of the Montagu and Lyttelton circle. His letters are interminably long; written in such small though neat writing, a magnifying glass is required for careful perusal. He was at this time a widower, with one married daughter, Charlotte, whose husband, William Alexander, was elder brother to the 1st Earl of Caledon. Mrs. Alexander had one child, a daughter, Jemima, who married the Rev. Edmund Rolfe, and was mother eventually of the 1st Baron Cranworth. Monsey's letters are so coarse one can hardly imagine the *bas bleus* putting up with them. Dr. Monsey begged Dr. Cruickshank, in case of his dying away from his own doctor (Dr. Forster), to dissect his body before the students, set up his skeleton for instruction, and put his flesh in a box and throw it into the Thames. He must either have been very swarthy, or disliked soap and water, as Torriano, in allusion to Monsey's threat of inventing a story about Stillingfleet and Mrs. Montagu, says, "Your fame, which was as fair as Dian's visage, will be soon black and begrim'd like the Doctor's own face!"

During this year Mrs. Montagu had also formed an acquaintance with an Armenian named Joseph Ameen, or Emin. He was the son of a merchant, and born at Hamadan, whither his father had been carried captive by the Persians. His father at last escaped to Calcutta, after being slave to Kouli Khan for many years. The Persians, ever since 1604, under Shah Abbas, had frequently made inroads into Armenia, captured the majority of the inhabitants, and carried them away as slaves into Persia. Emin grew up with a passionate desire to free his country from oppression and the yoke of unbelievers, for the Armenians were then, as now, Christians. Emin says of his father in a letter to his patron, the Earl of Northumberland *—

"My Father taught me like other Armenians only to write and read in our own language, and to get Psalms by heart to sing in Church, but he did not show me how to handle arms to fight for that Church, as my Uncle did who was killed at his Church door, nor anything to kindle up my heart to understand great affairs."

Burning to learn "the art of war" as practised by

* Hugh Smithson, the 15th Earl, made Duke of Northumerland in 1766; born 1714, died 1786.

the British soldiers in India, and his father opposing him, Emin determined on flight to England, and, taking what money he possessed, he "kissed the feet of Capt. Fox of the ship *Walpole* a hundred times to let me work * my passage to Europe before he would heed to me, but he did at last admit me, and I came to England with much labour." Arrived in England, he entered Mr. Middleton's Academy, and was first a scholar, and then, when his money was exhausted, worked there as a servant for his learning. His master becoming bankrupt, Emin lost his all, and was reduced to the streets. At last he obtained service with a Mr. Rogers, a grocer, as porter. "In this time I carried burthens of near 200 lbs. upon my back, and paid out of my wages to learn geometry, complete my writing, and learn a little French." Overstraining himself, he could no longer carry such heavy burthens, and was reduced to living on 1½*d.* a day, but a friend recommended him to a Mr. Webster, an attorney in Cheapside, with whom he got work for a time. His uncle sent £60 to Governor Davis to take Emin home to India, but after a while, meeting "by chance some gentlemen † who encouraged me and lent me books, and advised me to kiss Colonel Dingley's hands and show him my business, he was a brave soldier, took me by the hand, spoke to his own Sergeant, an honest man, to teach me Manuel Exercise, and gave me 'Bland's Military Discipline' and promised to help me learn gunnery and fortification." Unfortunately Colonel Dingley died, and Emin, in despair, and by the advice of the gentlemen mentioned before, who appear from the letters to have been a Calcutta lawyer and

* The passage took from February 3 (from Hoogley) to December 14, —ten months!

† The gentlemen were a Calcutta lawyer, Emin, or Joseph Ameen, and Edmund Burke, who at once protected Emin.

Edmund Burke, applied to the Earl of Northumberland in a long letter, passages of which I have quoted. Emin proposes that his lordship should apply to Governor Davis for some of the money his uncle had sent to pay for his passage back to India to enable him (Emin) to join the "black Armenians in the mountains, as I heard they had never been conquered," to teach him the art of war. The Earl of Northumberland at last—after Emin waiting at his house often from 10 a.m. to 6 p.m.!—took notice of him, and sent his servant to fetch him to see him, and on hearing his story, said, "Ameen, it is very hard to live in this country without friends and without money, almost four years, therefore the Lord is with you, be contented, I will from this time provide and furnish you with all necessaries," and, said he, "I will mediate to the son of our King, and after you have learned the art of war, I will send you to your Father and your Uncles: the noble lady * comforted me also likewise." Lord Northumberland introduced Emin to Sir Charles Stanhope,† and he in turn to Lord Cathcart,‡ who gave him great encouragement. Lord Northumberland now introduced him to the Duke of Cumberland, who henceforth took an interest in him. Emin applied for military service in a long letter to Heraclius II., King of Georgia and Armenia, who was anxious to shake off the yoke of the Persians, but evidently the reply was delayed, and the next we hear of him is that he had been sent to Woolwich Academy, "to Mr. Heaton's on Church Hill," to learn the "art of war." Having effected a reconciliation with his father, it is

* Elizabeth, only daughter and heiress of Algernon Seymour, Duke of Somerset.

† Sir Charles Stanhope, died 1759.

‡ 9th Lord Cathcart, aide-de-camp to the Duke of Cumberland, etc., etc.

interesting to read what presents he desired him to send this noble patron, the Earl of Northumberland—

"Send to my protector Nobleman, spices of the finest Pulam of Radnagar, 2 pieces of the finest Mul-mul, and 2 pieces of Madras red handkerchiefs, 2 pieces of Cuzombzar Silk handkerchiefs to be ornamented at both ends at Dacca."

So ends 1756.

On May 10, 1757, Emin writes from Woolwich to implore Mrs. Montagu to use her influence with her brother-in-law, Mr. Medows, who was intimate with the Duke of Marlborough, to get him a commission in the Royal Artillery, in order to enable him to join the British army then fighting to defend Hanover, and assist the King of Prussia against the inroads of the French.

This letter, speaking of Mrs. Montagu, addresses her as "My Queen of Sheba," and alludes to all "the noble ladies of her circle," and Dr. Monsey as "my honest, dear Dr. Monsey."

From a letter printed in my grandfather's collection of his aunt's letters, dated March 8, 1757, but which I do not possess, Mrs. Montagu writes to Dr. Monsey, then at Gog Magog, Lord Godolphin's Cambridgeshire seat—

"DEAR DOCTOR,

"That is because you have made me well! Dear Sir, because you make me laugh!"

In this letter, too long to insert here, she says "there have been great efforts to save Mr. Byng." She says Stillingfleet had left off his blue stockings, and was at gay operas and assemblies each night.

From Windsor Castle, where Lady Sandwich had

been granted apartments, and was living with her sister, Miss Fane, this interesting letter from Mrs. Montagu, who was on a visit there, is dated—

"Windsor Castle, Friday.

"MY DEAREST,

"I know you will be curious to hear how the famous election has been carried at Windsor, and the greatest pleasure I can have is to impart any to you. Mr. Fox* had a majority of 52, the Mayor, who is Mr. Bowles' friend, owns he had a legal majority of nine. The boxers and the bruisers Mr. Fox had on his side beat the Windsor mob out of the Field, but they had once the courage to attack Mr. Fox's person, and pulled off his wig, and threw it in his face. In short the affair has been very tumultuous. The town is quiet, none are actually dead, but four or five are dangerously ill, and the Doctors and Apothecarys had a great harvest of bruises and fractures. . . . The ladies wore party gowns, Fox's is partly yellow and green, and the others blue; our sex have a wise way of expressing their political principles."

On June 28, being returned to Sandleford, writing to Mr. Montagu, she mentions—

"The poor are very riotous on Market days, and it was rumoured, as I am told, that you had some corn in the granary,† and also the same of Mr. Herbert,‡ at which they were very angry; but I hope they will patiently wait its going to Market, for there is still a great while to Harvest. Corn fell last week, and bears but 8*s.* 6*d.* a bushell, but gin and idleness give the poor a riotous and licentious spirit. . . . Lady Sandwich has got a very pretty habitation in the Castle, we went into the little

* Henry Fox, born 1705, died 1774; afterwards Baron Holland.

† There was a great dearth of corn at this period, and a bill had to be passed prohibiting exportation.

‡ Mr. Herbert, of Highclere.

park in the evening, that and all I saw of the environs of Windsor delighted me extreamly."

Mr. Montagu thanked his wife on July 10 for telling him about the election, and says, "I hear it cost him (Mr. Fox) £3000, that he gave £50 apiece for many of his votes, and carried it by 31."

The first letter of Dr. Stillingfleet's * I possess is written on July 23 to Mrs. Montagu. His handwriting is clear, but he always uses a small "i" alone instead of a capital "I," except at the beginning of a sentence. Portions I copy—

"I have been at Malvern about twelve days, where with difficulty i have got a lodging, the place is so very full, nor do i wonder at it, there being some instances of very extraordinary cures in cases looked on as desperate, even by Dr. Wall,† the Physician, who first brought the waters into vogue. I do not doubt but that the air and exercise, which at present is absolutely necessary here, the Well being at over two miles ‡ from the town, contribute very much towards restoring the health of the patients. The road is very fine, and made on purpose for the drinkers. It is on the side of a hill, which i am told is found by exact mensuration in some part to be half a mile perpendicularly high, above a wide plain that lies at the bottom. Towards the well the road ascends considerably, so that i imagine the end of it is not much less than halfway up to the top. A gentleman in the neighbourhood has, at his own expense, made a walk a little above the well; this walk runs on a level for about 600 yards, winding with the breaks of the hill,

* Dr. Benjamin Stillingfleet, born 1702, died 1771. Wrote "Calendar of Flora," etc., etc.

† Dr. John Wall, an eminent physician. First made Malvern known as a Spa, and founded the porcelain manufactory at Worcester. Dr. Wall died in 1776.

‡ Matlock Bath now.

and makes the noblest terrace i ever saw, the plain over which you look being bounded by some fine hills, and on it, lying on one side, Worcester, on the other Gloucester. The hill is fed with sheep, here and there some cattle graze, overhead I see my favourite bird, the Kite, sailing, and all the while i tread on porphyry, the consciousness of which, you may guess, adds not a little to my satisfaction, when i consider that Princes are proud to have a few pillars of this material. . . . The town lies high on the side of the hill, and still on Porphyry. The church, which stands a little lower, was a Priory. . . . Not far below the Church is a spring of the same nature with that of Tunbridge. . . . I wish this place was nearer to London, for it seems exactly adapted to do you good. . . . There is a subscription going forward for building a large lodging-house near the Well. At present there is only one old house in the town, turned entirely to that purpose, which contains about fifteen persons, and one large room in it, where once a week there is a sort of public breakfast and dinner. We have had one public tea-drinking and card-playing in the afternoon, by particular invitation; to-day it will begin on another footing, and is to be weekly."

Soon after the receipt of this letter, Mrs. Montagu set out on a visit to Lady Bab Montagu and Mrs. Scott at Bath Easton, and Mr. Montagu, on July 28, writes to say he purposes driving to "Killum"* to see his friend Mr. Stevens.† "Killum" was Culham Court, Berks. George Stevens, a very eccentric character, afterwards, in 1766, published an edition of Shakespeare, and three years later some notes were incorporated in it of Dr. Johnson's. Mr. Montagu writes this description of "Killum"—

* This would place the building of Culham Court as taking place in 1707. See the first line of the next page.

† George Stevens, born 1736, died 1800.

"His house is a very good one, built about fifty years ago, the rooms large and wainscoated with oak, and three very good bedchambers with beds that at some time cost a good deal of money, but are the worse for time. He has been pulling down walls, and everything lyes rough and without order or neatness, and to finish the account of it, very much resembled its owner. Its situation is what I think fine and much pleases me, it is in a Valley which begins at the foot of that hill which we see on Maidenhead Thickett, and goes as far as Henley and further. The Thames runs quite through it, is of good breadth, and with a great number of little islands scatter'd here and there makes a most beautyfull appearance. On the bank of this river, on a terrass the house is built, it is of considerable extent, and if adorn'd with plantations and buildings would be very pretty and pleasant, but to do this may require a greater expense than may be convenient, so that all he at present thinks of doing is the improving the lawn. . . . You might blame me if I omitted giving you some account of one of a kind very uncommon. I mean Mr. Hart's * Chinese house. This stands in a beech wood of Mr. Stevens about half a mile from him. Consists of a suite of rooms pav'd with pantyles and hung with paper, and on the outside is embellish'd with very costly decoration of the Chinese manner. Mr. Stevens says the cost has been about two thousand pounds, but I don't believe three would pay for it. It seems to me no more than a whim, and so much money flung away. It stands very high, and has a more extensive view than Mr. Stevens'. It might be agreeable to entertain a company there in the finest and warmest weather, but one cannot think of it as an habitation without shuddering. At present no use is made of it; three servants are kept there who have no other business than to look after the house, keep the wood walks in order, and breed pheasants; in about 15 years the lease expires,

* This was Rose Hill, built by Governor Hart, now the property of General E. Micklem.

MRS. MARY DELANY.

[*To face p.* 105, *vol. ii.*

and then it comes to Mr. Stevens." Mr. Montagu says, "I have some other thoughts of taking another ramble about the middle of the week to Winchester, and perhaps Southampton."

Mrs. Montagu had written to ask for a pair of horses and a coachman to be sent to Bath Easton, in order to convey herself and sister to stay at King's Weston with Mrs. Southwell, "a man at Bath Easton will feed each horse at *6d.* a day!" Mr. Montagu sends them, but says, "They may possibly serve to carry you to King's Weston, and bring you part of the way home, but for any expeditions out of the Turnpike roads I fear they will not endure it."

In replying to her husband, the following character of Mr. Stevens is given:—

"I look upon Mr. Stevens as a man who has disfranchised himself from all slavery to custom and fashion, and who as seldom brushes up or new trims his modes of living as his coat, but wears both as long as they fit him, in spite of what fops and taylors may say. I hope he will come to Sandleford, for he has parts enough to make his singularities amusing. I dare say he was very happy in the visit you made him, both for the pleasure of your conversation and from a little vanity, for tho' the modes of singularity may give a man an air of designing to live alone and of contemplation, in the world, I believe one may venture to say, none are more desirous of regard and notice than those who affect to retire and be singular; they rather design their peculiarities for a badge of distinction than a line of separation between them and Society; and a man in low life may go ungarter'd or cross-garter'd, who in another station would have been ambitious of a blue garter, and their installment into a particular character is a matter of great wit. . . . We had a report that the Duke had killed 3000 French, but he is well off if he can keep on the defensive.

I had a letter from Mr. Emin that the Duke of Cumberland received him in the most gracious manner, and he is so pleased, I believe he thinks one more step will put him on the Persian throne. It is happy to be born of a hoping constitution; his day dreams are very pleasant. I wish his patriot spirit was communicated to a dozen or two of our great men."

Emin had joined the English army under the Duke of Cumberland, then fighting the French. On July 30 he wrote to Dr. Monsey, enclosing a letter to his patronesses, to be copied for each lady. In the postscript is the first mention of Edmund Burke.

"Now I would have you ask Mr. Burke's advice about this letter before you coppy it for my friends. Pray don't be mad because my friend is an Irish gentleman, but I can tell you that he is your beloved son-in-laws * countryman. I dare say you will be mighty pleased at being acquainted with him."

Emin's letter begins—

"Limburg, August 1, 1757.

"To all the ladies and Patronesses of Joseph Emin.

"MY NOBLE LADIES,

"I believe your ladyships have been in a long expectation to hear from this part of the world, more especially of the battle which began on the 23rd of July. In the morning we were ordered out with 25 horses and 200 foot irregulars to secure a post, where we found 300 husars and 700 foot soldiers, upon which we began immediately to fire, and they retreated very soon; and in the afternoon his highness, hearing that the French were advancing with their whole army,

* Dr. Monsey's only child married William Alexander, elder brother 1st Earl Caledon.

ordered that the part of his army were to advance also, but it was very unlucky for us that our infantry was too late; and before they could come up, the enemy begun from some distance to fire upon us with their cannon, with no manner of execution. His Royal Highness thought proper to return to his camp in Aferden. The next day, the enemy, still advancing from their camp at Halla all along the river Vizer,* and were retreating untill we halted upon a high hill with full of trees, and they on another; were the firing of cannon began again on both sides, and lasted till evening. Our situation not being so well as we could wish, we still retreated till we come to Hamelin,† there we posted the right of our army, and our left at Onsburg, and unfortunate Hastenbek ‡ between us and the enemy, which was soon burnt down. The 25th, about four in the morning, the enemy began to advance with their musicks and drums, making a very great noise, more like Indians than Europeans, and was soon silenced; as a few of our balls, and cannonading begun of both sides briskly. At that time your slave was upon a hill with no more than 200 irregulars, commanded by my friend, Major Freydag, a man of good conduct and judgment, where we could see the two armies very plain. It was a place had it not been so dangerous as the cannon balls were flying like so many flies over our heads, I would wish my noble friend ladies who are my patronesses and who are so fond of Heros and hearing of battles, to have seen it, which would really have been worth their while; then I would have wished again that the heavenly chariots where descended from the gods above, to have transported them to their native and blessed Island, peradventure they should have been in the greatest of dangers, for wee saw about eleven of the clock the enemy with no less than six thousand of Horses and Foot comming up to us of all sides with a great fury, except a little grass that led us down to our army, but this bravery of theirs was greatly owing to an information which they had of us a day before. Knowing

* River Weser. † Hamelen. ‡ Hastenbeck.

that we were no more than two hundred men, or else they woud not be so furious in their attack, for they are vastly like the black Indians, fire at a great distance and run away. However, we stood almost half an hour, our men ralyed three times and killed no less than 300 of them; for our men are brought up from their infantry (*sic!*) as huntsmen, they never miss their mark. I have seen them shoot at 300 yards' distance; they are like the mountiniers of Armenia and Dagastun, the French husars run away as soon as they see us. You see, my noble ladies, what great advantage it is to a Nation who has the liberty not only to kill the partridges but to kill as many deers and other animals as they please. The loss of ours was but 20 and 6 wounded, we could not support any longer and where obliged to retreat, and join the army, and about 2 a-clock in the afternoon, the enemy retreated with the loss of eleven cannon, and had taken some of ours, but we retaken them again, but the battle continued still and lasted from 4 in the morning to 6 in the afternoon, the loss of their side was about 3000 and about 1200 of ours, we don't look upon this as a battle in Persia, but as a scarmish (*sic!*). The inventor of gunpowder tho' he is cursed by many ignorant people but his invention has been a very great service towards preservation of Mankind, gunpowder is a thing which makes a great noise like lightning and thunder keep mankind distant with an awe. 'The thought of gunpowder,' says the great Marshal de Saxe, 'is more than the danger itself.' I woud wish to have no more than 1500 Persian Horse if it is not too bold and your humble servant the teacher of them, we could soon show the French that the effect of symiters (*sic*) would be greater than that of gunpowder tho' their number of what we hear is one hundred fifty thousand men and ours are you very well know. At present we are upon marches and countermarches."

At the end of the letter he says he has received nothing as yet from his royal master, and that if he does not, he must unwillingly return to his father in India, as he will not be a "begar" any longer on his noble patrons.

This battle was that of Hastenbeck. The Duke of Cumberland had placed the archives and valuable effects from Hanover in the town of Stadt, and from Stadt came a letter from Emin to Dr. Monsey, on September 13, just after the famous Convention of Kloster-Seven had, by the intervention of the King of Denmark, been signed, and peace arranged. In reply to Dr. Monsey's inquiry about the Duke of Cumberland's health, Emin says, "You are desirous to know how my royal master is. Mr. Andrews (*valet*), with his compts. to you, says his Royal highness's leg is quite well, so you may be easy."

To return to Mrs. Montagu, staying at Bath Easton, on August 1, writing to her husband, she expresses herself uneasy, as Admiral Boscawen was recalled from the fleet, for what he knew not. "Mr. Boscawen will be busy enquiring the cause of his being recalled, he has merit and a powerful family, and I hope his ennemies cannot oppress tho' they may oppose him. Do not mention this affair."

In July Mrs. Morris Robinson had presented her husband with a son and heir, who was christened Morris, after his father, and became eventually 3rd Baron Rokeby. "Morris' little boy goes on well. . . . Mr. Potter made a fine harangue to the Bath Corporation on Mr. Pitt's Election. The circus,* I am told, is but little nearer finish'd than when we were here."

In the next letter, after comments on the beauties of things at Weston, she writes—

"Yesterday morning Mrs. Southwell and I got into

* The circus at Bath.

her postchaise early, and went to the passage of the Severn, got into the Ferry boat and cross'd over to Chepstow in Monmouthshire, and from Chepstow we went to Mr. Morris' called Piercefield, a place so far exceeding any thing I ever saw or expect to see, I must reserve the description till I see you. A reach of the Severn of forty miles is one of the most inconsiderable advantages of the place, every beauty of land, sea, rocks, verdure, cultivation, old ruins, villages, churches are there in the highest perfection; the river Wye forms a most beautiful half island in one part as the Severn Sea adorns the other."

Mr. Montagu replies—

"On Tuesday night, as I was at Supper about 10 o'clock, who should come in to me but my cousin Wortley,* he had been making a visit to somebody near Wallingford . . . he missed his way, the roads were so bad and rough that two of the glasses of his new chaize were broken and he could not get any reparation at Newbury." In commenting on political subjects, he adds, "I suppose now everybody will be sensible of the folly we have been guilty of in so long suffering the Wild Boar of Germany to enter and destroy our vineyard."

Mrs. Montagu answers—

"I assure you it is with a melancholy pleasure I often look on this charming country, perhaps this is the last summer I may ever be an idle traveller thro' a peaceable country; however, I have one comfort, that as you are innocent of the evils that may overwhelm us, you will the better support yourself and me under them, and that the best we can hope is to be tributary vassals

* Mr. Wortley Montagu, senior, husband of Lady Mary Wortley Montagu, first cousin to Mr. Edward Montagu.

to France, perhaps they will invade and conquer us, but God forbid."

Mrs. Talbot,* writing from Barrington,† bids Mrs. Montagu to come and stay with her. The letter is not a remarkable one, but it says, "Have you heard lately from Lady Sandwich? I find the old Countess ‡ is dead at last at Paris." This was the eccentric Elizabeth Wilmot, sister of *the* Earl of Rochester, and grandmother of John, Lord Sandwich, widow of the 3rd Earl. It is said she governed her husband to such a degree that he was almost a cypher and a prisoner in his own house, she being, though an indifferent wife, a most brilliant spirited woman. After her lord's death in 1729, she lived in Paris, where she was the friend of Ninon de l'Enclos and St. Evremont. Both Pope and Lord Chesterfield have mentioned her as extremely spirited and having great intellectual ability.

Her daughter-in-law, Lady Hinchinbroke, *née* Elizabeth Popham, lost her husband, Lord Hinchinbroke, in 1722, and I have several curious letters written by her to Mrs. Montagu in 1739, respecting her son John, 4th Earl of Sandwich ("Jemmy Twitcher"). He was then eleven years old, and his mother sent him to sea. Probably he was even then very unruly, but he could not bear the sea, and through Mr. Montagu she applied to their common connection, John, Duke of Montagu, to get him a commission in the Army, buying it "as an ensign in a marching regiment." The duke's reply to this is singularly indifferent in expression, and his spelling terrible.

On August 6, writing from Bath Easton to her

* Mrs. Talbot, widow of Edward Talbot, Bishop of Durham.

† Barrington Park, near Burford, Oxon.

‡ She died July 2, 1757, at Rue Vaugirard, Paris.

husband, Mrs. Montagu alludes to the defeat of Frederick the Great at Kollin in Bohemia, on June 18, by General Daun. Emin had written to her, saying—

"The French seem afraid of us, tho' so much inferior in numbers. . . . I hear the King of Prussia takes to himself the whole blame of his disgrace in the late affair, and says if he had followed the advice of the Prince of Bevern, it had not happen'd; there is something more great perhaps in a Monarch owning his error than in gaining a victory, but it will not have the same effect in establishing his affairs in Germany, so that in his situation the least advantage over the Empress Queen* would have been of better consequence. Sir John Mordaunt, General Conway,† and Col. Cornwallis are going abroad with some forces as the Newspapers tell us, and the French seem again disposed to disturb us with the apprehension of an invasion."

Writing to Dr. Stillingfleet on August 7, in return for his description of Malvern, Mrs. Montagu gives this fine description of Emin—

"Mr. Emin was most graciously received by the Duke, had offers of money and all marks of regard from his Royal Highness, so that his letters express the highest satisfaction . . . there must be a nobler seat than the Persian throne reserved for that fine spirit which, born in slavery and nurtured in ignorance, aspired to give liberty, knowledge, and civil arts to his country. To compass this he risqued his life, and endured the greatest hardships, and ventured all dangers and uncertainties in a country whose very language he was a stranger to; how different from so many of our countrymen, who for little additions of power and greater gratifications of luxury, in spite of their pride of birth and

* Maria Theresa, Empress of Austria, born 1717, died 1780.

† Seymour Henry Conway, the cousin and bosom friend of Horace Walpole; born 1720, died 1795.

advantage of a liberal education and the incitements of the great examples of all ages and nations, will hazard enslaving us to a nation our forefathers despised."

In this letter we learn that Lord Lyttelton had returned from a Welsh tour very unwell, had spent two days with her and Mrs. Scott at Bath Easton, *en route* to Hagley, and that on her return to Sandleford she expected a visit from Dr. Monsey.

In a letter from Rev. Charles Lyttelton from Hagley of August 17, one catches a glimpse of the second Lady Lyttelton's temper. He says—

"My brother Lord Lyttelton returned from his Welsh expedition the same day I came home, and you will easily believe how welcome he was to Miss West and me, as we had nobody to converse with or rather to eat with, but ye amiable Lady of ye house, for she does not deign to converse or hardly say a single word to either of us. On Saturday, Hester * arrived, so we are now a strong party, and her Ladyship may be as sulkey and silent as she pleases. . . . Lord Lyttelton is got pure well."

This expression is often used in the eighteenth-century writings; apparently it meant perfect health at that time.

From Merton, on August 30, Lady Frances Williams † writes to Mrs. Montagu, and in her letter alludes with joy to Emin's safety, and then adds—

"By the accounts arrived from Lord Loudoun,‡ *the*

* Lady Hester Pitt.

† Lady Frances Williams was daughter of the Earl of Coningsby; her husband, Sir Charles Hanbury Williams, was a statesman, poet, and wit.

‡ Lord Loudoun, Commander-in-Chief of the English army in America against the French.

Mediterranean tragedy seems to be acting over again in the American seas. A Council of War was call'd to advise whether the 10,000 men brought to Louisburgh * should be landed or not; it was determined in the *negative* upon finding the French had 2 more ships than we had. Lord Charles Hay's only entering his protest, and they are returned to Halifax to wait a reinforcement.

"This brings to my mind the death of Admiral West, and the disgust given our friend Admiral Boscawen, which I look upon as a retaliation from the Pittites for the dismission of the former last Spring."

In a letter from Fulham on September 15 Mrs. Donnellan alludes to the expedition under Sir Edward Hawke † and Sir John Mordaunt against the French, which was kept very secret.

"They say Sir John Mordaunt said to the officers, 'You will have but a short bout, but it will be a brisk one, and I hope we shall all behave as we ought to.' 'Tis supposed we shall hear in less than a week something about it. . . . Whatever it is, Mr. Pit (*sic*) will either have the glory or disgrace of it, for every one calls it his scheme. The King, they say, had a fainting fit about a week ago as he sat at cards, but is now well and seems cheerful. . . . Lord Bolingbroke and Lady, were in such a hurry of passion they could not wait for settlements but were married upon an Article; may one not think of an old Proverb, 'Marry in haste.'"

Lady Bolingbroke was a daughter of Charles Spencer, Duke of Marlborough, and Mrs. Donnellan's

* Louisburg in Nova Scotia; the English were attacking the French Canadian Provinces.

† Sir Edward Hawke commanded the navy, and Sir John Mordaunt the army. It was against the French, and proved a failure, costing nearly a million.

prophecy came true, but not till 1768, when she was divorced, and married Topham Beauclerk, son of Lord Sydney Beauclerk.

On September 15 Mrs. Montagu wrote a long letter to Dr. Stillingfleet from Sandleford. In this she alludes to the humorous affection for her which Dr. Monsey had developed.

"You must know Sir, Dr. Monsey is fallen desperately in love with me, and I am most passionately in love with him, the darts on both sides have not been the porcupine's, but the grey goose quill. We have said so many tender things to each other by the post, that at last we thought it would be better to sigh in soft dialogue than by letter. We agreed to meet, and the rather, as all the lovers we had read of (and being in love with each other only *du coté de l'esprit*, you may suppose we woo by book) had always complained of absence as the most dreadful thing imaginable. He said, nay he swore, he would come to Sandleford, and twice had named the day, but each time his grand-daughter fell sick, and I know not whether he will keep the third appointment, which is for next Monday. These disappointments have made me resolve, and I really believe it will not be difficult to keep the resolution, never again to fall in love with a man who is a grandfather. In all other respects the Doctor is a perfect Pastor Fido, and I believe when we get to Elysium, all the lovers who wander in the Myrtle Groves there will throw their garlands at our feet."

Further on she alludes to Emin, who was at Stadt, and had written her a most devoted letter.

"I do not indeed hope to see him on the Persian throne, or giving laws to the East, but I know he sits on the summit of human virtue, and obeys the laws of Him who made that world the ambitious are contending for, and to such only my esteem pays homage."

In a letter to Mrs. Scott of this period occurs Mrs. Montagu's opinion of the character of her friend, Mrs. Boscawen.*

"She is in very good spirits, and sensible of her many felicities, which I pray God to preserve to her; but her cup is so full of good, I am always afraid it will spill. She is one of the few whom an unbounded prosperity could not spoil. I think there is not a grain of evil in her composition. She is humble, charitable, pious, of gentle temper, with the firmest principles and with a great deal of discretion, void of any degree of art, warm and constant in her affections, mild towards offenders, but rigorous towards offence."

I make extracts from a splendid letter to Mrs. Boscawen of October 25. Admiral Boscawen had just received a commission rather unexpectedly, owing to the failure of the Hawke and Mordaunt expedition.

"I am a little uneasy lest the surprize should have hurt you, satisfy me in that matter and my imagination will then sit down and weave laurel garlands for your husband's head, and I too will rejoice in the advantage which I hope his country will reap from his arms, but think me not ignoble if I own, glory is but a bright moonshine when compared to your welfare, and think me not below the standard of true patriotism, if I confess, it is for the sake of such as you, my country is a name so dear. I know you are too reasonable to wish Mr. Boscawen might avoid the hazards of his profession. The Duke of Marlbro' his kinsman, lived to old age and survived perhaps all the cowards that were born on the

* *Née* Frances Glanville, daughter of William Evelyn Glanville, of St. Clair, Kent.

same day, the accidents of life are more than the chances of war. Be not afraid, but commit it all to the great and wise Disposer of all events; a firm hope and cheerful reliance on Providence I do believe to be the best means to bring about what we wish, and that such confidence does it far better than all our anxious foresight, our provident schemes and measuring of security. I remember with sorrow and shame, I trusted much to a continual watching of my son,* I would not have committed him to a sea voyage, or for the world in a town besieged, I forgot at Whose will the waves are still, and Who breaketh the bow and knappeth the spear asunder. What was the reward of this confidence of my own care and diffidence of His who only could protect him? Why, such as it deserved, I lost my beloved object, and with him my hopes, my joys, and my health, and I lost him too, not by those things I had feared for him, but by the pain of a tooth. Pray God keep you from my offence and the punishment of it. I do not mean that you should be void of anxiety in times of hazard, but offer them to God every night and sleep in peace, the same every morning, and rise with confidence. . . . I am much pleased with his Majesty's confidence in Mr. Boscawen. . . .

"The Duke,† it seems, is gone to plant cabbages; as soon as these great folks are disgusted they go into the country; the indignant statesman plants trees upon which he wishes all his enemies hanged, his occupations are changed, but his passions not altered. The angry warrior rides a-hunting, 'mais le chagrin monte en croupe et galope avec lui,' nor can the hounds and horn 'that cheerily rouse the slumbering morn' content the sense that wants 'to hear piercing fife and spirit-stirring drum.'"

Not having been well, she adds she is moving to London to consult her doctors, leaving Mr. Montagu

* Alluding to her only child, John, *alias* "Punch's" death.

† The Duke of Cumberland.

to plant trees, etc., before joining her. "I expect a cargo of Morgans and good folk from Newbury to dine here; I always endeavour to depart the country in an odour of civility."

A letter from Mrs. Donnellan throws a light on the Mordaunt affair.

"All I can gather of this most shameful affair is that there will be no more known till there is a publick enquiry,* and then if the scheme is proved by the General Officers to have been impracticable, those who sent them on it must suffer, but if it is found that they might have made more of it, I suppose they will. . . . It will be defered (the enquiry, I mean) till the sitting of parliament. Sir J. Mordaunt and Admiral Hawke have both been to Court, the Admiral was received graciously, the other taken no notice of, 'tis said he stooped to kiss the royal hand, but it was pulled back from him; wou'd it not have been more kingly to have forbidden his coming? 'Tis said soon after some of the troops were in the boats in order to land; there was a council of war called, and when Hawke thought they were landed, they were ordered on board again; 'tis certain there were 5 or 6 days spent on councils of war, and then Hawke, who was not concerned in them, desired them to come to some resolution, for he wou'd either land them or return home. Colonel Conway, I hear, showed the most spirit, and that our commen men showed no unwillingness to action. . . . The Duke came thro' the city on Thursday at four in the afternoon. I saw some who saw him, there was no sort of notice taken of him; I think he was well off. I suppose you have seen the King of Prussia's letter to our King, 'tis denyed but believed to be genuine. I think your remarks on the correspondence between the King of Prussia and Voltair (*sic*) very just; however, I forgive

* The Mordaunt enquiry warrant was not signed till December 3, 1757.

ALLERTHORPE HALL.

[*To face p.* 120, *vol. ii.*

J. G. Eccardt. Pinx. Faber. Mezzo.

Conyers Middleton D.D.

Emery Walker Ph. So.

him some levity when conversed with a wit, and part since he knows when 'tis proper to the King. . . . I have got since I came home, Taylor's Sermons, he is so good he frightens me, and so witty he makes me laugh."

Mr. Montagu, writing from Sandleford on November 6, to his wife, mentions Hawke being sent out again with Boscawen, "was a clear proof that they had nothing to impute to him which was faulty." He was busy planting at Sandleford, and said he must get chestnuts and acorns when he came to London, as the last sown had been rotten, "according to Millar the way of trying them is somewhat like that formerly us'd in the case of witches, such of them as swim are to be rejected and those that sink esteem'd good."

Mrs. Montagu, with the advice of Dr. Shaw and Dr. Monsey, gradually recovered her health. Wormwood draughts were prescribed; her illness appears to have been a nervous fever, with weakness and loss of appetite. Of Dr. Monsey she says, "He has given me as much attendance as if I was a Princess of the blood, tho' I have never given him a fee." Dr. Shaw had been called off to the Duchess of Newcastle at Claremont, who was suffering in the same way. Great discussion is given as to giving of the "bark" without danger, and when to do so. "Dr. Shaw has had six guineas of me, I shall give him no more, I had difficulty to make him accept the last, but he attended me at first twice a day." The Mordaunt affair is alluded to in each letter. In one occurs the following—

"Lord Chesterfield in a letter from Bath to Lady Allen writes thus: 'Your ladyship may believe all the circles here think they have a right to form a court-martial to sit on Sir J. M. For my part I wait for information. I can never believe he wants courage or capacity, as I imagine he will show the scheme was impracticable and they must answer who sent him.'"

On November 7, Mr. Montagu writes to announce his intention of joining his wife, and adds—

"I see by the *Gazette* that the King of Prussia has obtained a great victory over the combined army under Prince Soubise. This is an unexpected event, and must give a turn to his affairs. One thing seems to be collected from it, that this enterprising courageous Prince has not made peace nor flung himself into the arms of France as we were given to believe."

This was the Battle of Rosbach in Saxony, won against the Austrians and French by Frederick the Great of Prussia on November 5, 1757. The year's correspondence ends with a letter to Emin of Lady A. Sophia Egerton, enclosing a letter of recommendation of him to her uncle, Mr. Bentinck, then in diplomatic service in Holland. Emin was going to rejoin the Prussian Army.

CHAPTER III.

1758, 1759—BEGINNING OF CORRESPONDENCE WITH MRS. CARTER, WITH DR. JOHNSON, AND WITH BURKE.

1758 commences with a letter on March 2, from Mrs. Montagu to her husband, who had left London for Sandleford. In it she says—

"I shall enclose an *Advertizer* in which you will find a curious article from Warsaw. It astonished all Europe to find the King of Prussia had got copies of the plans of the Imperial Court and Dresden, the means by which he obtained them are now discover'd. To this contrivance his Prussian Majesty and his Country owe their present being, but one cannot envy the state of a King if it is necessary to take such means for preservation as would startle a vulgar man of Honour. To get false keys to cabinets is but a poor low trick, and it is very strange to see a hero guilty of burglary, but as Mr. Pope observes, 'the story of the great is generally a tale that blends their glory with their shame.' Mr. Stanhope call'd on me as I was writing, and I am to dine with my brother Morris, so must abridge my letter. I can't hear what pass'd in the House of Lords yesterday in Delany's trial. . . . I was at the Oratorio last night, where I heard the Dublin man-of-war was sent to Mr. Boscawen to supply the loss of the *Invincible*. I am to be at Lady Hillsborough's assembly to-night."

The Delany trial had lasted for nearly ten years.

It was on account of Dr. Delany, in inadvertence, having burnt a paper of importance belonging to his first wife. Sometimes it appeared to be at an end, but it was as often renewed. At last, on March 5, Lord Mansfield,* after an hour and a half's speech, decided in favour of Delany. The cost of the suit exceeded the disputed sum, but the relief to the good dean and his wife on its decision balanced everything.

On March 9 Mrs. Montagu writes—

"I met Mrs. Delany to-day at Mrs. Donnellan's, and she is very happy, the Irish decree is reversed, tho' even as matters stand, they will have little left when the £7000 is paid. Lady Frances Williams is still in grief for her husband,† who in his madness has writt (*sic*) letters to half the crowned heads in Europe. I am going to the play to-night, to-morrow I shall give up the Oratorio to stay with Lady Frances Williams as comforter.

"That bright luminary of the Church, Dr. Clayton, Bishop of Clogher, is dead. . . . The Bishop has left his wife his whole fortune, which is very considerable. It is thought we shall not send troops to the King of Prussia, but whether he will accept of our money ‡ we shall not know till the return of the Express. The King of Pegu has wrote a letter to the King on a gold plate, and the stops are made with rubies; I should be glad of his correspondence tho' his letters had no wit in them."

Emin, anxious for re-employment, now addressed Mr. Pitt. The letter was addressed to Mr. Pitt, Secretary of State.

* "Silver-tongued Murray."

† Sir Charles Hanbury Williams, poet and writer, had been attacked with madness.

‡ Another letter says the King of Prussia will not accept money.

"SIR,

"Though I never had the honour to be known to you, yet I have the boldness to write. I have been over a great variety of the world, and have seen much people, but I wanted to see men; for the Design of my Travel was knowledge, and I thought knowledge of real men was better than books, therefore I have turned my Eyes upon all ways and at last had the great happyness of seeing and hearing you in that potent House of Commons, and there I discovered like the light breaking upon me, what my Friends had often told me, of your great love to your Country and your wise Eloquence that conquers more than the Sword of a Hero. I own I grew a little envious; for I thought no man loved his country better than I have mine, but I confess it that I am nothing, tho' I have been sailor, porter, slave, and suffered everything in every shape, to make my country what you have made yours. This is my small merit and the only recommendation I can make to you. Sir, I will observe that a cloudy day in winter is light enough to see what is about us and to serve common business, but permitt me to say no man is happy nor in good spirit untill the sun shines out. Then there is joy upon all men's faces. Thus it is, great Sir, with me in this country, I along with the rest in this happy land, find Benefit of the Light you give us all by your great wisdom of governing, but I am not happy, and my Life is dead untill I see the Vezirazam of England.

"If you do me this high Honour, you will see a poor soldier whose only Fortune is a character with all people which I have been amongst. I was a Porter for learning not for livlihood, and I was honest in that low way. This is known when by the goodness of great Souls I was raised from that. I was not idle nor ingreatefull; I have been high and low and I was not bad. When I served the last campaign in Germany, all the officers, both English and the German, will say more of me than I dare think of myself. I have, Sir, in my studies for my country, found the way to advance it, and do some service to your noble Nation at the same time. My humble plan for this good design I will do myself the Honour to show to you and be instructed by your great Wisdom and to give me new rights in this great matter. My scheme has two Qualities which make some laugh at me, others seem to like me for it. Whatever it is, it is little without your assistance. If you approve of it, I laugh at those that laugh at me, at any rate I am resolved and nothing shall stop me but Death, which is common to everybody, and an honest Heart need not fear any. I am, with the greatest Respect and Veneration,

"Great Sir,

"Your most obedient most obliged devoted humble Servant,

"J. EMIN.

"In the Month of March, 1758,

"To the R. H. William Pitt, etc., etc."

In her next letter to her husband Mrs. Montagu says—

"Emin dines with Lady Medows to-day, if joy can give appetite, he will make a good meal, for by the solicitation of Lady Yarmouth,* Mr. Pitt has received him, and promised to see what can be done for him, as great minds are akin. Mr. Pitt was much pleased with him. Emin repeated to me his discourse to Mr. Pitt, and it was full of Asiatick fire and figure—if it did not touch the man, it must the Orator. Mr. Pitt made him great compliments. I hope they will be realized, and they surely will if Lady Yarmouth continues her desire to serve him."

Emin was sent to join the English army under the Duke of Marlborough in their attempted invasion of France at St. Malo, and wrote on June 11 to say that Captain Howe had burnt 73 ships and from 10 to 16

* Amelia S. de Walmoden, created 1740, Baroness Yarmouth, mistress of George II.

guns, besides small vessels." After this expedition, Emin joined the army with the King of Prussia.

Writing to Dr. Stillingfleet on June 13, after alluding to the attack on St. Malo, Mrs. Montagu says—

"So much for war and war's alarms; as to our civil occurences, they have been so boisterously carried I need not change the tone of my narrative; the Judges, the Lord Keeper, the Chief Justice, and the late Lord Chancellor gave their opinions against the Habeas Corpus bill.* Lord Temple, much in wrath, insulted the Judges in some of his questions; Lord Lyttelton warmly and sharply reproved him upon which words rose high, the House of Lords interfered. The last day of this bill, Lord Mansfield and Lord Hardwicke † spoke so full to the matter, even Tory Lords, and these most violent in their wishes for it, declared they were convinced the new bill was dangerous to liberty in many respects, in many absurd; so that had there been a division there would not have been four votes for it, but Mr. Pitt's Party discreetly avoided a division. This affair has not set the legislative wisdom of the House of Commons in a very high light, but the great Mr. Beckford,‡ whom no argument can convince, no defeat make ashamed, nor mistake make diffident, did on the motion for a vote of credit stand up in the House of Commons and say he would not oppose that measure, as he had an opinion of the two Commoners in the administration, but in the Peers that composed it, he had no confidence, and ran in foul abuse of them and then ended with a severe censure of the House of Lords in general. Lord Royston § answered him that this was unparliamentary

* This was occasioned by a gentleman having been impressed for service in the Navy and illegally detained prisoner. The motion was to administer the Act more decisively.

† Philip Yorke, 1st Earl of Hardwicke, born 1690, died 1764.

‡ Alderman Beckford, a remarkable city man and father of the great millionaire and author.

§ Son of the Earl of Hardwicke, eventually 2nd Earl.

where personal, and indecent in regard to the House of Peers in general, to which Mr. Pitt answered with great heat that he was sorry to hear such language from a gentleman who was to be a Peer; he set forth the great importance and dignity of Mr. Beckford personally, and above all the dignity and importance of an alderman, concluding it was a title he should be more proud of than that of a Peer. This speech has enraged the Lords, offended the Commons, and the City ungratefully say was too gross. Those who wish well to this country, and consequently to a union of parties at this juncture, are sorry for these heats; it is well if they do not unsolder the Union. . . . I began Islington Waters to-day. . . . You make a false judgment of your own letters. I will allow you to say it gives you some trouble to write them, but pray do not assert that I have not great pleasure in reading them; it becomes not a descendant of the great Bishop Stillingfleet * to tell a fib."

Mention has been made of Mr. John Rogers, first cousin on his mother's side to Mr. Montagu, also of Mr. Montagu becoming his trustee in 1746, when he was pronounced a lunatic. At first it seems that he suffered from epileptic fits, which increased to lunacy, but of a mild order. On June 23 Mr. Edward Steuart wrote to say Mr. Rogers was seriously ill, and his death expected hourly; he was being attended by Dr. Askew, then a famous north-country doctor, and several surgeons, for a mortification in his leg.† On the 24th he expired, in his seventy-fourth year, at his house in Pilgrim Street, Newcastle-on-Tyne. Mr. Montagu was his principal heir. Mrs. Montagu, in a letter respecting the estate of East Denton, etc., wrote in later days, "Mr. M.

* Edward Stillingfleet, Bishop of Worcester, author of "Eirenicon," born 1635, died 1699.

† Mr. Rogers' leg swelling, the doctors feared dropsy, and made him drink two bottles of Hock daily.

BENJAMIN STILLINGFLEET.

[To face p. 128, vol. ii.

has half the estate by descent, a share by testamentary disposition, and a part by purchase." Mr. Rogers' lunacy seems to have been made worse by the death of his wife, Anne Delaval, daughter of Sir John Delaval, whom he married in 1713, and who died in 1722–23. His will was made in 1711, and a codicil added 1715, in which he left his property, after the death of his mother, Mrs. Elizabeth Rogers, to his wife, and failing issue by her, to the Montagus and Creaghs, all first cousins. Mary Creagh had married Dominick Archdeacon, and her sister Margaret, Anthony Isaacson; Mr. Montagu's two brothers, Crewe and John, being dead, the only other heir was Jemima, Mrs. Medows, afterwards Lady Medows. The estates were very large; besides Denton, with its coal-mines, houses in Newcastle, and in Bramston, Lamesley, Harburn, Parkhead, and Jarrow, in the county of Durham; lands at Hindley, Sugley, Throckley, Newbiggin, Scotswood, etc., etc.; collieries and saltpans in Cullercoats, Monkseaton, Whitley, and Hartley, etc., etc. Mrs. Montagu was at Ealing with the Bothams when the express came. She writes to her husband, "It gives me pleasure to think I shall see you with unblemished integrity and unsoiled with unjust gain, enjoying that affluence many purchase with the loss of honesty and honour."

Her brother Morris fetched her from Ealing in order to accompany her husband to the north. Mr. Rogers was embalmed and buried on July 5 at St. Nicholas' church in Newcastle. The Montagus did not start for the North till Tuesday, August 1. A letter from Dr. Monsey of June 26, while staying with the Garricks at Hampton, congratulates Mrs. Montagu on her inheritance, but scolds her for leaving her friends to go North. This contains the first mention of his acquaintance with the Garricks, who were great friends of Dr. Monsey's, and he says, "Mr. Garrick * was very near in a apoplectic fit when he found you were gone. . . . Mrs. Garrick † also abus'd herself for not pressing you to return to the Temple ‡ and enjoy another half-hour."

The next letter is the first I possess to Elizabeth Carter, whose learned translation of Epictetus was first printed in April of 1758. Miss Carter, or *Mrs.* Carter (as courtesy termed her), was the daughter of a clergyman, the Rev. Nicholas Carter, D.D., Perpetual Curate of Deal, Kent, where he resided; he had been twice married, and Elizabeth was his child by his first marriage. To his children by both marriages Mr. Carter gave an excellent education, and at an early age Elizabeth studied Latin, Greek, and eventually Hebrew. She was a proficient in French, and taught herself Italian, Spanish, and German; later in life Portuguese and Arabic were added. Her application to study produced severe headaches, principally brought on by drinking green tea and taking snuff to keep herself awake. It appears that Mrs. Montagu had met her in 1757, but Mrs. Carter had rather avoided such a brilliant acquaintance, being herself of a most humble and unambitious character, despite her learning. From the following portions of Mrs. Montagu's letter we learn that Miss Carter had been paying her a visit:—

"Hill Street, July 6, 1758.

"What must my dear Miss Carter think of the signs of brutal insensibility which I have given in not answering her obliging letter? As my heart has had no share in the omission, I have no apologies to make for it; no

* David Garrick, born 1716, died 1779; famous actor.

† Eva Marie Veilchen, or Viegel, known as "la Violette," once an opera *danseuse*.

‡ The temple at Hampton, on the lawn by the river, still existent; once held Roubilliac's bust of Shakespeare.

day has passed since you left us in which I have not thought of you with esteem and affection; I look upon my introduction to your acquaintance as one of the luckiest incidents of my life, if I can contrive to improve it into friendship; this is, and has been the state of my mind and I am proud of it: as to my conduct in the commencement of our correspondence, I am ashamed of it. I was ill when I received your polite and agreeable letter. I have ever since been drinking Islington waters, from which I receive some benefit, but with this inconvenience, that I am unable to write till late at night, and even then not without headache. The death of a relation of Mr. Montagu's in the North, which happened about a fortnight ago, with a large accession of fortune, has brought me the usual accompaniment of riches, a great deal of business, a great deal of hurry, and a great many ceremonious engagements. The ordering funeral ceremonies, putting a large family in mourning, preparing for a journey of 280 miles, and receiving and paying visits on this event, has made me the most busy miserable creature in the world. As the gentleman from whom Mr. Montagu inherits had been mad above 40 years and almost bed-ridden the last ten, I had always designed to be rather pleased and happy when he resigned his unhappy being and his good estate. I thought in fortune's as in folly's cup, still laughed the bubble joy; but though this is a bumper, there is not a drop of joy in it, nor so much as the froth of a little merriment. As soon as I rise in the morning, my housekeeper with a face full of care, comes to know what must be packed up for Newcastle; to her succeeds the Butler, who wants to know what wine, etc., is to be sent down; to them succeed men of business and money transactions; then the post brings twenty letters, which must be considered and some answered. In about a week we shall set out for the North, where I am to pass about three months in the delectable conversation of Stewards and managers of coal mines, and this by courtesy is called good fortune, and I am congratulated upon it by every one I meet; while in truth, like a poor Harlequin in the play, I am acting a silly part *dans l'embarras des richesses.* I would not have troubled you with this detail, but as part of my defence for not having written to you. I can perfectly understand why you were afraid of me last year, and I will tell you, for you won't tell me; perhaps you have not told yourself. You had heard I set up as a wit, and people of real merit and sense hate to converse with witlings, as rich merchant-ships dread to engage privateers, they may receive damage and can get nothing but dry blows. I am happy you have found out I am not to be feared; I am afraid I must improve myself much before you will find I am to be loved. If you will give affection for affection *tout simple* I shall get it from you. . . ."

Mention is made of Emin's joining the King of Prussia, so he was known to Mrs. Carter, probably through Lord Lyttelton.

"I have the pleasure of hearing infinite commendations of Epictetus every day; from such as are worthy I taste a particular pleasure; from the multitude I take it in the gross, as it makes the sum of universal fame. Some praises I heard a few days ago at the Bishop of London's I put in the first class."

A most amusing letter from Lord Lyttelton to Dr. Monsey of July 24 now occurs, in which he returns a letter of Mrs. Montagu's to the doctor, and summons him to a duel of words in her praise on Hagley turf. He teases Dr. Monsey with the idea of her going north, and advises him "to quit Lord Godolphin to follow love, follow him over the Cheviot Hills and down to the coal-pits at Newcastle." After a great deal of chaff it ends, "Your most affectionate, humble Servant,—LYTTELTON."

This frightened Monsey, so on July 30 he writes

from St. James's and gives her strings of advice as to her health.

"I know the generality of Physicians will be cautious of blooding you, as being what is called nervous; I know nothing of nerves in the usual sense of the word, if indeed it has any precise meaning at all, it is used by the wise to quiet fools, and by fools to cover ignorance." Then he adds in high fever she may be blooded, "5, 6 or 7 ounces, and if you flag a blister! will set matters to right. I say nothing of vomits, you can't bear 'em, but you will gentle purging, your lemon mixture and contrayserva with a little saffron, be cautious of hot medicines, but do not wholly throw them away, as to spasms and cramps they are such Proteuses, one does not know how to catch or hold them, Valerian and Castor are in such reputation for vanquishing those Hussars. . . . Assafœtida you can't bear, I wish you cou'd . . . if feverish 3 spoonfuls of a decoction of the bark by boyling one ounce and half in a quart of water to a pint, and if your stomach flags put in from 5 to 10 drops of Elixir of Vitriol, so arm'd a common cold will not have courage to attack you."

Finally he consigns her to a Dr. Ramsay's care, should she require a physician!

On August 1 Mrs. Boscawen wrote from Hatchlands a long letter describing a visit to London. Her letters are sprightly, but too much larded with French words and phrases; the end is interesting—

"*Enfin* we left this dear odious London at 4 in the afternoon, *chemin faisant* I thought within myself, what if I should meet an express from America, and sure enough upon Cobham Common I met a post-chaise containing an officer, on him I star'd attentively, he star'd again; then he cry'd 'Stop,' I echoed 'Stop,' *enfin* I heard him ask 'is Admiral Boscawen's * lady in that coach?' I make quick reply in the affirmative, and soon he produced himself at my coach window, and told me he was express sent by the Governor of Nova Scotia with news of our troops having taken the Forts of Beau Sejour and Chignecto, that he attended Admiral Boscawen for his orders twenty-three days ago, and left him in perfect health; he added that Admiral Boscawen had saved North America, where all our Colonies were in the utmost danger, as well as consternation till he came. Papers having been found which showed the French had a design to destroy Halifax, where the people imagin'd the French wou'd let in the Indians to massacre them. . . .' He added, 'Mr. Boscawen had taken, or as the phrase there is *detain'd*, six French merchant ships, and had blocaded Louisbourg.'"

She adds that her letters from her husband were with Mr. Cunninghame (the Officer), addressed to Mr. Cleveland, so she let them go, and sent on her black servant "Tom" next day to fetch them, and was going to Portsmouth to meet the Admiral, who thought he should soon be back.

To return to the Montagus, they set out on August 1 for the North, and the first letter is from her to Lord Lyttelton on August 6, from Darlington—

"I am now about 25 miles short of Newcastle, having travelled above 250 miles since last Tuesday, and am better to-night than I was when I left London, so I will no longer endure that Dr. Monsey shall call me flimsy animal, puny insect, and such opprobrious names. I have had a surfeit of being in a post-chaise, that I have not made many excursions to see the fine places that lay in the road. In my way to Nottingham I went to see

* Admiral Boscawen, Major General Amherst, and Brigadier-General Wolfe were combined in this campaign.

Sir Robert Clifton's,* which appears to me for beauty of prospect equal to any place I ever saw. You are led to it from the turnpike road by a fine terrace on the side of the Trent. From a pavillion in the garden you see the town and Castle of Nottingham standing in the most smiling valley imaginable, in which the Trent serpentizes in a most beautiful manner. . . . I return your Lordship many thanks for having lent me so agreeable a companion as Antonio de Solis." †

To this Lord Lyttelton writes from Hagley on August 17, to say how glad he is she bore the journey so well, and the book entertained her. He had been drinking the waters at Sunning Hill, Berks, and found benefit. In the end of a long letter he writes, "Miss West and Captain‡ Hood will be as happy next Monday as mutual love can make them." Miss West was Gilbert West's sister, and her future husband, Captain Hood, became afterwards first Viscount Bridport. Mary West lived till 1786, but had no children. Lord Lyttelton alludes to her not being very young and "having no time to lose."

In another letter of August 22, written from Lindridge Vicarage, Worcestershire, where the Vicar, Mr. Meadowcourt, was a great friend of his Lordship's, he writes—

"Tom and I came this afternoon to this sweet abode on our way to Hampton Court. . . . I told you in my last that Miss West was to be married to Captain Hood. Yesterday I had the pleasure to give her away to him at Hagley Church, after which we made a party to Mr. Shenstone's § Arcadian Farm in very fine weather. The

* Clifton Hall.

† "The History of the Conquest of Mexico," by Antonio de Solis, a Spaniard; born 1610, died 1686.

‡ He became the celebrated Admiral Hood.

§ William Shenstone, poet, born 1714, died 1763. His place, the "Leasowes," adjoined Hagley.

pastoral scene seemed to suit the occasion, and the bride owned to me that the cascades and rills never murmured so sweetly before. . . . The Dean * came to Hagley just time enough to give Hood and her the Nuptial Benediction."

Further on, alluding to Mr. Montagu's going north to take possession of the Rogers' estate, he says—

"I suppose this will find you, like Guyon in Mammon's Cave, got down the bottom of your mines,† and beholding your treasures with all the indifference that the Knight of temperance showed when the Demon of Riches revealed to him his hidden wealth. I paint to myself the wonder and admiration of the subterraneous inhabitants when you first came among them. Since the time that Proserpina was carried by her husband to his Stygian Empire, the infernal regions have not seen such a charming goddess. But is it sure they will let you return again to daylight? Upon my word I am afraid you are in some danger, as the Habeas Corpus Bill was thrown out; for all the women of the upper world will make interest with the Judges to let you stay there. Yet I verily think Baron Smith will release you in spite of them all, and even if he should fail, you have still a resource, Emin shall come back and deliver you from the Shades as Hercules did Alcestis."

The best description of the Montagus' arrival in the north is contained in a letter to Dr. Stillingfleet at "Robert Price's, Esqre., Herefordshire," sent open to Dr. Monsey, who forwards it with a few words of his own. It is dated, "Carville, ye 22nd day of August." Carville Hall had been hired by them; it was situated at the end of the Roman Wall, called Wallsend. Portions of the letter I give—

* Charles Lyttelton, Dean of Exeter.

† Denton was, and is, full of coal-mines, copper, etc.

"I desired Dr. Monsey to acquaint you with the death of Mr. Rogers. Many letters were to be written in order to procure him most pompous funeral obsequies, according to the fashion of Northumberland, as he was allied to the people of the first rank in the county, and they were all to be at the funeral. . . . The 7th of August at noon we got to Durham, and there began hurrys and ceremonies that have continued to this day, and I know not when I shall see a quiet hour. At Durham we were met by a great number of Mr. Rogers' relations, and the Receivers and Agents of his estate, who attended in great form till we got to Newcastle, where we were to stay two or three days, with a relation of Mr. Montagu's till our house was aired. We had not been an hour at Newcastle before we had the compliments of the principal persons of the Corporation and in the town. The next morning visits began. . . . We had fifteen people to dine here on Sunday, a family yesterday, people about business to-day, and three families to dine here to-morrow; in the morning I am up to the elbows in dusty parchments and accounts, after dinner as busy as an hostess of an Inn attending her guests, at night as sick as an invalid in Hospital, and these are the woes of wealth, and I am not *une malade imaginaire*. . . . Mr. Rogers' family Mansion * having been uninhabited many years, was not fit for our reception, his house † in Newcastle was not agreeably situated for the summer, so we hired a house on the banks of the Tyne for the occasion. It is a very pretty house, extreamly well furnished and most agreeably situated, ships and other vessels from Newcastle are sailing by every hour. The river here is broad and of a good colour, and we have a fine reach of it: we have a very good turnpike road to the sea-side, where I should pass a great deal of my time if it was not all engross'd by company, but we are in the midst of the largest neighbourhood I ever saw, and some of these gentlemen by means of coal mines have immense fortunes."

* Denton Hall.

† In Pilgrim Street.

In a letter to her sister, Mrs. Scott, Newcastle is described.

"The town of Newcastle is horrible, like the ways of thrift it is narrow, dark and dirty, some of the streets so steep one is forced to put a dragchain on the wheels: the night I came I thought I was going to the center. The streets are some of them so narrow, that if the tallow chandler ostentatiously hangs forth his candles, you have a chance to sweep them into your lap as you drive by, and I do not know how it has happened that I have not yet caught a coach full of red herrings, for we scrape the Citty wall on which they hang in great abundance. There are some wide streets and good houses. Sir Walter Blackett's seems a noble habitation."

Mention is made of the Claverings, Bowes, and Lord Ravensworth calling.

In a letter of August 25 to Mrs. Carter, Mrs. Montagu tells her, that *en route* to Newcastle, she had visited "Althorpe, the seat of Mr. Spencer, worthy of regard only on account of a very fine collection of pictures. The park is planted in a dull uniformity, the ground flatt (*sic*), little prospect, has not the advantage of a river or lake." After repeating the details of her journey, she adds that Denton Hall

"had not been inhabited for 30 years, the poor gentleman having long been a lunatick, so I imagined the rats and ghosts * were in such full possession, it would require time to eject them, and I am now placed as I could wish, being within 4 miles of Tinmouth. . . . We have a very good land as well as water prospect. We see from our windows the place where once lived the Venerable Bede,† some little ruins show still, I

* Did she know? It is supposed to be haunted to this day.

† The monk Beda, or Bede, born 672, died 735.

believe, where the Monastery stood: the place is called Jarrow, the estate belong'd to Sir Thomas Clavering and the late Mr. Rogers. I shall visit it more from respect to the old Historian than curiosity to see a new possession."

On August 27 Mrs. S. Montagu wrote to young Tom Lyttelton a long letter describing the country round Newcastle.

"After dinner I ferried over the river Wear to Sunderland, a good sea-port town. They are making a new pier there, which is done at the expense of the coal-owners, who have mines near the Wear. I got a very pleasant walk on the sea-shore; several ships were sailing out of the harbour fraught only with the comforts and conveniences of life, they carry out coal and salt and bring home money. I question whether those who carry out death and bring home glory are concerned in so good merchandize, though they account their occupation more honourable. On Thursday I went to see Lumley Castle; it is a noble habitation, but so modernized by sash windows and other fashionable ornaments, I admired it only as a good house. There are many family pictures in the Hall, a succession of 16 Lumleys, all martially accoutred, the Lumley arms on their shields, their figure and attitudes make them look like scaramouches. They hang so high I could not read the inscriptions, but I imagine it is intended one should suppose each picture was taken from life; but from the dress and character, I am sure they have been done by one hand from the genealogical tree. There are many old pictures in the house, and many fair testimonies of the ancient nobility of the family, but I cannot pass them sixteen * generations. There are large plantations of firs at Lumley Castle, a large park behind the Castle, to

* She was wrong; the Lumleys descend from Liulph, a Norman nobleman of merit in 1060.

the front a good prospect, and the river Wear at a due distance."

Mrs. Montagu was connected with the Lumleys, her cousin, Mrs. Laurence Sterne, being the daughter of the Rev. Robert Lumley, of Lumley Castle. At the end of the letter she complains of the tediousness of the post —three weeks before she had any letters from her friends!

This accounts for the news of the taking of Louisburg on July 27, under Admiral Boscawen, General Amherst, and Wolfe, not having reached her when she wrote, as Lord Lyttelton wrote to congratulate her on August 22, "upon the glorious success of Admiral Boscawen. I wrote last post to his lady, whom I love for a thousand good qualities in herself and because she loves you. Had her husband commanded in the Mediterranean, and Amherst or Wolfe at Fort St. Philips, we had not lost Minorca."

In another letter of August 31, Lord Lyttelton having had a pleasant tour to Lady Coningsby's,* where he met Sir Sidney Smith, and to Lord Oxford's,† Brampton Brian,‡—

"I carried Tom with me through the whole tour, and a more delightful fellow traveller I never can have, unless his Mother was raised from the dead or Heaven would give me another Lucy! Wherever we went he won all hearts, and you may believe mine beat with joy at the sight of his conquests, my only fear is that hereafter he may please the ladies too well. You must instruct him, Madonna, as Minerva did Telemachus to avoid the dangers of the Calypsos he may meet with in his travels, and let him learn by admiring you that no charms are

* Hampton Court, Herefordshire, built by Henry IV.

† Edward Harley, 24th Earl of Oxford.

‡ In Herefordshire.

truly amiable, but those that are under the government of wisdom and virtue."

Tom was fifteen at this time, having been born January 30, 1743-4. His father's fears as to his attractions for the fair sex were prophetic.

Tom writes to Mrs. Montagu on September 9, giving her an account of his travels. Here is a description of Hampton Court, Herefordshire, the seat of Lady Coningsby—

"The house stands at the end of a line of regular planted trees, and looks more like a Monastery than a nobleman's house. The garden is very large, and would have been pretty enough if Nature had been left in it unmolested. In the middle of it is a piece of water of about an acre, cut into two square lines, in which, to the astonishment of the beholder, you see Neptune upon his throne, and twenty Tritons waiting behind him. The carver has express'd great fierceness in his countenance, and well may the god who shakes the earth with his Trident, be angry at being confined in a Pool, which would scarce hold two hundred fish. From the garden one might see a noble lawn bounded with an amphitheatre of wood, was it not for the high Yew Hedges clipt into a thousand ridiculous shapes which hinder the eye from passing them, the park, too, is very large, but so overrun with Bushes that some of the Lawns resemble bogs. . . . From my Lady Coningsby's we went to my Lord Oxford's, a place where nature has done a great deal, which by a little money judiciously laid out may be made the prettiest *ferme ornée* in England. My Lord's House is a very good one, built in a remarkable good taste for the times of Queen Anne."

Lord Lyttelton, as usual, adds a few words at the end of the letter, and congratulates Mrs. Montagu on the King of Prussia's "most glorious success, but I am in pain till I hear what has become of Emin.'

Dr. Monsey writes from Claremont on September 6—

"DEAR MADAM,

"I should be asham'd of myself to be in the house of a Prime Minister, and not let you know the King sent a long letter from the King of Prussia hither this evening, giving a long detail of his last victory * over the Russians, but it being in French and the Duke of N(ewcastle) not being the best reader, I am unable to give you an account, though my Lord G(odolphin) heard it as well as I, and wou'd have interpreted for me, if he cou'd. However there is an English account too of which I will give you some particulars. Eighteen thousand killed by their own account, 6 generals killed, I don't remember how many wounded, 7 Generals prisoners in the King's Camp, 73 pieces of cannon taken, the military chest with 850,000 Rubles. General Brown killed, refusing quarter. The Russian infantry as they had behaved like Bears, fought like Lyons, part of Count Dohna's foot gave way, or else it had been a most compleat victory. The King himself took the colours in his hand and brought 'em on again, sure this is too bold for anybody but an immortal and invulnerable. He had two aide-de-camps killed."

Monsey picked up the cover to the letter, addressed—

"A Monsieur mon frère,
"Le Roy de grande Bretagne."

This he intended to send Mrs. Montagu, but the Duke asked for it. It was sealed with two large seals, the arms and royal Crown under a camp canopy in black wax.

On September 9 Emin wrote a long letter from the Duke of Marlborough's Quarter in Germany, whither he had retired disconsolate at not being allowed to fight in the battle by General Yorke, Lady Anson's

* Battle of Zorndorff, fought August 25.

brother, to whom he had been recommended by her. Meanwhile he had marched four days with the Army, and the King of Prussia had taken notice of him, staring at him hard and saying to Mr. Mitchell he wished he had 12,000 men like him. Emin wished he had a letter to the King, and was furious at General Yorke's forbidding him to fight; probably the General was too anxious for his safety. The following description of the King of Prussia is so interesting I insert it, the whole letter to Mrs. Montagu, a folio sheet closely written, being too long:—

"I will do my endeavour to describe the King of Prussia's person, and his way of living. He is no taller than Emin the Persian, he has a short neck, he has one of the finest made heads ever I saw in my life, with a noble forehead; he wears a false wigg, he has very handsome nose. His eyes are grey, sharp and lively, ready to pearce one through and through. He likes a man that looks him in the face when he is talking to him. He is well made everywhere, with a bend back, not stupid (*sic*, stooped?) at all, like many Europeans. His voice is the sweetest and clearest ever I heard. He takes a great quantity of Spanish snuff, from his nose down to the buckles of his shoes or boots is all painted with that confounded stuff. His hands are as red as paint, as if he was a painter, grizy all over. He dines commonly between twelve and one, and drinks a bottle of wine at his dinner. I was told that he was very unhealthy in the time of peace, but since this war he has grown healthy, and left off drinking a great quantity of coffee, which he did formerly. All the satisfaction that I have, which is great enough that I have seen Cæsar alive, nay twenty times greater, he is more like King Solomon, for he rules his nation by wisdom and understanding. . . . His armies are not only disciplined to the use of arms, but very religious, and say their prayers three times a day: it is never neglected, even when they are on the march."

Emin winds up with a message of apology to Mr. Burke at not having written to him from want of time.

Meanwhile his adored Mrs. Montagu had nearly lost her life through the carelessness of a maid. It happened on September 3. Writing to Sarah Scott, she gives this description—

"On this day sennight at 4 in the morn I was seized with a fainting fit, in which I lay some time, my maids in their fright let the *eau de luce* fall into my eye, nostril and mouth, my eyes were enflamed and nostril, the mouth and uvula of the throat excoriated. After a long and cruel struggle for life,* a most sharp contention with this medicine, I awaken'd to find myself in this terrible condition. Dr. Askew unhappily lay at Durham that night, so had no assistance till 2 at noon, then I was blooded, which abated the inflammation so far I could articulate. The Doctor told me my safety depended on frequent gargling and drinking, so for, four days, I was never a quarter of an hour without doing so, the spitting was more violent than from a mercurial salivation. . . . When I came out of my fit, to see blood running from eye, nose and mouth drove Mr. Montagu almost distracted, and I knew not which way my agonies would end. . . . Mr. Montagu has shown on this occasion the most passionate love imaginable. Dr. Askew has been very careful, and an excellent apothecary has watched me night and day."

In a second letter she says, "On the fourth day when I was able to look up I was surprized at the impression concern had made on Mr. Montagu, and I should hardly have known him, he looked 20 years older at least."

In a letter of Monsey's we learn *eau de luce* was made of strong sal ammoniac and quicklime.

Mr. Montagu's sister, now Lady Medows, wrote on

* For two days her life was despaired of; for four days she could swallow no solid, and was salivated for a week.

September 14 to say her brother-in-law, Sir Philip, had been nearly killed in the same way by hartshorn. At the end of the letter she says, "Lady Bath dyed at two this morning of the Palsy." This was the wife of Pulteney, Earl of Bath, soon after this to become one of Mrs. Montagu's most intimate friends. Lady Bath's maiden name was Maria Gumley, daughter and heiress of a great glass manufacturer. She had the character of great penuriousness, and her husband was credited with the same character, but I hope to show later that he could be very generous. When the news of Mrs. Montagu's accident spread amongst her numerous friends, many were the letters of condolence and rejoicing at her safety from Lord Lyttelton and a host of others. Dr. Monsey had been staying with the Garricks; he was a great admirer of Mrs. Garrick, whom he often quotes in his letters. It was whilst staying with them he heard of it. Both he and Lord Lyttelton were quite frantic at the risk she had run, and distressed at her fainting fit. Monsey was suffering from a bad cough, for which, when staying with Sir John Evelyn at Wooton, he tried bleeding, cathartics, and syrup of white poppies. He returned to St. James's, where Mrs. Garrick came to sit with him, and cheer him up. In a letter of his to Mrs. Montagu of September 23, mention is made of Lady Burlington's death. "Lady Burlington is dead. Mrs. G(arrick) gets nothing, but rid of her, and that's a great deal, I think. She gives the Duke of D. £3000 per annum . . . not a farthing to any one servant, she had some lived with her 20 or 25 years."

Lady Burlington, widow of the 3rd Earl, the celebrated amateur architect, was the daughter of William, Marquis of Halifax. On Eva Marie Viegel's * arrival

* Eva Maria Viegel, or Veilchen, born at Vienna, 1725; married David Garrick on June 22, 1749.

in England from Austria, the Empress Queen, Maria Theresa, gave her a recommendation to Lady Burlington, who received her at Burlington House as an inmate. It is said "La Violette," as she was called from her exquisite dancing in the operas, had attracted the Emperor of Austria's attention so much as to alarm the Empress, and that she therefore sought to remove her from Austria. Lady Burlington strongly objected to Garrick's attachment to La Violette, having more ambitious projects for her *protégée*, but it was a true love affair from the beginning even to the end, and not one word could ever be said against Mrs. Garrick; theirs was indeed a love match, and after fifteen years of married life Garrick presented her with a ring on her birthday, with the most touching love verses. From the letters, I gather it was Dr. Monsey who brought Mrs. Montagu into personal intercourse with the Garricks.

Dr. Monsey was so disturbed at Mrs. Montagu's accident that he wrote almost daily to her, and no one who reads his letters could imagine, however eccentric he was, that he was a free thinker in religion, as is asserted in the "Dictionary of National Biography." His letters are so long that it is impossible to print them in full in this book. He had a bad cough and a sort of vertigo at this time, in the midst of which he was called to the Earl of Northumberland, who was desperately ill, whose sufferings Monsey succeeded in alleviating. In a letter of October 8 we learn that his birthday and Mrs. Montagu's were on the same day, viz. October 2.* He promises in joke to marry Mrs. Stuart, a widow lady who had nursed Mrs. Montagu with the greatest attention. To add to Mrs. Montagu's troubles, her faithful housekeeper, Mrs. Crosby, a lady

* Monsey, in a letter, said he was sixty-four then.

by birth, but reduced to poverty, died of a quinsy in twelve days.

In a letter of Dr. Monsey's of October 27, mention is made of Lord Godolphin drinking "absent friends" as a toast, coupled with special mention of Mrs. Montagu, and also of Allan Ramsay,* the artist. "Ramsay is one of us, he was born on October 2. I jumped for joy, but hang it, 'tis the old October. I tell him he must be regenerated, become a child of grace, and then he shall be adopted into our family. . . ." Dr. Monsey's little grand-daughter "loves Missy Montagu dearly."

A letter of Atkinson, the farm bailiff at Sandleford, on October 3, to Mrs. Crosby, the late housekeeper, shows the current price of food: "Everything continues dear for ye pour, and will do so all this winter, I am afraid, befe is sold in our market for 3*d.* for a pd. Muton 4*d.* to 4½*d.*, it is beyond prise wich I never heard before at this time of ye year, pork and veal 5*d.* a pound."

Mrs. Donnellan wrote from Fulham on October 21 condoling with Mrs. Montagu on her accident, and the loss of Mrs. Crosby. She says—

"I told you how near we were losing our respectable friend Mrs. Sherlock, she is now quite recovered . . . they say there never was a more moving scene than between her and the Bishop,† who would be carried up to her in the worst of her illness; he got hold of her hand and it was with difficulty they could get him to let it go and separate them." (Bishop Sherlock was born in 1678, so was then eighty years of age.) "I went yesterday *pour égayer* a little to see Mrs. Spencer ‡ after

* Eminent portrait painter; son of the Scotch poet of the same name; born 1709, died 1784.

† Thomas Sherlock, then Bishop of London.

‡ *Née* Georgina, daughter of Stephen Poyntz, of Midgham, Berks.

her lying in, and there is nothing but joy and magnificence; the child * is likely to live tho' it came, they reckon, six weeks before its time. Mrs. Poinne showed me all the fineries; the pap boat is pure gold, etc., etc. I like Mrs. Spencer, she is a natural good young woman, no airs, no affectation, but seems to enjoy her great fortune by making others partakers, and happy with herself."

This was Georgina, *née* Poyntz, who had married Mr. John Spencer, afterwards 1st Earl Spencer, by whom she had Georgiana, afterwards the beautiful Duchess of Devonshire; George John,† who was born on September 1, 1758, was the owner of the gold pap boat. and Lady Besborough. Mrs. Donnellan adds—

"Mrs. Poinne (Poyntz) has the practical moral virtues, and when I see her good works I think she is worth a hundred such poor spectators as I am; her present business is attending the foundling Hospital, and she has six and twenty children nursing under her care. . . . The Duchess of Portland and her family are at Bath."

The next letter is from Lord Lyttelton on October 10, full of anxiety as to Mrs. Montagu's health, and urging her to return South as soon as possible. In this he says—

"You inquire about my new house,‡ and my History,§ both are going on but the first much faster and better than the other. When the History will be finished I cannot tell, and when it is, I fear it will be little better than a *gothick house modernised.* The Goths

* Became Earl Spencer, born September, 1758.

† Became 2nd Earl Spencer in 1783.

‡ He was rebuilding Hagley.

§ His "History of Henry II."

will think it too Græcian and the Græcians too Gothic." He winds up with, "Adieu, best Madonna, take great care of yourself, your late danger has shown you how dear you are to your friends. Don't try their affection that way any more."

Writing on October 20 to Dr. Stillingfleet, who was exploring Wales with Charles Lyttelton, the Dean of Exeter and brother of Lord Lyttelton, Mrs. Montagu says—

"Carville * is just at the end of the Picts' Wall, it makes part of our enclosures, and we have a Roman Altar in the stables. The din of War has so frightened the rural Deities that even the long time that has passed since the Union with Scotland, has not brought them to make their residence with us. Pan, Ceres, and Pomona, seem to neglect us; we are under the domination of the god of mines. There is a great deal of rich land in this country, but agriculture is ill understood. The great gain made by several branches of the coal trade has turned all attention that way. Every gentleman in the country, from the least to the greatest, is as solicitous in the pursuit of gain as a tradesman. The conversation always turns upon money; the moment you name a man, you are told what he is worth, the losses he has had, or the profit he has made by coal mines. As my mind is not naturally set to this tune, I should often be glad to change it for a song from one of your Welch Bards."

Mrs. Lowther had asked her to spend some time at Lowther Hall,† of which she says, "Lowther is much greater than Gibside, which is too great for me." In the next letter of Lord Lyttelton's he mentions Mr. Anson and Mr. Steward being at Hagley—

* Carville, the house they had hired.

† Now Lowther Castle.

"Stuart seems almost as fond of my hall as of the *Thessala Tempe*,* which I believe you heard him describe when I brought him to see you. . . . He is going to embellish one of the Hills with a true Attick building, a Portico of six pillars, which will make a fine object to my new house, and command a most beautiful view of the country. He has also engaged to paint me a Flora and four pretty little Zephyrs in my drawing-room ceiling, which is ornamented with flowers in Stucco, but has spaces left for these pictures. He thinks all my Stucco work is well done."

This was James Stuart,† nicknamed "Athenian Stuart," traveller and antiquary, author of "The Antiquities of Athens." Alluding to Tom, he says, "Dr. Bernard‡ offered to putt him into the Remove, but rather advised him to stay in the fourth form in order to learn more Greek, which advice he has prudently and cheerfully followed."

Mrs. Montagu, being attacked by a choleraic disorder, which kept her in her room a week, and being still very hoarse from the *eau de Luce*, Mr. Montagu insisted on her returning to London before himself, so as to be in reach of Dr. Monsey. On November 6, from Wexford, she writes to Sarah Scott to inform her she is returning to London. Mr. Montagu had accompanied her three days' journey; he then returned to Carville. She had left behind the post-chaise, and travelled in the "body coach, but my horses are so stout I believe they will perform the journey from Carville to London in seven days." *En route* she picks up Mr. Tom Pitt,§

* Mr. Bower's place.

† James Stuart, born 1713, died 1788.

‡ Head-master of Eton.

§ 1st Lord Camelford, Thomas Pitt, junior, son of Lord Cobham's brother Thomas and his wife, *née* Christian Lyttelton.

nephew of Miss Pitt and a friend of his, and carries them to Durham, putting her maid into their post-chaise. "My gentlemen leave me at Stilton, from whence they go to Cambridge." She mentions that Mr. Montagu had bought all the jewels belonging to Mr. Rogers for her, "and to-day intimated he should give me a great purse of old gold which fell to his share in the division; some of the pieces are curious, but there will be between £60 to £70 of money that one may spend with a good conscience."

Arrived in London, Mrs. Montagu writes to her husband that his sister, Lady Medows,* was in very bad health, and she had recommended her to take "Viper broth!" if her doctor approved it, "as it is a nourishing food, and by its quality supplies deficiency of food." I believe vipers are still used as medicine in France, but whether in England I know not; perhaps "Brusher Mills,"† the famous New Forest snake-catcher, could inform one; it does not sound inviting! In the same letter she mentions having secured a berth as midshipman for Montagu Isaacson,‡ Mr. Montagu's cousin, with Admiral Boscawen. The Admiral had been most graciously received by the King, "and nothing can exceed the honours the Admiral meets with from all quarters."

A Scotch gardener had been hired for Sandleford, and she adds, "The Scotch Gardener was tired a little, so I thought you would not dislike his recreating himself and resting his horse a little. I have sent him to the play to-night."

In the next letter she writes, "The Carville gardener will set out to-morrow, he is more happy in London

* She was suffering from cancer and dropsy.

† Since this was written, "Brusher" died.

‡ Son of Margaret, *née* Creagh, and Anthony Isaacson.

than a young toast, he has seen St. Paul's, Westminster Abbey, etc., and sees them with taste; his mind was made for a higher condition of life." Mentioning the horses, she says she shall send three to Sandleford, "it is a shame for a little animal as I am to keep 7 horses in town." The team for a big coach was then six, but a seventh was ridden alongside by a servant in case of accidents on the way.

George II. had been very ill. "Princess Emilia not well, and the Duke * has got the gout. . . . Sixteen thousand pounds a year of annuities on the Duke of Marlborough † expire with him, so there are many sincere mourners; the Duchess ‡ bears her loss better than could have been imagined. Lord Bath § is so apparently rejoiced at his deliverance, it makes people smile, he ordered a plentiful table to be kept as soon as she was dead, and is gay and jolly, and at the Bath like a young heir just come to his estate. . . . It is thought Mr. Charles Montagu ‖ can live but a few days."

Great anxiety reigned for some days about the health of little Morris Robinson, Morris's son. Dr. Monsey stayed with the child four days and nights, and he pulled through, but it painfully reminded his aunt of her loss in little "Punch," Morris being much of the same age. Dr. Monsey wrote to Mr. Montagu to say he had insisted, when the child was at its worst, that Mrs. Montagu should not come to see it. Mention is made

* Cumberland.

† 3rd Duke of Marlborough, died October 20, 1758, at Munster in Westphalia.

‡ Elizabeth, daughter of 2nd Baron Trevor.

§ William Pulteney, Earl of Bath, had just lost his wife.

‖ Charles Montagu, son of the Hon. James Montagu, cousin of Mr. Edward Montagu. He died in 1759.

of young Mr. Pitt "just come to town, not so well as when you saw him; he was here on Tuesday night, and I thought looked ill; his chairmen were drunk and threw him in the street, and cut his face and hurt him a little, and he had a bad fit that night from the surprise." This was Thomas Pitt, junior, son of Thomas Pitt, of Boconoc, Cornwall, brother of Mr. William Pitt, and afterwards 1st Lord Camelford.

On November 23 both houses of Parliament met at Westminster, and Mrs. Montagu writes on the 28th to her husband—

"Mr. Pitt opened the session on Tuesday with a very fine speech, Mr. Beckford stood up and said the turn things had taken of late had put him in good humour, so that he was willing to give two millions towards the war on the Continent; he thought it too little to be of service, but rather more than could be got. Mr. Pitt answered the sum must not be limited, a great deal indeed would be wanted, he knew not how it would be raised, for he did not concern himself with Treasury business, but the honourable gentleman, signifying Mr. Legge, understood these matters, and he did not doubt would raise a proper sum. Poor Legge looked distressed. No one knows how these great sums are to be raised, taxes on Dogs and publick diversions are talked of, the King is much pleased with his Secretary's declaration of a support of the continent interest at any rate. I hear Mr. Pitt's speech was much admired, and nowhere more than at St. James's. . . . Mr. Pitt has a personal dignity that supports open measures, and I am glad he does not learn the political art of prevarication. He has the people's intire confidence, and I hope he will use it to good ends."

On December 2, writing to Mr. Montagu, she says—

"Emin is come home, he has a great loss of the

Duke of Marlborough, who called him his Lion and kept him always with him. He has been a sort of aide-de-camp to Count Schullenburg; he has lately been in Holland where the Armenians have promised to assist his schemes. Lady Yarmouth has him with her in a morning and promises him her interest with a very great man; Lord Northumberland, Lord Anson, and General York are to be his advocates with Mr. Pitt. He is an astonishing creature to take thus with all kinds of people. He hopes to go home in January in a sort of public character. He is full of anecdotes of the King of Prussia. He says his eyes and forehead are just like mine, and he is as particular in his description of him as a portrait painter would be. He marched with him seven days, the Prussian Hero is as easy and familiar as a private man, knowing his character will give him more respect than his rank: it is not advisable in general for Princes to lay aside their rank lest they should not otherwise gain respect, but a truly great man is above all respect that is not personal."

A set of verses sent by Dr. Monsey from North Mimms to Lord Lyttelton is amusing, but too prolix to insert. Lyttelton had a bad cold, and wanted to go to Eton to see his boy—

"*L.* I *must* go to Eaton."
"*M.* You shall *not* go to Eaton."

Much allusion is made to Mrs. Montagu in the verses, which are rank doggerel.

Louisburg had been taken on July 27. On December 7 Mrs. Montagu writes, "The House of Commons yesterday returned thanks to Admiral Boscawen and General Amherst for their services at Louisburg, and to Admiral Osborne for his conduct in the Mediterranean."

Dr. Monsey had been reading the "Memoirs of Madame de Maintenon," in whom he sees a strong likeness to Mrs. Montagu.

"I take her into my hand and you into my mind as I go along . . . tho' Lewis was a scrub of a scoundrel and not worthy a crown which he would not put upon her head, he now and then thought right about her, instead of a foreign Princess whom he must study to please, he chose a woman who made it her whole business to please him, the only one who could inspire him with a lasting passion, and so revered that in the admiration which the recital of her vertues occasioned he cried, 'Let us go and shut ourselves up to talk of this woman.' That's my Lord (Lyttelton), and I!"

On December 17 the Earl of Arran died; he had married Mr. Montagu's relation, Elizabeth, daughter of Lord Crewe of Stene, who brought him a large fortune. It was an unhappy marriage, and Mrs. Montagu hints that, had Lady Arran treated her husband as he deserved, her money would have come to Mr. Montagu and Lady Mary Gregory. He died at eighty-eight. His sister, Lady Emily Butler,

"is a surprising woman, healthy and lively at past 99! Mr. Boscawen yesterday show'd us a box of horrid implements with which the French cannon was charged at Louisbourg, rusty locks, pieces of pokers, curling tongs, nails in abundance and all sorts of iron instruments, and this not for want of ammunition, but wanton cruelty. He found the cannons loaded with these as well as ball. General Wolfe had a gridiron shot at him; it fell short of him, but he had it taken up and straiten'd and eat a beef steak broil'd upon it."

In a letter undated, but presumably at the end of December, Mrs. Montagu says—

"Lord Bath said there had been but three speeches in Parliament this year; one was Lord Middleton's,*

* 3rd Viscount Middleton.

who said he would give all he was worth to support the war; the other Sir Michael Grosvenor's,* who said he would lend all he was worth; and the third, Mr. Pitt's, who said he would take all they were both worth. . . . If Mr. Isaacson wants any enquiries made at Cork, I can get good intelligence by means of Mr. Burke, a young lawyer by profession, tho' an author by practice, for he wrote Natural History † preferable to Artificial; he has several acquaintance of credit at Cork, you have often heard me mention him."

This is the third mention of Edmund Burke, the first being in a letter of Emin's, whose patron he was, to Dr. Monsey.

On December 28, writing to her husband, who was still at Carville, Mrs. Montagu says—

"The Parliaments meet on the 16th . . . the ardour for carrying on the war is such it will be rather a point of contention who shall give most money. Some people think Mr. Boscawen will be sent against Quebec. General Conway is taken into favour again, he is going to settle ye dispute between us and the Dutch concerning the ships we have taken. The Princess of Orange is thought in a desperate state of health . . . My Father call'd on me on Monday; he was not well, which put him a little out of sorts, he seems uneasy that he is not immortal, however, he takes the best means for long life, and I daresay will attain it unless fears of the inevitable moment should hurt his spirits. Life has been to him one long play day, he must not expect the rattles and sugar plumbs will hold good to the last. He has never tasted business, care, or study; *vivre du jour la journée,* as the French saying is, has been his moral maxim; it may make a merry day, but it does not make

* Sir Richard Grosvenor, afterwards 1st Earl Grosvenor.

† "Vindication of Natural Society," his first avowed work copied for him by Emin, and published in 1756.

the best evening; the mind that has employ'd itself in study and application or in active life has more to look back upon, and old age's joy is in the retrospect."

This ends the letters for 1758.

On January 2, 1759, writing to Mr. Montagu, who was still in the north, his wife says—

"I am now reading a very ingenious, pernicious French author, his name is Helvetius,* a descendant of the famous Helvetius;† he is a man of fortune in France, very amiable in his private character, good-natured, liberal and witty, so has many disciples at Paris from respect to his person; I fear he will have many here from respect to his doctrines well adapted to the corruptions of the human heart. He endeavours to show it is custom makes virtue and vice, like Epicurus, placing his good in pleasure but not his pleasure in good. He thinks a less strict observation of some moral rules would make man in general happier. He would trust everything to laws, Legislature is to be the god and conscience of mankind. He does not consider how many by their situation are above laws, how many one may say are below it, and how many more by fraud, evasions, concealment would hope to escape it. I hope conscience, call'd by Mr. Pope 'the god within the mind,' will keep her empire in spite of Mr. Helvetius. . . . The church has obliged him to a retractation, which indeed may in some measure mortify the author but will not alter the argument of his book. . . . Lord Clarendon's other volume‡ will soon be published. . . . I forgot to tell you I have receiv'd great compliments from Mr. Pitt, the Secretary, since I came to town,

* Claude Adrien Helvetius, born 1715, died 1771. Published "De l'Esprit" in 1758.

† John Claude Helvetius, his father, celebrated physician and author; died 1755.

‡ His "History of the Rebellion."

congratulations on your accession of fortune, congratulations on my recovery from the *eau de Luce*, high expressions of esteem and friendship, but being a person of moderate ambition, I have not ask'd for a place at Court."

In the next letter of January 4 she says—

"I was last night at Lady Cowper's concert, where there was much good company and good musick. The night before I was at an assembly at Mrs. Pitt's, where I found Sir John Mordaunt playing at cards with Lady Hester Pitt; this might be accident, but among political folks one is apt to look deeper perhaps than the truth lies, but this and General Conway being received into grace and sent to Le Cas * to settle the cartel for exchange of prisoners, makes me suspect some coalition may be designed between the folks at Leicester House and the D(uke). . . . I am to go to the play with Miss Pitt to-morrow night. Mr. Garrick is to act Anthony, he will make but a diminutive hero; I should not think it a part he would shine in, but he has taken great pains about it."

On January 18, writing to her husband, Mrs. Montagu says—

"It is apprehended the loss of the King of Spain † will be a misfortune to Great Brittain. There is a great conspiracy discovered in Portugal; it was at first surmised that the assassination ‡ of the King arose from jealousy, but people now think there was more of ambition than jealousy in it. The Marquis of Tavora's family had a nearer claim to the crown than that Duke of Braganza who got it, but not being

* He was sent to Sluys, for which the French is L'Ecluse, not Le Cas, to meet Monsieur de Bareil.

† Ferdinand VI.

‡ Attempted assassination of Joseph I., led to the expulsion of the Jesuits.

personally so well qualified for so great an attempt, or for want of alliances or other means, they were quietly governed by Spain, but when the Braganzas gained the Royal dignity, they grudged it to them, and ambition and envy may easily form conspiracy and assassination. Twelve of the first nobility will be brought to the scaffold."

On the 24th occurs a very long letter to Mrs. Carter. In this mention is made of Rousseau: "There is a letter from Rousseau to Mr. D'Alembert * upon the project of settling a theatre at Geneva, which treats of Dramatical performances in general; it is ingeniously written and with great eloquence." She also adds that she is sending Mrs. Carter Dr. Newton's "Dissertation on the Prophecies," Leland's "Life of Philip of Macedon."

"Lord Lyttelton's History is not yet ready to appear; the work goes on slowly, as the writer is scrupulously exact in following truth. His delicacy in regard to characters, his candour in regard to opinions, his precision in facts, would entitle him to the best palm history can claim, if he had not added to these virtues of History (if I may call them so) the highest ornaments of style, and a most peculiar grace of order and method. . . . I shall send you a treatise on the 'Sublime and Beautiful,' † by Mr. Burke, a friend of mine. I do not know that you will always subscribe to his system, but think you will find him an elegant and ingenious writer. He is far from the pert pedantry and assuming ignorance of modern witlings; but in conversation and writing an ingenious and ingenuous man, modest and delicate, and on great and serious subjects full of that respect and veneration which a good mind

* Lettre à d'Alembert (Sur les Spectacles), Amsterdam 1758; translated into English in 1759.

† First published in 1757.

and a great one is sure to feel, while fools mock behind the altar, at which wise men kneel and pay mysterious reverence."

Soon after this letter, Mrs. Carter paid her first visit to Mrs. Montagu in Hill Street. Mrs. Carter had been much troubled by the severe illness of Miss Talbot, her bosom friend, and of Archbishop Secker, with whom the Talbots lived. Mrs. Montagu, writing to condole about this, mentions that Lord Waldegrave * was going to marry the illegitimate daughter of Sir Edward Walpole, and she continues—

"Miss Kitty Fisher modestly asked Earl Pembroke † to make her a Countess; his family love forms, so perhaps the fair one thought he would approve the legal form of cohabitation; but he hesitated, and so the agreement is made for life, a £1000 per annum, and a £1000 for present decorations."

Mr. Montagu had now returned to his wife, having bought another portion of the Denton estate from Mr. Archdeacon, his cousin. He made a codicil to his previous will of 1752, leaving his wife the whole property, as well as all he possessed besides. The codicil was witnessed by Ben Stillingfleet, William Archdeacon, and Samuel Torriano, on April 12, 1759.

On June 7, writing to Mrs. Carter, who was drinking the waters at Bristol, Mrs. Montagu chaffs her as to her surroundings. "Do you like pompons or aigrettes in your hair? if you put on rouge, dance minuets and cottillions? that I may describe and define you in your

* 2nd Earl Waldegrave, married Maria, daughter of Sir Edward Walpole, on May 15, 1759. She survived him, and married in 1766 the Duke of Gloucester, brother to George III.

† Henry, 29th Earl of Pembroke, born 1734, died 1794.

MRS. ELIZABETH CARTER.

[*To face p.* 160, *vol. ii.*

Bristol State." Mention is made of Mr. Mason's "Caractacus."

"It is a Drama not dramatized; his Melpomene is too chaste, too cold for the theatre. She is a very modest virgin, pure in sentiment and diction and void of passion; her sober ornaments are a Greek veil and some Druidical Hieroglyphicks, all which I mightily respect and do not like at all. . . . Lord Northampton had a fine suit for the birthday, the wastecoat silver and gold, the coat gold and silver."

On June 9 occurs the first letter of Dr. Johnson * to Mrs. Montagu.

"MADAM,

"I am desired by Mrs. Williams to sign receipts with her name for the subscribers which you have been pleased to procure, and to return her humble thanks for your favour, which was conferred with all the grace that elegance can add to Beneficence.

"I am,

"Your most obedient
and humble servant,

"SAM. JOHNSON.

"June 9, 1759."

This letter is printed in Boswell's "Life of Johnson," † vol. ii. p. 113; but who introduced him first to her I have not yet been able to discover, but I fancy it might be through Mrs. Carter. His mother had died at the age of ninety in January of this year. His "Rasselas," published in the following April, is said to have been written to pay the expenses of the funeral of his beloved

* Dr. Samuel Johnson, born 1709, died 1784; the famous lexicographer and critic.

† By John Wilson Croker revised, and by John Wright published, 1880.

parent. Mrs. Williams was one of Dr. Johnson's *protégées*, a woman of talent and literary attainments, who had been a constant companion of his late wife. Her eyes being affected with an incurable cataract, she became blind, and Dr. Johnson was trying to raise money enough to buy an annuity for her. In 1766 she became a permanent inmate of Johnson's house, and on Mr. Montagu's death in 1775, Mrs. Montagu settled £10 per annum on her.

Dr. Johnson's writing is singularly clear, and, once seen, is unmistakable, from his peculiar long *s*'s.

On June 9 also, Emin wrote on board the *Prince Edward*, from the Mole of Genoa, where they were in quarantine. The letter begins, "To the most learned and most magnanimous Mrs. Montagu." He was on his way to see Prince Heraclius with letters of recommendation from his father and all the principal Armenians of Calcutta and India to the Prince and the Archbishop of Armenia. At last his transcendent merit as a leader had been acknowledged by his own countrymen, who now designated him "their chief, their Shepherd and Protector." Emin's affectionate heart was rent at the thought of parting with his kind English protectors, and in this letter he says he was almost glad when he found most of them out or away from home when he called to bid adieu. He was to cross Turkey by land to get to Armenia, a most dangerous journey, and on the way out two ships had chased them for four or five hours off Spain.

Writing from Sandleford on July 25 to Mrs. Carter, Mrs. Montagu narrates the sad death of Lady Essex, carried away at the early age of nineteen by puerperal fever and throat disease. She was the daughter of Lady Frances Williams, who was bowed down with this affliction, added to the terrible lunacy of her husband.

Mrs. Carter was at Bristol drinking the waters for her constant violent headaches. At the end of the letter we read—

"I am glad you agree with me in detestation of Voltaire's Optimism. Are not you provoked that such an animal calls itself a Philosopher? What pretence can he have to philosophy who has not that fear of God which is the beginning of wisdom? This creature is a downright rebel to his God. Some good may arise indeed from the division of Satan's household; Voltaire directly opposes Lord Bolingbroke and those who affirm whatever is is right, and that there wants not a future state to make the system just."

Lady Medows writes that her appetite has been mended by drinking "Calves Pluck water!"

On August 3 Mrs. Montagu thanks Lady Barbara Montagu for "the great favour you have done me in behalf of Mr. Burke," but what that favour was I know not. The letter proceeds thus—

"I conducted Mrs. Pitt to Maidenhead Bridge on Tuesday, and on Wednesday dined at Mrs. Clayton's * at Harleyford.† I think it the most agreeable situation I have seen on the Thames, I mean as a place of residence, every object speaks peace and plenty, the silver Thames glides at the foot of their garden, lofty trees crown the summit, they have fine prospects, sweet lawns, fine cornfields and distant villages. . . . I could not get permission from Mr. Montagu to stay a day or two, but had barely leave for a dining visit; to my great mortification, my Landlord at the Bridge told me that to go by Marlow would carry me 8 or 9 miles out of the Road, so I gave up my scheme, but met Mr. Amyand,

* Presumably the widow of Bishop Clayton, and sister of Mrs. Donnellan.

† Now the seat of Sir William Clayton.

who was travelling through Maidenhead town: he jumped out of his post-chaise, got into the coach to tell me all the news of the town, and on my complaining of my disappointment in regard to Mrs. Clayton, he assured me if I would go two miles out of my road I should find myself on the bank of the river opposite Mrs. Clayton's house, that then I might go on board a flat-bottom'd boat and invade her territories. I followed his directions, but as my coach could not pass the river, I proposed only to drink a dish of Chocolate, walk round her gardens, and proceed to Reading. She kindly desired to carry me thither early in the afternoon, said she would get Mrs. Southwell * of the party, that my coach should go on to Reading and I should find my horses refreshed and ready to set forward for Sandleford : no magical wand could have made a metamorphosis more to my advantage than converting the rose Parlour at the Inn in Reading into an elegant *salon*, and my Landlord and his wife into Mrs. Clayton and Mrs. Southwell; and an empty coach into one filled with good company. A most incomparable dinner appeared, and Mrs. Southwell; we went together to Reading, and by 11 I got back to my darksome pines."

Soon after her return to Sandleford, Mr. Montagu fell ill of a bad throat, caught, she thought, at a place built by a Mr. Cottington near Newbury, on such a hill that, as she says to Lyttelton,

"it would have made a good situation for a college of Augurs, for here they might conveniently make observations on the flight of Birds; the ascent is so steep a goat can hardly climb to it; he built a Belvidere at the top of the house, where perhaps he hoped to sit as umpire in the battles between the cranes and the pigmies, for as to looking down from it, it is rather horrible."

* Of King's Weston.

DR. SAMUEL JOHNSON.

[*To face p.* 164, *vol. ii.*

Fortunately, Dr. Monsey was at Sandleford, and promptly "blooded" and doctored Mr. Montagu. Mention is made of a "magnificent epistle of Emin to the noble daughters of Brittain," too long to be inserted here.

Lord Lyttelton and "Tom" were taking a tour to the Highlands, having gone from Hagley to Durham, thence to Lord Ravensworth's and Morpeth, "on our way to Alnwick." Lord Lyttelton alludes to the Battle of Minden, fought on August 1, between the English, Hessians, and Hanoverians, against the French. Prince Ferdinand * of Brunswick commanded, and under him Lord George Sackville,† who commanded the English and Hanoverians, and incurred some obloquy on the score of disobeying orders; but Lyttelton says—

"The necessity the French will be under of restoring their army in Germany by large reinforcements must, I think, putt an end to their intended invasion, and you Ladies of Britain will not be exposed to the outrages and brutalities which the poor Ladies of Hildesheim have suffered from the rage of those polished barbarians. . . . I had writt thus far at Taymouth, Lord Breadalbane's fine seat, but was forced by some interruption to delay ending my letter till I came to Inverary, from whence I now write. The House deserves to be call'd, as it was stil'd by Lord Leicester, 'the Royall Palace of the King of the Goths.' He reigns here in great state, but Nature reigns in still greater. I have scarce ever seen her more sublimely majestick; nor does she want some sweet graces to soften her dignity and make it more amiable. As the Duke of Argyll ‡ is one of your admirers, and, I think, a favoured one too, you ought to make him a

* Brother of the Duke of Brunswick.

† Afterwards Lord George Germaine.

‡ Archibald Campbell, 3rd Duke of Argyll, born 1682, died 1761, ætat 79.

visit here when next you return to your northern dominions."

Tom Lyttelton, who was travelling with his father in Scotland, writes on September 10 from Edinburgh to Mrs. Montagu. Some portions of his letter I copy—

"The first place I shall mention to you is Alnwick, the seat of the Earl of Northumberland. The Castle is very gracious, and stands on the brow of a hill; it was formerly very strong. His Lordship has shown great judgment in the manner of fitting it up, for instead of using the modern stile of architecture (as Mr. Lumley has done at Lumley Castle), he has left it for the most part as it was in Harry Percy's time, with this difference, that two or three rooms which were before ill proportioned and quite unfurnished, are now much enlarged and fitted very handsomely in the Gothick stile. He will add many more rooms on the other side of the court, and will make it in time a very good house, still preserving its original character. From thence we went to Berwick to Sir Hugh Dalrymple's. . . . The Bass Island is all a vast Rock broken into many rough and irregular pieces; it is inaccessible to very large ships, there is but one place where a boat may safely land; in the middle of the ascent there are still the remains of an old castle, which was a state prison with houses for soldiers built in the rock; they tell you that within these sixty years it was garrisoned, but it is now become the habitation only of an infinite number of sea birds, of which the Solan goose is the most remarkable. . . . We went to dine with Mr. Charters, and from thence the same night reached Edinburgh, and were lodged in the Royal Palace called *Holy Rood House*. . . . My next shall be from Bishops Auckland (a seat of the Bishop of Durham's). . . ."

As usual, Lord Lyttelton adds a postscript, and in it says—

"We dined to-day with the Magistrates and corporation of Edinburgh, and supped with the Duke of Argyll, who honoured me with his presence at the dinner, a distinction he never paid to any other than upon this occasion. Tom and I had our freedoms given us, as we have had from many other towns with as great compliments as if I had been a minister of State, or the Head of a faction."

Young Edward Wortley Montagu writes on September 13 to Mr. Montagu from "Mrs. Lyster's in Hyde Street, Bloomsbury Market," to say—

"I am really greatly concern'd that it has hitherto been out of my power to wait upon you, and I am afraid will be so the whole summer, for my book is sold off, and Millar presses me for a second edition, which I am now about, and since I wish it should appear in the world as perfect as possible, I must beg the favour of you to let me know what corrections you think it may want; the world received the first edition with great indulgence, but the second will have a right to approbation when it has received a greater degree of perfection from the corrections of a gentleman of your abilities."

In an answer to Lord Lyttelton's letter from Inverary, too long to be inserted, Mrs. Montagu mentions that she is sending the letter to York—

"I shall be glad to hear that your Lordship and Mr. Lyttelton like York, to which perhaps I am partial as to the place of my nativity. One of the strongest pictures in my mind is the funeral of a Dean of York, which I saw performed with great solemnity in the Cathedral when I was about 4 years old. . . . I know, my lord, you will rejoice with me for Mr. Boscawen's * victory, both from public spirit and private friendship."

* Admiral Boscawen defeated the French off Cape Lagos on August 18.

Emin, after a serious illness, was setting off on his dangerous journey through Turkey, and on September 20 wrote "To the Montagu the Great," ending up with, "My dearest, brightest and the wisest Queen of the East, your very affectionate and faithful, obedient, humble servant and soldier, Emin of Hasnasari in Persia."

Lord Lyttelton and his son travelled from Edinburgh to Lord Hopetoun's place, Hopetoun House. In a letter to Mrs. Montagu of September 21, Tom says, "There is one chimney piece done by Risback that cost £600, my father thinks it the finest he ever saw.' Thence they proceeded to Stirling, and paid visits to Lord Cathcart and Lord Kinnoull; thence to Glamis Castle, which he describes "as a very old castle, but has not a tolerable apartment, and can never be altered much for the better." He does not mention the ghost; probably he was not told about it. From thence to the Duke of Athole's at Dunkeld, where he is enraptured with the country, and mentions the window at the Hermitage,* "through which the falls of the Braan appear as a surprise to the visitor." The Lytteltons accompanied the duke to his other seat, Blair Athole, after which they proceeded to Taymouth, Lord Breadalbane's splendid place, which enchanted Tom.

He now gives Mrs. Montagu a sort of character sketch of the Scottish nobility—

"The characteristical virtues of the Scotch are courage, temperance, prudence, economy and hospitality. This last is not only peculiar to the nobility, but is universally practised by all kinds of people. *Good breeding*, though it cannot be properly styled a virtue, is of the highest *consequence* to Society. This the Scotch universally possess, and there is not in the North such a character as that of an English country Squire, whose whole life

* Ossian's Hall.

is spent in the laudable customs of hunting, drinking, swearing and sleeping. . . . Scotch ladies are very handsome and very sweet tempered. It is their general character to be rather too free of their favours before marriage; however that may be, they are very chaste after that ceremony. They breed up their children in a particular manner, for they are accustomed from their infancy to go without shoes and stockings, nor in the coldest weather do their parents permit them to wear a great-coat; if they are of a puny constitution they die, if not, they are the better for it all their life."

He also remarks that "few of the nobility omit going to Church on a Sunday, and what is of more importance, when they are there they do not trifle, but seem seriously to reflect upon the duty they owe their Maker." This description from a boy of fifteen is remarkable, and throws light upon English manners of that period. After several other visits, Tom returned to his studies at Eton.

Next to this comes a letter from Mr. Burke, which, being the first, is given *in extenso*. His handwriting is beautiful and very even, but of a feminine cast.

"MADAM,

"I have now the honour of writing to you for the first time, and the subject of my letter is an affair that concerns myself. I should stand in need of many more apologies than I know how to make both for the liberty I take and for the occasion of it, if I had not learned by experience that I give you a pleasure when I put it in your power to exert your good-nature. I know it is your foible to carry this principle to an extream, and one is almost sure of success in any application, or at least for pardon for having made an improper one, when we know judiciously to take advantage of a person's weak point. I do not know anything else which could give me confidence enough to take the Liberty I am now going to use. The Consulship of Madrid has been vacant for several months; I am informed that it is in the gift of Mr. Secretary Pitt, and that it is valuable. I presume, however, that it is not an object for a person who has any considerable pretensions, by its having continued so long vacant, else I should never have thought of it. My interest is weak, I have not at all the honour of being known to Mr. Pitt; nor much to any of his close connections. For which reason I venture to ask your advice whether I can with propriety proceed at all in this affair, and if you think I ought to undertake it, in what manner it would be proper for me to proceed. If my little suit either in itself or in the persons through whose hands it must necessarily pass, should be attended with any circumstances that may make it disagreeable to you to interfere in it, I shall take it as a favour equal to that I have asked, if you will be so good to tell me you can do nothing in it. I shall think such a declaration a great mark of your confidence. I am sensible that there are in all people's connections many points that may make a person of delicacy unwilling to ask a favour in some quarters, and yet more unwilling from the same delicacy to tell the person for whom it is to be asked that they have such difficulties. There are undoubtedly many circumstances of propriety in every person's situation, which none can feel properly but themselves. I am not, however, if I know myself, one of those expectants who think everything ought to be sacrificed to their Interest. It occurred to me that a letter from you to Miss Pitt might be of great service to me. I thought too of mentioning Mrs. Boscawen. The Admiral has such great merit with the Ministry and the Nation, that the want of it will be the more readily overlooked in any person for whom he may be induced to apply. But these are crude notions and require the understanding they are submitted to, to bring them to form and maturity. To say the truth, I am quite ashamed to have

EDMUND BURKE.

[*To face p.* 170, *vol. ii.*

dwelt so long upon so indifferent a subject. Your Patience is almost equal to the rest of your virtues if you can bear it. I dwell with far more pleasure on my acknowledgments for what you have done for my friend * in so obliging and genteel a manner. He has but just now succeeded after a world of delays, and no small opposition. He will always retain a very grateful sense of what you have done in his favour. Mrs. Burke † desires me to present her respects to you, and her best wishes for your health. When last I had the pleasure of seeing Dr. Monsey, he told me that the country still agreed with you, else I should most wickedly wish this fine weather over that you might be the sooner driven to town. This fine weather suffers nothing good to be in Town but itself. We are much obliged to the Doctor for the satisfaction he gave you in uniting his care with yours for Mr. Montagu's recovery. I congratulate you very sincerely on that event. If I could find some agreeable circumstance in your affairs for congratulation as often as I wish I should be the most troublesome correspondent in England, for nobody can be with greater respect and gratitude,

"Madam,

"Your most obliged and
obedient humble servant,

"EDMUND BURKE.

"Wimple Street, Cav. Sq., Sep[r] 24, 1759."

In a letter to Lord Lyttelton of October 23, Mrs. Montagu mentions visiting Lady Townshend to congratulate her on the taking of Quebec, which had happened on September 13, and in which her son, General Townshend, had taken a prominent part. In this she says—

* This was Emin.

† Mrs. Burke's maiden name was Nugent. She was a Roman Catholic.

"The encomiums on Mr. Wolfe run very high, a great action is performed and every one can endure to give praise to a dead man; and there was certainly something very captivating in his character; he took the public opinion by a *coup de main*, to which it surrenders more willingly than to a regular siege. The people had not time to be tired of hearing him called the brave; he is the subject of all people's praise, and I question whether all the Duke of Marlborough's conquests gained him greater honour."

In answer to this Lord Lyttelton says—

"I wish that a French invasion from Havre de Grace, which I have particular reasons to be more afraid of than ever, may not correct the extravagance of our joy for our unexpected success at Quebec, and the false security it has produced in the minds of our ministers. . . . Mr. Bonus, the picture cleaner, has come down and has restored my old family pictures to such a state of perfection that I can hardly believe my eyes when I see them. Few gentlemen, I assure you, have a finer collection than mine appears to be now. If Lady Coventry ever comes here, she will cry at the sight of some of the beauties of Charles the Second's court, which by Mr. Bonus' help exceed hers as much as she does my milkmaids. There is particularly a Duchess of Richmond whom you have read of under the name of Mademoiselle Stuart in the 'Memoirs of the Count de Grammont,' whose charms are so divine that my nephew Pitt is absolutely falling in love with her and does nothing but gaze upon her from morning till night. What would you living beauties give if twenty years hence, when you begin to suffer by time, there could be found a Mr. Bonus to restore you again, as he has done this fair lady and others at Hagley? Pray come and see the miracles of his art. . . .

"Pitt sends his best compliments, and we both agree you have indeed a great deal of a witch about you, but nothing of a Hag."

Mrs. Montagu evidently refused to exert her influence in favour of Mr. Burke's desire to obtain the Madrid Consulship, as on October 6 he writes—

"MADAM,

"For many publick as well as private reasons I am sorry that you have not an influence on Ministers of State; but the qualities which some persons possess are by no means those which lead to Ministerial influence. The reasons you have been pleased to give me for not making the application are very convincing and obliging. Before I applied I was well aware of the difficulties that stood in my way."

Further down in the letter (which is not sufficiently interesting to be given *in extenso*) he says—

"It is not very easy to have access to Mr. Pitt, especially for me, who have so very few friends. I mentioned those methods, not that I was satisfied of their propriety, but because I would try every method which occurred to me."

On December 17 Dr. Johnson writes—

"MADAM,

"Goodness so conspicuous as yours will be often solicited and perhaps sometimes solicited by those who have little pretension to your favour. It is now my turn to introduce a petitioner, but such as I have reason to believe you will think worthy of your notice. Mrs. Ogle who kept the music room in Soho Square, a woman who struggles with great industry for the support of eight children, hopes by a Benefit Concert to set herself free from a few debts, which she cannot otherwise discharge. She has, I know not why, so high an opinion of me as to believe that you will pay less regard to her application than to mine. You know,

Madam, I am sure you know, how hard it is to deny, and therefore would not wonder at my compliance, though I were to suppress a motive which you know not, the vanity of being supposed to be of any importance to Mrs. Montagu. But though I may be willing to see the world deceived for my advantage, I am not deceived myself, for I know that Mrs. Ogle will owe whatever favours she shall receive from the patronage which we humbly entreat on this occasion, much more to your compassion for honesty in distress than to the request of, Madam,

"Your most obedient
and most humble servant,
"SAM. JOHNSON.

"Gray's Inn, Dec. 17, 1759."

This letter is printed in Croker's edition of Boswell's "Life of Johnson," vol. ii. p. 115, published in 1880 by George Bell and Sons. He probably received the copy, as he did a former letter, from my grandfather, the 4th Baron Rokeby, as he would have been too young to obtain it from Mrs. Montagu, who died in 1800, and John Wilson Croker was not born till 1780.

Though undated, the following letter of Laurence Sterne may be placed here. Early in 1759 he had been writing the first two volumes of "Tristram Shandy," towards the end of the year he was in London arranging for their publication with Dodsley the publisher, who declined the venture. They were printed for and sold by John Hinxham, bookseller in Stonegate, according to Mr. Traill's volume on Sterne in the "Englishmen of Letters" series. The allusions to the Dean of York, etc., referred to a dispute between a Dr. Topham and Dr. Fountayne (Dean of York), in which Sterne sided with the Dean when he wrote his "History of a Good Warm Watchcoat," "a sarcastic apologue," as Mr. Traill terms it. I have not time or knowledge enough to enter into the details of this affair, but hope the letter may throw light upon it to students of Sterne's character.

"MADAM,

"I never was so much at a loss as I find myself at this instant that I am going to answer the letter I have had the honour and happiness to receive from you by Mr. Torriano; being ten times more oppress'd with the excess of your candour and goodness than I was before with the subject of my complaint. It was entirely owing to the Idea I had in common with all the world of Mrs. Montagu's that I felt sorrow at all—or communicated what I felt to my friend; which last step I should not have taken but from the great reliance I had upon the excellency of your character. I wanted mercy—but not sacrifice, and am obliged, in my turn, to beg pardon of you, which I do from my soul, for putting you to the pain of excusing, what in fact was more a misfortune, than a fault, and but a necessary consequence of a train of Impressions given to my disadvantage. The Chancellor of York, Dr. Herring, was, I suppose, the person who interested himself in the honour of the Dean of York, and requested that act of friendship to be done to the Dean, by bringing about a separation betwixt the Dean and myself—the poor gentleman has been labouring this point many years—but not out of zeal for the Dean's character, but to secure the next residentiaryship to the Dean of St. Asalph, his son; he was outwitted himself at last, and has now all the foul play to settle with his conscience without gaining or being ever likely to gain his purpose. I take the liberty of enclosing a letter I wrote last month to the Dean, which will give some light into my hard measure, and show you that I was as much a protection to the Dean of York—as he to me. The answer to this has made me easy with regard to my views in the Church of York, and as it has cemented anew the Dean and myself beyond the power of any future breach, I thought it would give you satisfaction to see how my interests stand, and how much and how undeserved I have been abused: when you have read it—it shall never be read more, for reasons your penetration will see at once.

"I return you thanks for the interest you took in my wife, and there is not an honest man, who will not do me the justice to say, I have ever given her the character of as moral and virtuous a woman as ever God made—what occasion'd discontent ever betwixt us is now no more—we have settled accounts to each other's satisfaction and honour, and I am persuaded shall end our days without one word of reproach or even Incivility.

"Mr. Torriano made me happy in acquainting me that I was to dine with you on Friday; it shall ever be my care as well as my Principle ever to behave so that you may have no cause to repent of your goodness to me.

"I am, Madam,
"With the truest gratitude,
"Your most obliged and aff[te]
"Kinsman, LAUR. STERNE."

A fragment, also undated, from Mrs. Sterne may be placed here, but I have failed to find any allusion to it in other letters—

"Cou'd Mrs. Montagu think this the way to make a bad husband better, she might indeed have found a better, which I have often urg'd, though to little purpose, namely some little mark of kindness or regard to me as a kinswoman, I meant not such as would have cost her money, but indeed this neither she or any one of the Robinsons vouchsafed to do, though they have seen Mr. Sterne frequently the last two winters, and will the next, so that surely never poor girl who had done no one thing to merit such neglect was ever so cast off by her Relations as I have been. I writ three posts ago to inform Mrs. Montagu of the sorrow her indifferation had brought upon me, and beg'd she wou'd do all that was in her power to undo the mischief, though I can't for my soul see which way, and must expect to the last hour of my life to be reproach'd by Mr. Sterne as the blaster of his fortunes. I learn from Mr. Sterne that there was both letters and conversations pass'd betwixt them last winter on this subject, and though I was an utter stranger to that and every part of this affair till ten days ago, when the Chancellor wrote his first Letter, which Mr. Sterne communicated to me. Yet in several he wrote to me from London he talk'd much of the honours and civilities Mrs. Montagu show'd him, which I was well pleas'd to hear, as the contrary behaviour must have wrought me sorrow. I only wish'd that amongst them she had mixt some to her cousin, but that I heard not one syllable of. I beg you will give me one gleam of comfort by answering this directly. Mr. Sterne is on the wing for London, and we remove to York at the same time, so that I fear thy letter will not arrive before me. Direct to Newton. Mine and Lydia's love,

"Thine most truly and affectionately,

"E. STERNE."

Commenting on Mrs. Sterne's character some years after this date, Mrs. Montagu said she was a woman of good parts, of a temper "like the fretful Porcupine, always darting her quills at somebody or something!"

Lady Medows, Mr. Montagu's sister, who had long been suffering from cancer, died at the end of October. Horace Walpole says in his letter to George Montagu that she left Lady Sandwich's daughter £9000, after the death of her husband, Sir Sydney Medows.

CHAPTER IV.

1760 TO THE DEATH OF GEORGE II.—IN LONDON, AT TONBRIDGE, AND IN NORTHUMBERLAND—CORRESPONDENCE CHIEFLY WITH LORD LYTTELTON.

THE year 1760 opens on January 1 with a letter to Lord Lyttelton from Mrs. Montagu, a portion of which I copy—

"Can I begin the new year more auspiciously than by dedicating the first hours of the New Year's Day to that person from whose friendship I hope to derive so much of the honour and happiness of every year of my life? Among the wishes I form for myself, not the least earnest are those of seeing Lord Lyttelton and his son enjoy all the health, felicity and fame that can be attained in this world, with the chearing prospect of a better state. . . . The world much admires the Pamphlet,* and Lord Bath does not deny he is the author as I am told. I ordered Mr. Bower to send it to your Lordship, but it is out of print. . . . The Hereditary Prince† is gone to the King of Prussia with 18,000 gallant men. I was at Lady Hervey's last night, she is very well."

The next letter of January 15, to the same, is as follows:—

* Probably the "Letter to two Great Men" of Walpole's Memoirs of George I. Ed. 1847. Vol. iii. p. 250.

† Prince Ferdinand of Brunswick.

"My eyes have at last served me to read the collection of letters which have afforded me much entertainment, those from the illustrious I consider as written in their theatrical character, for though they are written behind the scenes, which gives them an air of reality, they are made to suit the assumed character. Lord B(ath) is Patriot and Philosopher, after the manner of the Ancients, his letters bear a consular and stoical dignity, and when I expect to see them signed Marcus, Cato or Caius Cassius, he surprises me with a Christian name and modern title. Those of another eminent person appear more natural, though perhaps they are not more sincere, but the modes we are used to by their familiarity appear less constrained and artificial. . . . I will send Mr. Lyttelton the Gazette extraordinary from Quebec next post, it is from the Indian Savages, and expressed in hieroglyphicks; it will give him an idea of the expresses sent by the Mexicans and Montezuma. I will send him the explanation with it. . . . Mr. Stewart gave me this curious piece this morning. . . . I did not say Lord Bath own'd, but that he did not stoutly deny the pamphlett. Mr. Pitt and his party are angry at it, and I hear H. Walpole has answer'd it."

Tom Lyttelton writes from Eton, March 8, to Mrs. Montagu, to beg her to write to him. Her eyes had been very weak lately, and writing was an effort. In this Tom says—

"I hear my cousin Pitt is gone abroad with Lord Kinnoul. . . . I wish his tour may afford him as much pleasure as it will improvement. But nothing can ever hinder a mind like his, active and desirous of knowledge from improving itself everywhere, but particularly in foreign countries. . . . I only wish the eyes of the handsome Spanish Ladies may not make a greater impression on his heart than the beautiful Vales of Arragon and Castile."

Thomas Pitt had gonė to Lisbon with the Embassy under Lord Strathmore,* which England sent after the attempted assassination of the King of Portugal. In a letter to Lord Lyttelton from Lisbon on March 27, 1760, Mr. Pitt describes Lisbon—

"The Tagus is extremely noble, and the shore on the other side is covered with woods of pine and fir. The city is quite destroy'd, and though they talk of magnificent plans for the rebuilding it, there is little likelihood that it should rise out of its ruins for many years."

He then alludes to the late attempted assassination of the king, but his account is too long to copy *in extenso*—

"The story of a conspiracy is universally disbelieved, the whole is attributed to the malignity of the Duke of Aveiro, and the resentment of the old Marquis and Machioness of Tavora for the dishonour † done to their family since the late dreadful execution, which is followed by the erection of the Bastile, into which people of the first rank are committed without any cause assigned, makes them afraid to be even seen with one another. . . . I hear my little friend Tom has not forgot me in my peregrinations, has apprehensions from the impressions I may receive from the Spanish ladies. Pray give my love to him, and assure him if they resemble those of Portugal I never was in less danger."

In his next letter of April 14, to Mrs. Montagu, he says—

"I am going in about a week or ten days into the

* John Lyon, 7th Earl of Strathmore.

† The king had opposed the marriage of the Duke of Tavora's son to a sister of the Duc de Cadaval.

true country of Knight Errantry. I shall set out for Spain and pass through Andalousia and Granada before I go to Madrid, but instead of Rosinante and the Barber's basin I shall provide myself with side-creeping mules and a heavy crazy old coach that has outlived the earthquake. I propose being at Madrid about the time the King makes his public entry, which is to be extremely magnificent. I shall dispute the prize at every tilt and tournament, and expect to send you a lock of hair plucked as a trophy from the forehead of a wild bull that I have laid dead at my feet. We have a very good chance of escaping the Corsairs, and sea-sickness, as the French Ambassador * here has had the goodness to write to his Court for a passport to enable us to get to Italy through the South of France."

The next letter is from Lord Chesterfield † to Lord Lyttelton.

"Blackheath, May 7, 1760.

"MY LORD,

"I return you my sincerest and warmest thanks for your most entertaining and instructive present.‡ When I heard that you had undertaken that work, I expected no less, and now that I have it, without a compliment I could wish for no more from you. You have applied History to its best use, the advantage of morality; you have exposed vice and folly, but with so noble a hand, that both fools and knaves must feel that you would rather correct than execute them. You have even shown mercy to one who never showed nor felt it; I mean that disgrace to humanity, that sanguinary monster of the North, distinguished only by his Barbarism and his Barbarity, Charles the 12th § of Sweden.

* Monsieur de Merle.

† Philip Dormer Stanhope, Earl of Chesterfield; born 1694, died 1773.

‡ His "Dialogues of the Dead," just published.

§ Allusion to Dialogue No. 20 on Charles XII. and Alexander the Great.

I would fain have homicide no longer reckoned as hitherto it has been, a title to Heroism, and the infamous but fashionable traffick of human blood, no matter for or against, who, if they pay but well, called by its true name *assassination.* Your Lordship has still a great field left open to you for another and yet another volume, which nobody can range in so usefully to mankind as yourself. I must take the liberty of troubling your Lordship with a petition to your brother the Governor of Jamaica,* whom I have not the pleasure of being acquainted with myself. It is to recommend to his protection and favour a relation of mine, one Captain Stanhope, who is now there, and, I believe, has some little employment given him by the present Deputy Governor, Mr. Moore. My kinsman was formerly an Officer of the footguards, but being a man of wit and pleasure, shared the common fate of that sort of gentleman, and was obliged to leave England and go to Jamaica, for (I doubt) more than suspicion of debt. I am assured that he is now quite reformed, and has a mind to be an honest man.

"I am with the greatest honour and esteem,
"Your Lordship's
Most faithfull, humble servant,
"CHESTERFIELD."

Lord Chesterfield's handwriting is beautiful, and the easiest possible to read.

Lord Lyttelton's "Dialogues of the Dead" had just appeared. Of these Mrs. Montagu wrote three, viz. Dialogues 26, 27, 28. Writing to Mrs. Carter, she says—

"I have just received my dear Mrs. Carter's letter, and am very happy in her approbation of 'the Dialogues.' With her encouragement I do not know but

* William Henry, son of Sir Thomas Lyttelton; he was created Baron Westcote of Ballymore in 1776; died in 1808.

at last I may become an author in form. It enlarges the sphere of action and lengthens the short period of human life. To become universal and lasting is an ambition which none but great genius's should indulge; but to be read by a few, a few years, may be aspired to. . . . The Dialogues, I mean the three worst, have had a more favourable reception than I expected. Lord Lyttelton's have been admired to the greatest degree."

Mrs. Montagu had vainly tried to conceal her part as joint author of the "Dialogues." Mrs. Donnellan immediately challenged her as to whether she or Mrs. Carter had written them, and Mrs. Montagu was fain to confess Mrs. Carter was not responsible for them. The fine ladies were much offended at Dialogue 27, between Mercury and "Mrs. Modish," a modern fine lady, in which they were taken off. The authoress was disgusted at the fine ladies' conduct in going to the trial and sentence of Lord Ferrers* for murdering his steward. She says to Mrs. Carter—

"I own the late instance of their going to hear Lord Ferrers' sentence particularly provoked me. The Ladies crowded to the House of Lords to see a wretch brought, loaded with crime and shame, to the Bar, to hear sentence of a cruel and ignominious death, which, considering only this world, casts shame back on his ancestors and all his succeeding family."

The Rev. William Robinson had become engaged to a Miss Mary Richardson, daughter of Mr. Adam Richardson; she had a portion of £10,000. The poet Gray called her "a very good-humoured, cheerful woman." From other letters it appears she was not good-looking, but amiable. This letter, written by Mrs.

* Laurence, Earl Ferrers, was hanged at Tyburn, on May 5, 1760.

Montagu to her sister Sarah, describes the wedding, which appears to have taken place at the end of June.

"Saturday night, after ten.

"MY DEAREST SISTER,

"'I'll tell thee, Sall, where I have been,
Where I the rarest sights have seen,
Oh! sights beyond compare!'

"The Bride triste, the Bridegroom tristissimo; but to the order of the nuptials, Pappa Robinson and Mr. Richardson* in Pappa's postchaize, bride and bridegroom, Mrs. M(orris) Robinson and Sister Montagu in her coach and six. Brother Morris Robinson and Mr. Montagu in Brother Morris' postchaise, so went we to Kensington Church, the neighbours gazing, the children running, the mob gathering; from Church we went to Greenwich, where the Bridegroom gave us a very elegant and splendid dinner: then we walk'd in Greenwich Park, return'd to the Inn to drink tea, after tea the Bride and Bridegroom and Mr. Richardson got into my coach, I carry'd them to Kensington, and there I left the lovely loving pair. . . . William smiled and looked in high beauty as we went, as we return'd he was grave, angry perhaps, that Phœbus did not gallop apace his fiery-footed steeds and hasten on the happy hour. Never was wedding so decent, so orderly, so unlike a wedding, none of your fulsome fondness, I assure you, a few fond glances, but not a syllable addressed to each other. I believe William will behave well, and she is sensible and good-natured. . . . I am glad the wedding is over that I may depart on Monday to Tunbridge. I have been disappointed of my lodgings, the lady who was to have left them being ill, but I have got a house for a week till I can have that I had hired."

From Tunbridge Wells on Tuesday, June 30, Mrs Montagu writes to her husband, then in Hill Street—

* The bride's brother; her father was dead.

"MY DEAREST,

"I had a very agreeable journey hither, but found my present lodging too small to receive the maids who are to come in the postchaise, so cannot send for them till Lady Fitzwilliam is well enough to leave Dr. Morley's. I can give but little account of Tunbridge as yet. I drank the waters at the well this morning, and have now taken leave of the walks till to-morrow, as this fine weather will be better spent in an airing than on the Pantiles. . . . Lord Bath was on the Walks, and General Pulteney,* and Mr. and Mrs. Torriano and Mr. Marriott. Many of the ladies are too lazy to come down in a morning, and those that do come to the well are an hour later than when I was here last."

Miss Botham now joined Mrs. Montagu, who was looking out for a house for Lord Lyttelton.

"I believe your Lordship must accept of a house on Mount Ephraim, which Lady Pembroke laid in last year, for I do not believe I can get you a better. Order your postillion to stop at Mr. Dowding's on Mount Ephraim when you come, and there your Lordship shall be inform'd of the certain place of your abode."

On July 14, Dr. Stillingfleet writes from Stratton to Mrs. Montagu to thank her for a letter, and says he was out of health and spirits;

"this has hindered me from receiving so much pleasure from the unexpected kindness of Lord Barrington † as might naturally have been expected." He then comments on her disappointment "at the smallness of the favour conferred upon me, for it seems to me much superior to anything i would have expected. However favourable you, dear Madam, may judge me, i cannot

* Lord Bath's brother.

† 2nd Viscount Barrington, Secretary for War in 1755, etc.

rate my talents so highly as to think they are undervalued at £100 per ann., when no business is to be done for it." This was his appointment as Master of Kensington Barracks, which took place on June 12. "I had a letter from Dr. Monsey dated Wotton, that gives me much concern, for by his account he seems to be in a bad state of health, and i should think by no means qualified to travel in the *pais* (*sic*) *du tendre*, but he is a thorough-paced hero, and can be romantic in the midst of pain. Should you lose your knight errant i do not think the world can furnish you with a successor, for amongst all your other admirers you will not perhaps meet with one who at seventy is capable of all the tenderness which they have at twenty. . . ." After this he alludes to the inflammation of the eyes Mrs. Montagu was suffering from. "If you cannot see to write he and all your friends will lose one of their greatest pleasures. Has he prescribed the Vitriol Water?"

Miss Anne Stanley, daughter of Mr. Stanley, of Paultons, Hants, and grand-daughter of Sir Hans Sloane, now joined Mrs. Montagu from "Clewar," near Windsor.* Anne and Sarah Stanley lived with their mother, Sarah Stanley, and were the intimate friends of Lord Lyttelton, whom Anne mentions in a letter of July 29. "Lord Lyttelton returned to us yesterday, and has had a bad night with the pain in his back, which has made him resolve to give up Sunning Hill Waters." Anne eventually married Welbore Ellis, afterwards Lord Mendip. Sarah married Christopher D'Oyley, M.P. Their one brother was the Right Hon. Hans Stanley,† Lord of the Admiralty from 1757 to 1763.

On August 2 Lord Lyttelton writes from Hill Street—

"Monsieur des Champs brought me his translation

* Now known as Clewer.

† He died in 1780.

of your three Dialogues. They are as well done as the poverty of the French tongue will admit. But such eloquence as yours must lose by being transposed into any other language. . . . There is great mourning in the gay world for poor Lady Lincoln.* I have seen her so lively, so cheerfull, so happy, that it shocks me to think of her sudden dissolution, and it frights me when I think that I have very dear friends who may as suddenly die, and especially some whose spirits, like hers, exceed their strength. Monsey says he cannot tell what was the cause of her death."

In the next letter to her husband, who was going to Sandleford, Mrs. Montagu says—

"I went to the ball last Friday, it was the first time I had been to the publick rooms, and it had like to have been fatal to me; for the coachman not being acquainted with the place, the night dark, and having no flambeaux, had like to have overturned just coming out from Joy's Rooms, down a place where the coach would have been entirely topsy-turvy; the footmen were thrown off from behind, but several people being by, the coach was held up, and I got safe out, and no hurt done to the persons or machine. My fright was such I did not get my rest till six o'clock in the morning. I had many civil messages in the morning, and Lord and Lady Feversham came up the hill to inquire after me; my nerves are still a little the worse. If the coach had fallen it would have gone down some feet, but the standers-by behaved with great humanity, bearing a very heavy load on their shoulders. I believe our new coachman is too lazy to serve us. The danger I was in when John and the postillion were drunk and had like to have overturned us on a gallop against a post when we came from Windsor, and my second

* Catherine Pelham, daughter of Henry Pelham, brother to the 1st Duke of Newcastle; she died July 27, 1760.

peril on Friday, makes me tremble whenever I get into the machine."

To this Mr. Montagu replies—

"MY DEAREST,

"I am more concerned than j can express at the peril you were in. I tremble and shudder when j consider how fatal the consequences might have been if you had been actually overturned. . . . I have inquired after the cause of this unhappy affair, and though Ned says he cannot say the coachman was drunk, still he had been at the Ale House, and when he came home said there was no danger, and that the boys made almost as much noise as his Mistress. I find he is a lazy, proud, and what they call a gentleman coachman, and such as j would very soon get rid of."

Ned was the head groom, and Mrs. Montagu proposed substituting him for the coachman, as he was honest and sober. To this her husband replies, "I wish he had more experience, but j should with all that think j run no great hazard in trusting him, besides he might practise to go out with the six horses of times when you did not want him." To turn a lumbering coach and six must have been a most intricate affair. Ned was promoted to be coachman, but only to practise with the coach and six; "a coachman to a Mr. Lambard, and afterwards to Captain Pannel's heir," was employed when the coach went out, being then under a job-master, one Mr. Jarret, and a chaise and pair conveyed Mrs. Montagu to the Wells.

"The gentleman here ordered the place of my danger to be mended and acquainted me he had done so, and hoped I should not be frighted away from the balls.

"Sir Roger Twisden inquired much after you and

my Father. He stays but a few days here. Lord Bath was ill again yesterday, he told me he was mortified that he had never been able to wait on me, but he was so weak he could not venture to trouble any one with a visit. I think he is in a bad way, but has a great deal of witt whenever he is tolerably well. His Lordship, I know, has been prejudiced in my favour by some of his friends, who are also friends of mine and Mr. Domville in particular, which I believe has given him a desire to be acquainted with me, but I believe he will hardly be able to make a visit this season, and in London he never visits any one who does not inhabit a ground floor. He has still a fine countenance, and those piercing eyes that denote a mind extraordinarily lively and penetrating."

William Pulteney, Earl of Bath, was born in April, 1684, hence he was at this period turned seventy-six. He had lost his wife, *née* Anna Maria Gumley, in 1758. Mrs. Montagu must have known him in a superficial society way, as a description of a great rout given by Lady Bath some years previously is in this book. But now was to commence that tender intimacy and affectionate friendship between them that lasted to his death, and which prompted him, even in the act of dying, to stagger from his bed and write a few lines of adieu to her as his last effort—sacred lines which I possess and treasure! For his political character I must refer the reader to history, and the "Dictionary of National Biography." As regards his private character I cannot do better than quote Elizabeth Carter's account of him in "Memoirs of her Life." It was probable that through Mrs. Carter, who was a great friend of his, he began to appreciate the manifold charms of Elizabeth Montagu. This is what Mrs. Carter says—

"None of his friends, I believe, will remember him

longer and very few with equal affection. Indeed, there was something in his conversation and manners more engaging than can be described. With all those talents which had so long rendered him the object of popular admiration, he had not the least tincture of that vanity and importance which is too often the consequence of popular applause. He never took the lead in conversation, or even assumed that superiority to which he had a claim, as he was blessed with an exemption from many of the pains and infirmities of old age; he had none of its defects. In so many months as I was continually in his company last year (1763), I do not recollect a single instance of peevishness the whole time. His temper always appeared equal. There was a perpetual flow of vivacity and good humour in his conversation, and the most attentive politeness in his behaviour, nor was this the constrained effort of external and partial good breeding, but the natural turn of his mind, and operated so uniformly on all occasions that I never heard him use a harsh or even an uncivil expression to any of his servants."

At the end of Mrs. Montagu's letter she states that Lord Mansfield * had shown her

"great civilities the few hours he was here . . . an old quaker of four-score, who was reckoned one of the greatest Chymists in Europe, and is a man of witt and learning and who was connected with all the witts of the last age, has taken a great fancy to me because he will believe, in spite of all I can say, that I wrote certain 'Dialogues,' and he sits by me so cordially and attends on me so much, that if he was forty and I was twenty years younger it would be scandalous. . . . Torriano will be kill'd by the Archbishop's † sumptuous fare, who

* William Murray, Earl of Mansfield, born 1704, died 1793; eminent statesman, Lord Chief Justice, etc.

† John Gilbert, Archbishop of York, 1757 to 1761. Torriano seems to have been then his secretary.

feeds more like a pig of Epicurus than the head of a Christian Church."

Mr. Montagu had been at Sandleford, where Morris, his wife, and little boy were spending some time. The little Morris was a great favourite, and delight to poor Mr. Montagu, who loved children. He was now preparing to set off northwards to Northumberland, having two collieries which he was going to work, or, as the expression was, to "win," viz. Leamington and "Denton." The first would cost a £1000, the latter, now called "Montagu's main," £5000. He consults his wife about all this, and adds, "I think j shall not while j live get rid of the trouble my succession has brought upon me, and have only one object, who, j hope, will reap the benefit of all my labour." This meant his wife. At Tunbridge his wife, with "all our fine ladies and gentlemen," was attending Mr. Ferguson's lectures on Philosophy. In a letter of Lord Lyttelton's he mentions his brother Richard. "Sir Richard, or rather 'Duke Lyttelton's'* Royall villa at Richmond, a finer room I never saw, and he seems made to sitt in it, with all the dignity of a gouty Prince. But though I greatly admired it, I would not have his gout to have his room."

To this letter a long answer is returned by Mrs. Montagu, and she informs Lord Lyttelton that, despite her eyes being very weak, she had been reading

"the new translation of Sophocles. . . . The Œdipus Coloneus affected me extreamly, and would have done so more if it had not been for the constant presence of the Chorus, but the passions are awed and checked by a crowd. I am more than ever averse to the Chorus because, though the translator tells us the Choruses of

* He had married the Dowager Duchess of Bridgewater in 1745. She was second wife to Scroop, 1st Duke of Bridgewater.

Sophocles are less alien to the subject of the Drama, than those of any other tragedian, yet here they hurt the interest of it very much."

She adds that she has "sent 4 sets of dressing boxes from hence as your Lordship desired. At the same time I took the liberty to send on a cheap set of tea-cups and coffee cups for a Tunbridge faring." Lord Lyttelton returns answer, saying, "I dined at Dicky Bateman's half gothick, half attick, half chinese and completely fribble house." There he met "my old Love, Lady Hervey,* and my new love, Mrs. Hancock† not to mention Lady Primrose,‡ for whom I have a great friendship." Lord Lyttelton was highly delighted with a favourable criticism of his first volumes of his "History of Henry II." by the great Earl of Hardwicke,§ too long to be inserted here. Lord Lyttelton had been rebuilding ‖ Hagley House, his seat in Worcestershire, which was about to be publicly reopened. On August 18 he writes from there to say he has had to put this off till September 1.

"I have the pleasure to tell you that I find everything done incomparably well, as far as is done, and that the Beauty and Elegance of my House, upon the whole, exceeds my expectations. The bed which is adorned with your handywork is so pretty that if you were to see it I think you would own your pains were not lost. And then the prospect out of that chamber is so delightful, and in case of a rainy day the prints it is hung with

* A celebrated beauty, *née* Mary Lepell, widow of John, Lord Hervey, Pope's "Sporus."

† Mrs. Hancock, sister-in-law to Mrs. Vesey by Mrs. Vesey's first marriage.

‡ Lady Primrose, widow of 3rd Viscount Primrose.

§ Philip Yorke, 1st Earl of Hardwicke, born 1690, died 1764; Lord Chancellor, etc.

‖ Mr. Millar was the architect.

are so amusing that if you were at Hagley I believe you would wish to lodge there yourself, and leave the best apartment to vulgar women of quality, who love finery better than the delicate beauties of Nature and Art. My lower print room in the Atticks is also much obliged to you for the boxes of its Toilette, which suit admirably well with the furniture of it."

He then points out to her that "the glass lustres and the feathers for my bedroom are wanting," and to order their despatch.

In reply to this Mrs. Montagu writes to Tom, to spare his father's writing, to say she delivered the girandoles herself to Mr. Griffith.

"I shall be mortified if they do not make part of the glories of the first. . . . My imagination will attend all the ceremonies of the day, and should my spirit appear it will not come like Banquo's ghost to frown on the banquet, and least of all to frighten and menace the noble Master of the feast to whom I wrote a long and happy enjoyment of his new palace."

Anne Stanley now left Mrs. Montagu, and her sister Sarah, afterwards Mrs. D'Oyley, took her place.

Mr. Montagu, who was contemplating going to Northumberland, paid his wife a short visit at Tunbridge, and started back to London on September 2. On September 4 his wife, in her letter to him, says—

"You may remember to have heard Lord Bath talk of a robbery here which a gentleman was suspected to have committed, of Bank bills to the amount of £300; this person, finding he was suspected, it is supposed, threw them this morning into the musick gallery on the Walks, where one of the Fidlers found them, and is entitled to £30 reward. The person who was guilty of this theft is a gentleman, and his brother is an officer of credit in the army, so one is glad he escapes, but the circumstances almost amount to a conviction. The person robbed was so overjoy'd at finding his bills he seem'd in a fever this morning."

Dr. Monsey, seriously unwell, but anxious to see his beloved friend, paid Mrs. Montagu a short visit at Tunbridge to take farewell of her before her setting out to join her husband in Northumberland. In a letter to Lord Lyttelton of September 7 she says—

"The great Monsey came hither on Friday and stays till Thursday, he is an excellent piece of Tunbridge Ware. He is great in the Coffee house, great in the rooms, and great on the Pantiles. Bucks, Divines, Misses, and Virtuosi are all equally agreeable to him. Miss Sally Stanley leaves me on Friday. There is no abatement of Lord Bath's * passion and I have had two sides of folio paper from the Bishop of London,† so affectionate, so polite, so badine it would surprise you. I answered his Lordship's first letter, concerning the 'Highland Poems,'‡ and with great deference urged the reasons which induced me to esteem them genuine. His Lordship pays great compliment to what I had said on the subject, answering other parts of my letter with spirit and gaiety, and at last concludes that, in spite of 83, without a voice, and with shaking hands, he had endeavoured to follow my train of thought, which he should always look upon as a very good direction."

She then informs Lord Lyttelton—

"I shall take leave of Tunbridge to-morrow sennight,

* Lord Bath had become an ardent admirer of her.

† Thomas Sherlock, born 1678, died 1761.

‡ Macpherson's "Fragments of Ancient Poetry," from the Gaelic.

the 15th of September. I shall take two days' rest in London, and propose to set out on Thursday, 18th. . . ."

Mrs. Montagu had invited Mr. and Mrs. Allan Ramsay to visit her at Tunbridge. Allan Ramsay was a portrait painter of note, son of Allan Ramsay * the Scotch poet, who wrote "The Gentle Shepherd" and other poems. He writes on September 11 thus—

"MADAM,

"By a letter from my wife last post, I learn that you have been so good as to renew your invitation to us to be your guests at Tunbridge—an offer so advantageous that my not availing myself of it sooner must put my understanding in a suspicious light, from whence I should be glad to have it extricated and not to write so long an Apology as Colley Cibber's for my life, thus it is. Two small daughters were inoculated; it was necessary for me and mine to perform quarantine at a distance from many of our most respectable friends, particularly from you; I had some business to settle in Scotland, and my friend Wedderburne † was going thither alone. Having finished my business within my fortnight of Quarantine, I have been detained from day to day in hopes of seeing his Grace of Argyll, of whose setting out we got the first certain account yesterday by a letter from Grantham. Whether this relation will give you a more favourable opinion of my sense than you would have had without it, I don't know, but by much drinking with David Hume and his associates, I have learnt to be very historical; and am nightly confirmed in the belief that it is much easier to tell the *How* than the *Why* of any thing, and that it is, moreover, better suited to the state of man; who, we are satisfied from self-examination, is anything rather than a rational animal. I am sorry to hear that you propose to leave

* Allan Ramsay, the poet, born 1686, died 1758.

† Sir John Wedderburne, born 1729, died 1803.

Tunbridge so soon as the 15th. If you happen to have such heavenly weather there as we have in this place, you will be probably tempted to stay some days longer; in which case my wife and I may still enjoy the pleasure, with which we flattered ourselves, of passing a day or two with you. I see by the newspapers that Admiral Boscawen is come safe home, and when you write to the Lady, be so good as to transmit my hearty congratulations, who am, with the greatest respect,

"Madam,

"Your most obliged
and most faithfull Servant,

"ALLAN RAMSAY.

"Edinburgh, Sept. 11, 1760."

On September 15 Mrs. Montagu returned to Hill Street. On Thursday, the 18th, she enclosed Bishop Sherlock's * letter to her for the Duchess of Portland to read.

"Hill Street, Thursday.

"MADAM,

"I have enclosed the Bishop of London's letter, which I beg of your Grace to keep till you have a leisure hour in which I may receive it from your hands, either here or at Whitehall; in the mean time I am perfectly satisfied as to the letter being safe, and shall not wish to have it return'd till it is most convenient to your Grace to pay me for any pleasure it may have given you, by that I shall have in its procuring me an hour of your company. I think indeed the letter will afford you a good deal of pleasure, it must be a great comfort to every good mind to see how religion can impart not only patience but even cheerfulness under the greatest bodily infirmities. I find it will be necessary to trouble your Grace with some explanation of the Bishop's letter. Before I went to Tunbridge,

* Thomas Sherlock, born 1678, died 1761.

I sent his Lordship the 'Highland Poems,'* by the Dean of York, and the day before I went to Tunbridge my Lord sent them back with a very obliging note to thank me for them, but express'd his opinion that they were not genuine. I was a little distress'd by this favour, as I had not an opportunity to wait on the Bishop before my journey. I thought to write to him and assume the air of being his correspondent would have too much appearance of presumption, and not to thank him for his note might look like neglect, so I waited till the season allow'd me to send him some wheatears and to assure him I wrote only as his poulterer. As it was natural to take notice of what his Lordship had said concerning the poems, I ventured with the utmost deference to give the reasons why I should have believed them to be genuine and original, and then return'd back to my character of Poulterer and desir'd his Lordship to forgive my presumption and order my letter to be put on the wheatears when roasting to preserve them from being burnt. I ask pardon for this long story, but it was necessary as a key to the Bishop's letter. Your Grace will find some mistakes made by his Secretary.

"I was misinform'd the other night when I told your Grace Mr. Wortley Montague was gone abroad, he is in England, but where is a secret even to his lawyer, and those who are imploy'd on his affairs. I thought it right to let your Grace know this, as it appears to me very singular, as he is now under the protection of privilege. I know you will be so good as not to mention I told your Grace this unless it be to Lady Bute, who I should think had better know this circumstance. I beg my best respects to my Lord Duke, and Lady Harriet Bentinck.

"With the greatest regard,

"I am, Madam,

"Your Grace's

most obliged most obed[t]

and faithful humble Serv[t],

"E. MONTAGU."

* "Fragments of Ancient Poetry," translated from the Erse or Gaelic language, by James Macpherson.

This is the Bishop's letter—

"Fulham, ye 1st Septemb^{r}, 1760.

"MADAM,

"When I was a boy at Eton school, I remember it was a Principle of the Law Marshall (practised there): that he who gave the second blow was the beginner of the Fray; and there is something in it, if you consider it; however at this time, it will help to excuse me from the Presumption and folly of inviting you to a Combat, in which I can have no hopes of success. When I read on, and observe with what accuracy and finesse you trace the motions of the Heart, and call Nature from the inmost recess's to discover plainly what arts is usually employ'd to conceal; I am confounded.

"It is true indeed that you have named the Passions and Qualifications of the person to be Described, but what Work will a man make, who should think that he had got all the Secrets; tho' he was unacquainted or incapable to understand it, to such a man. Alexander the Great and *Diogines* (*sic*) are Characters alike, for they were both Actuated by the Spirit of Ambition, one who wanted a new World to display himself in, the other valued nothing beyond the Tub he lived in. In the midst of this Philosophical enquirey about the Passions, you very artfully turn to your Family Affairs and give (I doubt not) excellent directions to the Cook wch shows you to be as great in the Kitchin as in the Closet, which indeed is the only way of being great in either.

"Nothing, I think, is more disagreeable than Learning in a Female, when the Mistress studys Newton, which perhaps she neither does nor ever will understand, to the absolute neglect of her Children and Servants. You conclude by putting in your claim for the Lady's Privilege, which is a very extensive one; give me leave to tell you a short story.

"There was a poor Printer who had got a little sum

of Money, by publishing the last words of a dying Criminal, and he grew so fond of last words, that after the Man had been long dead, he published another paper called MORE last words. Thus you see, Madam, that I have in spite of eighty-three, without a Voice, and with shaking Hands, endeavoured to follow your Strain of thought, which I shall always look upon to be a very good direction. My time of Life calls upon me to think of other Subjects, and the greatest of all to *Justifie the ways of God to men.* This theme can never wear out, it takes in the whole of God's Dispensation, with respect to the Religion of the World, and shows by the connection in the several parts that the whole is the work of perfect Wisdom.

"But I am going to preach instead of Answering a short letter, you will pardon me for looking back upon my old profession, and believe me to be, with the greatest Sincerity,

"Madam,

"Your most obedient Humble Serv[t],

"THO: LONDON.

"P.S.—Mrs. Sherlock and Mrs. Chester desire their respectfull compliments."

The Bishop's amanuensis' spelling and capital letters are singular. The letter is signed in trembling characters, "Tho: London."

On September 19 Mrs. Montagu set out from Hill Street on her journey to Northumberland, starting in a postchaise and picking up Ned and her own horses at Baldock, and so reached Buckden on the same day. She writes to Mr. Montagu—

"I call'd on Dr. Young at Welling and staid about two hours with him, he received me with great cordiality, and I think appears in better health than ever I saw him. His house is happily opposite to a church yard, which is to him a fine prospect; he has taught his imagination to sport with skulls like the grave-digger in Hamlet. He invited me to stay all night, and if my impatience to see you had not impell'd me on, I had been tempted to it. His conversation has always something in it very delightful; in the first place it is animated by the warmest benevolence, then his imagination soars above the material world, some people would say his conversation is not natural. I say it is natural of him to be unnatural, that is out of the ordinary course of things. It would be easier for him to give you a catalogue of the Stars than an inventory of the Household furniture he uses every day. The busy world may say what it pleases, but some men were made for speculation, metaphysical men, like jars and flower pots, make good furniture for a cabinet tho' useless in the kitchen, the pantry and the Dairy."

In a fragment of a letter to Lord Lyttelton, Mrs. Montagu describes her visit to Dr. Young. She had heard "the Dialogues of the Dead praised to the highest degree, and with taste and judgment in a most delicate sense of their moral merits."

Through Mrs. Montagu, Dr. Monsey sends to Dr. Young a powder for his rheumatism. From "Hog Magog" on September 26, Dr. Monsey writes a long letter to Lord Lyttelton, describing his visit to Tunbridge to see "dear Amadissa," meaning Mrs. Montagu. In it he says—

"It may be new to your Lordship tho' not strange, that the Earl of Bath is fall'n desperately in love with one who seems not insensible of his passion, and I think 'tis time for you and I to look about us, for an Earl is better than a Baron or a quack Doctor . . . it is impossible for me to tell your Lordship with what warmth he talk'd to me about her, and so now there are 3 fools of us. 'She is the most extraordinary woman in the world' with a nod of the head and a grave face, 'she beats a french Duchess with an hard name all to pieces, upon my word, Doctor, she is——' 'Ay, so she is, my Lord, but neither I nor you know what.' 'Suppose we say angel.' 'No,' says I, 'Devil, for she leads us all into temptation.'"

On receipt of this, Lord Lyttelton wrote to Mrs. Montagu, and says—

"I wish Lady Hervey * mayn't poison you for stealing Lord Bath from her, as for myself, I will not plead against him as my Rival that I am a younger man (for that plea you will not regard) but that I am an older friend. Adieu, inconstant woman, I feel horribly jealous, but if you won't love me better, pray love me next to Lord Bath."

He also chaffs her for spoiling Miss Stanley's chance of marrying Lord Bath.

From Newcastle, on September 26, Mrs. Montagu writes to her father—

"Sir,

"I arrived here last night and had the pleasure of finding Mr. Montagu very well. He went this morning to Gibside to attend Mr. Bowes' † funeral obsequies, which according to the custom of this county are to be very pompous. Lord Ravensworth, Sir Walter Blacket and all the gentlemen of Northumberland and the county of Durham are to be at it, and I fear it will be late at night before it is over, tho' they are to set out about 4 from Gibside to go to the church. My cousin Rogers' funeral we had order'd to be as private as decency would permit, as he had been so long dead to Society, but even that was attended by 38 gentlemen's

* Lady Hervey was a great friend of Lord Bath's.

† George Bowes, of Gibside and Streatlam Castle.

coaches, so I suppose a publick funeral must be three or four hundred. In the South people live with more pomp and dye with less. I hope not to outlive all my vanity, for I have seldom seen a good and never an agreeable character without it, but I think it should not survive one, and I should desire not to go to the grave with all this bustle, not that I should be afraid any one should say of my funeral, as Pope does of Sir John Cutler's—

> "'When dead a thousand lights attend
> The wretch who, living, sav'd a candle's end.'

I love a blaze of wax lights and my friends about my living person very well, but the torches and the crowd about my dead body would give me neither light nor amusement. Sir Walter Blacket call'd here this morning, and said he hoped to ride in Hyde Park with you about the 15th of November. I had a very pleasant journey, for fine weather, like a good-humoured companion, makes ordinary scenes appear chearfull and pleasant, but from the time I left Hertfordshire till I got to Doncaster, the counties I pass'd through were dreary and barren, but if these prospects in the other counties were brown, these in Northumberland are bleak, the people in them a parcel of dirty Savages, so that I cannot say with the Psalmist that my lot is fallen in a fair ground, it is some comfort it is in a rich one, as I shall see its produce at Sir James Colebrooke's in Threadneedle Street with great pleasure. . . . I met Sir Thomas Clavering just before I got to Darlington; he desired me to present his best respects to you and beg your vote and interest, he sets up for the county of Durham in the room of Mr. Bowes. Mr. Montagu gives him all his interest. If the Bishop of Durham should declare for Mr. Shaftoe (a very young man whose Father formerly served for Durham), Sir Thomas will be hard press'd. Lord Darlington will support Mr. Shaftoe, and most people imagine the Bishop of Durham will do so too. When applied to for Sir

Thomas Clavering, he answered he should act as he found most agreeable to the majority of the county gentlemen. Now I imagine Bishops as well as women (both wear petticoats and a character of gentleness) command while seeming to submit, 'and win their way by yielding to the tyde,' and that my Lord Bishop in a mild way of suggestion will bring the gentlemen to that side he likes best, while he persuades them he follows their inclination. I must say his Lordship is much beloved from his liberality and affability, which are fine moral qualities, as to Xian graces, no doubt but he has them in a higher degree, so that as Prince Palatine or Bishop he must influence many. The Dean of Durham is strongly engaged to Sir Thomas, and there will be a sort of schism in the church."

The Montagus were residing in Pilgrim Street, at the town house of the late Mr. Rogers; "an exceeding good house" it is called. In conclusion Mrs. Montagu says, "I shall send you some fatted moor game by the first opportunity."

On October 11 Lord Lyttelton writes a long letter to "Madonna" from Hagley, commenting on Mr. Bowes' death.

"As his vanity descends with his estate to his daughter, I don't wish to see her my daughter-in-law, though she would make my son one of the richest and consequently, in our present ideas of greatness, one of the great peers of the Realm. But she will probably be the prize of some needy Duke, who will want her estate to repair the disasters of Newmarket and Arthur's, or if she marries for love, of some ensign of the Guards, or smart Militia captain."

Lord Lyttelton had just lost his clerical friend, Mr. Meadowcourt, of Lindridge, to whom he pays a high tribute.

"His house was the abode of Philosophical quiet and disinterested friendship. The scene about it was elegant, mild and beautifull Nature. The Hills on each side and the vale underneath it were covered with orchards, with Hop yards, with corn or fine grazing grounds thro' which wound a river. . . . Now the Master is dead it is fall'n to the dullest of all dull Divines, one Stillingfleet, cousin to him you know, who has not taste enough to live there himself, but leaves it to a curate. He desires his compliments to Dr. Gregory, who was staying with the Montagus, and adds, 'I am glad the Scotch like my Dialogues.' He also desires if the Bishop of Ossory (Richard Pococke) is with them to send him on to Hagley, and assures Mrs. Montagu he is very well and grown quite plump. His thinness was a constant joke with his friends, who called him nothing but bones, and he contends if weighed in the balance with Lord Bath, he would be found 'very wanting.' The Devil take him for having so much witt with so much flesh. He commends his new house and his daughter, now living with him."

Dr. Monsey writes to Mrs. Montagu from St James's on October 12, beginning the letter at 10 a.m., continued at 9 p.m., and finished the next day at Claremont. At the end of this letter he says that he has been very unwell and reported dead; he had made his will.

"While I am writing I have your letter come in, which gives an account of my death, which is true, but save yourself the trouble of an epitaph for me or your funeral sermon, for I have *really* given my body away by will to a Surgeon at Cambridge, who is to make a skeleton of my bones for the use of students in Physic, so if you have begun your epitaph with 'Here he's interr'd, etc.,' change it to 'Here hang the bones, etc.,' and convert your sermon into an Osteological Lecture."

Mrs. Montagu, in a long letter to Lord Lyttelton upon Euripides' and Sophocles' plays contrasted with Shakespeare's, says—

"I am actually an inhabitant of Newcastle, and am taking out my freedom, not out of a gold box, but by entering into all the diversions of the place. I was at a musical entertainment yesterday morning, at a concert last night, at a musical entertainment this morning. I have bespoken a play for to-morrow night, and shall go to a ball on choosing a Mayor on Monday night"

To this Lord Lyttelton replies from Hagley on October 18—

"You tell me, good Madonna, that you are grown *as robust as a milkmaid.* If you are so, I have no objection to your going to Balls, Plays or Poppet Shows if you please every night; but you have sometimes the spirits of a milkmaid without the strength. However, I believe Diversions are better for you than too much reading, and therefore I am not sorry you have no time to committ excess with your books. If I were to live with you, I would not trust you in a Library or alone in your Room but at stated hours with proper Intervals of exercise and conversation. . . . I am glad to hear we shall have another volume of Highland Poems. To stay your stomach (for, as I know, your appetite is eager towards them), I send you a copy of four of a later date than the others now printed, and not much inferior to them in the Natural Beauty and Force of Description, tho' not, I think, so bold and sublime. Being purely descriptive, they could have nothing dramatic or passionate in them as most of the others have. But at the end of these you will find some objections I have as a Chronologist and Historian to the authenticity of the printed ones which it will be hard to get over. Yet I am not persuaded myself they are not genuine, for who can write so now? Mr.

Rust * was so struck with them, he read them every morning and evening aloud to the Family as a Chaplain does Prayers. And the more I consider them, the more I admire them. I have seen some specimens in a Latin translation of the Poetry of the two most admired Welsh Bards, but they don't in any degree approach to the greatness and the Beauty of these. I am charmed with your comparison between the Greek Plays and Shakespear. He is indeed unequalled in the power of painting Nature as she is and giving you sometimes the utmost energy of a Character of a Passion in short Stroke and Dash of his Pen. I also agree with you that the moral Reflexions in Shakespear's Plays are much more affecting by coming warm from the Heart of the interested persons, than putt into the mouth of a chorus, as in the Greek Plays. I am glad you like my favourite Philoctetes. The faults you find with the Ajax are perfectly just, yet I feel the grief of that hero when he returns to his Reason, and especially in the scene between him and Termessa. Suppose Belisarius had gone mad with the unjust Disgrace he had suffer'd, and in his Distraction had done actions which dishonoured and exposed him to the Ridicule of his enemies, what a fine subject would it be for a play if he had killed himself upon recovering the Use of Reason. Setting aside the poetical Fiction, Ajax is Belisarius, and Sophocles has painted the horrors of a great mind so overwhelmed and confounded with shame in a very masterly manner. . . . I am glad your three Dialogues are well liked in Scotland, where the Author is not known. Those who know you and believe they are yours are hardly fair judges. Your form and manners would seduce Apollo himself in his throne of criticism on Parnassus itself. . . ."

Alluding to her visit to Tunbridge and the society there, he says—

* Mr. Rust was travelling companion to the son of Mr. Hoare, of Stourhead, the great banker.

"There is Envy and Malice enough against Beauty alone, but Beauty, Wit, Wisdom, Learning and Virtue united (to say nothing about Wealth) are sure to excite a Legion of Devils against the Possessor. It is amazing to me that with all these dangerous things about you you have not been driven out of Society a great while ago."

In a fragment of a letter Lord Lyttelton writes, "I presume Lady Hervey really likes them (the Dialogues), Lord Chesterfield's warmth in their Praise has secured her vote in their favour, in spite of Horace Walpole and of Lord Bath."

From Newcastle, on October 24, Mrs. Montagu writes to Mrs. Carter, telling her she had been suffering from toothache.. She mentions a sonnet sent to her by Mrs. Carter, "which would have given me a pleasing melancholy if it had not represented your state and condition as it did; it cost me some tears and obliged me to go from table where I received your letter. Teach me to love you less or imitate you better. I admire the resignation with which you submit to your pain.' Mrs. Carter suffered from excruciating headaches at this period. Lord Bath said that if she would drink less green tea, take less snuff, and not study so much, they would disappear.

Mrs. Montagu says the house at Newcastle was very comfortable, and instead of an equipage, she could pay visits to her neighbours in a Sedan chair.

"That I might not offend here I enter'd into all the diversions of this town, visits, concerts, plays, and balls. The desire of pleasure and love of dissipation rages here as much as in London. Diversions here are less elegant and conversation less polite, but no one imagines retirement has any comforts, so that in a little while if one would enjoy retired leisure one must dwell amidst inaccessible mountains and unnavigable rivers."

Dr. and Mrs. Delany had just paid a visit to Hagley, which pleased them much. Dean Lyttelton, writing on October 25 from Hagley, regrets that Bishop Pococke (of Ossory) had not visited Hagley on his return from Northumberland, where he had been staying with the Montagus. Evidently old Mrs. Pococke, the Bishop's wife, was dead, as the Dean says it is fortunate for the Bishop his sister has made up her mind to remain at Newtown.*

"Such a low-bred, narrow-spirited woman would disgrace an episcopal house . . . Mr. Palgrave spent two days here last week, and brought us some new Erse poems which Lord Lyttelton sent you a few days since. His strange figure and awkward silent behaviour did not recommend him greatly to the inhabitants of Hagley, or do much honour to my nephew's taste in his friendships."

On October 25 King George II. died suddenly. Dr. Monsey wrote to inform Mrs. Montagu of this event, from St. James's, and that—

"The suddenness of his Death made people call it an apoplexy, but I conclude otherwise from it. An apoplexy, except when a vessel breaks in the brain, is not so very rapid. People live four or six days or more, that is, they breathe and have a pulse. The King died in an instant, and from some strange odd faintnesses and oppressions upon his breath, I was almost sure 'twas in his heart or the great vessels near. And upon opening him, the Aorta, the canal which receives the Blood directly, was found burst (a very uncommon case), the

* Her mother's house near Newbury.

Duke of Leeds says. I have known and seen it thickened, cartilaginous (crusty), and ossified, but I never met with a broken one; however, 'tis a species of Death he wished for, sudden, and nothing could be more so than this, for the instant that vessel breaks, the heart stops for ever and for ever. . . .

"The King* had a levee to-day at one o'clock at Leicester House, and the Duke of Leeds, who with Mr. Godolphin dined with us to-day, says he so designs every day. No women are to appear at Court yet, so you may finish your affairs without being in a hurry. The Court goes into mourning on Sunday next 'tis said, and about a month hence the King is to be buried."

From Hagley, on October 26, Lord Lyttelton writes—

"MADONNA,

"The sudden death of the King will make me leave this place to-morrow, a week sooner than I had intended, and I propose to be in town on Tuesday or Wednesday. This is only to notify you, as I have not a moment to spare. I suppose all things will go on as they did for some time in the Court and the Nation. Certainly it is no season for any great changes. As to my own situation, I doubt not it will be as it is. The Dean received an admirable letter from you last Post. I have read it over and over with infinite pleasure. Come well to London, and let all the world go as it will. Adieu, you shall hear from me again as soon as I have seen my friends in Town, and can tell you any news. I am perfectly well, and am, Madam,

"Your most faithfull
and obedient humble Servt,
"LYTTELTON.

"My respectfull compliments to Mr. Montagu."

* George III.

To this Mrs. Montagu replies—

"Newcastle, ye 31st October, 1760.

"MY LORD,

"It would be perfect sacrilege and robbing the mighty dead of his due rites, if one began one's letter with any subject but the loss of our sovereign; on which I condole with your Lordship, in whom the virtue of Patriotism, and the antequated one of Loyalty still remain. I know you had that veneration for our late King which the justice and prudence of his government so well deserved. With him our laws and liberties were safe; he possessed in a great degree the confidence of his people and the respect of foreign governments; and a certain steadiness of character made him of great consequence in these unsettled times. During his long reign we never were subject to the insolence and rapaciousness of favourites, a grievance of all others most intolerable when persons born only one's equals shall by the basest means perhaps possess themselves of all the strength of sovereign power, and keep their fellow subjects in a dependance on illegal authority, which insults while it subjects, and is more grievous to the spirits than even to the fortunes of free-born men. If we consider only the evils we have avoided during his late Majesty's reign, we shall find abundant matter of gratitude towards him and respect for his memory. His character would not afford subject for Epic poetry, but will look well in the sober page of history. Conscious, perhaps, of this, he was too little regardful of sciences and the fine arts; he considered common sense as his best panegyrist. The monarch whose qualities are brilliant enough to entitle him to glory, cultivates the love of the Muses, and their handmaid arts, painting, sculpture, etc., sensible that they will blazon and adorn his fame. I hope our young Monarch will copy his predecessor's solid virtues, and if he endeavours to make them more brilliant by the help of poetry, eloquence, etc., etc., the happiness and glory of Britain will be great. His present Majesty's religious disposition, and decent moral conduct, give us hope we shall not be plunged into riot, and lost in debauchery and libertinism, which, if it were to take place at Court, would soon affect a rich and luxurious nation, and the profaneness and immorality of Charles the Second's days would, from the more prosperous state of our nation at present, be outdone. . . .

"I will now thank your Lordship for your letter and the Highland compositions. Your remarks go far in staggering my faith as to their authenticity. I think they convince me the poems cannot be as ancient as pretended. It seems to me possible, that some great bard might from uncertain and broken tradition, and from the scattered songs of former bards, form an epic poem, which might not agree with history. The pillars in the hall of Fingal struck me at first reading; but I imagined they might not refer to polished marble pillars, but to smooth lime or beech trees which one may suppose to have been used as supporters in very rude buildings, and which would look smooth and shapely to one not used to polished marble; and I imagine convenience taught the use of such supporters long before they were introduced as ornaments. . . . I hear Lord Marchmont says our old Highland bard is a modern gentleman of his acquaintance; if it is so, we have a living Poet who may dispute the *pas* on Parnassus with Pindar and the greatest of the ancients, and I honour him for carrying the Muses into the country and letting them step majestic over hills, mountains and rivers instead of tamely walking in the Park or Piccadilly. . . . The Bishop of Ossory tells me Mr. Macpherson receives an £100 per annum subscription while he stays in the Highlands to translate the poems; if he is writing them, he should have a thousand at least. . . .

"Dr. Gregory, in talking of Mr. Hume, said he had a great respect for your Lordship. The Dialogue of Bayle and Locke could not be agreeable to him. . . . Dr. Gregory says Mr. Hume told him he spent an evening with me at Mr. Ramsay's, and he had received very favourable impressions of me, and, I find, said much more of me than I deserve. The Doctor told him I was not of his freethinking system, but Mr. Hume thinks that no fault in a woman. . . . Dr. Monsey is revenging my coquetry with Lord Bath by an assiduous courtship of Miss Talbot, but he can no more be untrue to me than the needle to the pole!"

The same day, October 31, Lord Lyttelton writes from his house in Hill Street—

"MADONNA,

"According to my promise, I now write to tell you the news of the town; and it is with great pleasure that I can assure you all parties unite in the strongest expressions of zeal and affection for our young King, and approbation of his behaviour. Since his accession he has shown the most obliging kindness to all the royal family, and done everything that was necessary to give his government quiet and unanimity in this difficult crisis. . . . There will be no changes in the ministry, and I believe few at Court. The Duke of Newcastle hesitated some time whether he should undertake his arduous office in a new reign, but has yielded at last to the earnest Desires of the King himself, of the Duke of Cumberland, and of the heads of all Parties and Factions, even those who were formerly most hostile to him. His friend and mine, Lord Hardwicke, has been most graciously talked to by the King in two or three audiences, and will, I doubt not, continue in the Cabinet Council with the weight and influence he ought to have there. . . . Lord George Sackville has been admitted to kiss the king's hand, and thus ends my *gazette extraordinary*. As for myself, I got well to town on Wednesday night, was at Court on Thursday morning, was spoken graciously to by the King, and am told by everybody that I grow fat." He then urges Mrs. Montagu to return from Northumberland at once. "I have often told you that you are a mere hot-house plant, fine and rare, but incapable of enduring the cold of our climate, if you are not housed the first day that the white frosts come in.

"I found Mrs. Pitt in pretty good health and spirits; she is *well-housed*, though she has left your palace in Hill Street."

This was Anne Pitt,* late maid of honour, who had been staying in Mrs. Montagu's house till her own was furnished. Further on in the same letter he says—

"The King has opened his grandfather's Will in presence of all the royal family, and it is said the Duke of Cumberland is heir to the much greater part of what his Majesty had to dispose of, but that is much less than was supposed. The next best share is the Princess Emilia's.† The sums are not mentioned. Mr. Pitt has just had a new and very extraordinary mark of the affection of the city, in an inscription they have put upon the first stone of the new bridge. I would have sent it you with to-day's paper in which it is printed, but somebody has stolen it out of my room. You will see it in the next Chronicle. It speaks of a certain *contagion* by which Generals, Admirals, Armies and Fleets catch valour and prudence from him, to the great benefit of our affairs."

From Hill Street, on November 5, Lord Lyttelton again writes to Mrs. Montagu—

"If I were to write the History of my own Times, I would transcribe into it your character of the late King, and should thereby pay my Debt of gratitude to his memory. I would only add to it that it appears from several Wills he has left, that he never had been such a Hoarder of Treasure as was generally supposed.

* Sister of Lord Chatham.

† Sometimes called Princess Amelia, daughter of George II.

And of what he had saved this war has consumed so much that he was able to leave no more to his three children than thirty thousand pounds in equal proportions, and I have heard that the Duke has given up his to his sisters. Princess Emily is come to live in my brother's House like a private woman. It is said the Princess of Wales will not come to St. James's. The great court offices are not yet settled, but I believe it is certain that Lord Bute * will be continued Groom of the Stole, and Lord Huntingdon † Master of the Horse."

In a later part of the letter he assures her that Emin, who had been reported murdered by the Turks, had got back safely to his father in Calcutta.

"I presume he will go to some Indian Nabob or Rajah, and then you may have the pleasure of tracing his marches on the banks of the Ganges, and over many regions *where the Gorgeous East showers on her Kings Barbaric Pearls and Gold;* and if he is successful, large tribute of those pearls and gold will come to you."

Mention is made of Mr. Vesey visiting Hagley, his wife too indisposed to accompany him. "Alas! in all that prospect I have not one glimpse of you. When will you come and dance on my lawns or sport on my hills with the Muses, or meditate in my woods with the pensive Goddess of Wisdom."

Mrs. Montagu started on her return to London on November 10. From Weatherby she answers the above letter on November 11, having journeyed "48 miles through the roughest roads in the gloomiest day in the dreariest month of the year." Mention is made

* John Stuart, 3rd Earl of Bute, born 1713, died 1792; married Mary Wortley Montagu.

† Francis, 10th Earl of Huntingdon, son of the famous Lady Huntingdon, the patroness of the "Huntingdon Connexion" branch of the Methodists.

of the King's funeral. "I approve much of your Lordship's prudence in not going to the King's funeral,* it is a ceremony for those who wish to catch a cold rather than for one who wants to get rid of one."

From Ferrybridge, on the 15th, Mrs. Montagu writes to her husband that the rain had been so heavy that the waters of Newark were said to be impassable.

Arrived at Grantham on Sunday the 17th, she writes—

"My Dearest,

"I got here very safe to-night, but the journey from Ferrybridge has been very unpleasant, from the great depth of the waters. Our coach is fortunately hung very high, all the people who passed Newark to-day got a great deal of water into their carriage, but I had very little. The waters were impassable till this morning, and it is now raining hard, so I had good fortune to get thro' in the short interval; some of the water near Barnby Moor was as deep as at Newark, and tho' this is only a long day's journey, I have got out every day as soon as it was light; the horses perform admirably. I shall get to Stilton to-morrow, and, I hope, get you some cheese."

Writing the same evening to Lord Lyttelton, she says—

"Do not figure to yourself that I sit like Aurora in her car drawn by the rosy-bosom'd hours, *les jeux et les ris*, but imagine Dobbin and Whitenose and their 4 companions all mire and dirt, dragging me through deep water, over huge stones, the winds blowing, the clouds low'ring and rain darkening the windows of the coach."

* The funeral of King George took place the same day, November 11, 1760.

In a letter to Mr. Montagu, from Stilton, is this amusing passage—

"Lord Panmure pass'd me on the road yesterday, and I hear all the Scotch are gone to town from Peers to Pedlars, and I suppose all with the same intention to sell something and to get money. I found that a Scotch countess had bought all the black cloth, crapes and bombazeen, black ribbons, and fans at Darlington before the poor shopkeepers knew of the King's death. She bought a great many suits of broad cloth and crape, which must be with an intention to sell them at a higher price in town, but surely nothing could be more mean than to enter into such a traffick and take advantage of the Shopkeepers' ignorance, and it seems to me not honest. This lady is wife to Lord C——t; I believe I mistook when I called her a countess. The town was soon inform'd of the reason she had bought such a quantity of mourning, and I wonder she was not mobbed. The ladies at Darlington and in the neighbourhood are very angry, for she left but two yards of crape in the whole town."

Lady Frances Williams, writing on November 19 to Mrs. Montagu from Bath, where she was drinking the waters, says—

"I no sooner heard of the loss of our good old King than I thought with regret of our friend Mrs. Pitt. I believe it has prevented her coming to this place, where I proposed much pleasure in meeting her. I hear the G—t minister's friends, the mob, have posted upon all the Palaces—

'*A Pittical administration,—no Sc—tch influence;*'

and on the Royal Exchange—

'*No petticoat administration, no Lord G. S—k—lle* * *at Court.*'"

* Lord George Sackville.

Writing on November 20 to her husband, Mrs. Montagu says—

"The young King spoke his speech * with great grace; his voice, they say, is very fine, and his delivery most remarkably good. The Princess Dowager is not to be at St. James's, and people think she looks chagrin'd; no doubt she had visions of power and authority which will probably not be answered; all people seem glad that she is not likely to have influence. Dr. Wilson made a very flattering sermon at Court, upon which the King express'd great displeasure, and order'd all the Chaplains should be told he did not come to Church to hear himself praised. Lord Egremont † made a fine speech in the House of Lords for the address. Lord Royston is to move for the address in the House of Commons to-day, and Sir Richard Grosvenor,‡ who is to be made a peer, it is said, seconds him. Mr. Pratt § is to be made Lord Chief Justice in room of Willes, whose son is to be Solicitor-General, and Mr. York attorney. Some say Pratt is to be made a Peer. There seems a very strong union between Pitt and the Duke of Newcastle, but as yet no one knows how things will combine. The whole Cocoa Tree ‖ and every human creature has been at Court, and this being said one day in a large company, I was ask'd when I should go. I said not till you came to town, but when you did you intended I should be presented. Mrs. Boscawen said she suppos'd I should be introduced by Lady Bute, as we were relations, and visited; I answered no, for I should not go as a courtier. . . .

"I should ask Lady Cardigan to carry me, who was the head of the Montagu family, and a person who went as a great independant lady to pay her duty to her

* Parliament met on November 13.

† Charles Wyndham, 2nd Earl of Egremont.

‡ Sir Richard Grosvenor, afterwards 1st Earl Grosvenor.

§ Made 1st Earl Camden, became Lord Chancellor and Lord President of the Council.

‖ A famous Whig coffee-house.

sovereign without being a courtier. It seems if I am to go to Court, I must not appear anywhere till I have kiss'd hands, which makes it necessary, if done, to be done soon, but I shall wait your orders, and I beg you to speak freely."

To this letter Mr. Montagu replies—

"The distance j am now at from you, unhappily hinders me from discussing an affair of this moment with you and consulting with myne or your friends. At present j can only say that if you mean nothing more than paying your duty to our new sovereign j see no harm in it, and j think Lady Cardigan of all others the properest person to introduce you; but if you go further, before you give your attendance at a Court, j wish you would take the consequences into your most serious thoughts. The principal reason of my absenting myself ever since j was Member of Parliament was that j did not concur in the measures that were then taking, and the Principal members in the opposition thought they had no business at St. James, and j believe neither the wifes of the Peers nor of the Members of the House of Commons were found there. If j should be still so unhappy as out of dislike for the present measures not to alter my way of acting, and not to appear at Court, would it be proper for you to be attendant? Indeed, it seems to me that it would not, but if you can make out the contrary upon any sound Principles of reason j will readily submit. I have for many years liv'd in a state of Independancy though j may truly call it of Proscription, so far as those could make it to those who thought not, and acted not with them where politics they thought endanger'd the Liberties and good of their country, am j to alter now, or maintain the same conduct j hitherto have done? Whilst j flatter'd myself that we were in the same way of thinking, and that my conduct met with your approbation, j did hardly suffer anything. I then thought and still reflect with the utmost sense of gratitude on the sacrifice you made me in your early bloom, by giving up all the pleasures and gaieties of a Court, and it was the greater because you had all the advantages of beauty and sense to shine and make a figure there. I think that capacity is not so far gone as you in your modesty are pleas'd to say, and j may add in some sense perhaps improv'd, either at a Court or anywhere else j wish you every thing that is good that you may long enjoy that good will and esteem which your merit has acquir'd you, and leave the rest to your own candid and impartial consideration."

To this his wife replies—

"I had yesterday your most kind and judicious letter, and my own way of thinking coincides so much with yours I have no merit in acquiescence. Your wonted independancy I hope in God you will ever preserve. . . . If you should be in opposition, I shall drop going at all; as to Peers, all who were not profess'd Jacobites, and also their wives, always went to St. James', even the most protesting Lords, till the Division between the late King and late Prince of Wales."

At the end of the letter Lord Bath is mentioned as urging her to kiss hands, and she declares she will only attend two drawing-rooms a year, and not those, if Mr. Montagu disapproves.

On November 22, from Hill Street, Mrs. Montagu writes to her husband that her toothache having been very agonizing, she had sent to Mr. Lodomie to examine her teeth. As he is often mentioned, he must have been the fashionable dentist of that period. In the same letter we read that—

"there has been a quarrel between General Townshend * and Lord Albemarle,† which had ended in a duel if Mr. Stanley ‡ had not carried the Captain of the Guards to take them into custody. The story is too long for a letter. Mr. Townshend appears to have been too hasty: Lord Albemarle behaved very well, and all is now made up. Mr. Beckford in the House of Commons the day before yesterday call'd our German campaign this year a *languid campaign*, for which Mr. Pitt gave him a notable threshing, repeating languid and languor several times, and once how rash must that gentleman be, how inconsiderate, if he calls this languid, after repeating what had been done, and after enlarging on everything, again, again, and again, retorting the *languid* upon Beckford, who himself made a languid campaign, not returning to the charge. I heard of a good piece of witt of Mr. Pitt on my Lord Mayor of London's absurdly asking him in the Drawing-room, where the secret expedition was destined. He ask'd his Lordship if he could keep a secret, which the grave Magistrate assured him he could upon his honour, and expected to be inform'd, on which Mr. Pitt only made a low bow and said, *so can I, Sir*, a very proper reproof for his impertinent question."

December 2. Mrs. Montagu writes to Lord Bath—

"Mrs. Montagu presents her compliments to my Lord Bath, and has the pleasure to send him the Bishop of London's letter to the King, which she had never been able to get till yesterday; she begs of his Lordship not to give any copy of the letter. If the Bishop should have any human vanity still subsisting, it must be of such a kind as will be gratified by the approbation of Lord Bath, but would disdain common and ordinary applause. Mrs. Montagu hopes my Lord Bath remembers he was so good as to promise her the honour

* George Townshend, 4th Viscount and Marquis, born 1723, died 1807.

† George Keppel, 15th Earl of Albemarle.

‡ Hans Stanley, of Paultons, Hants.

and pleasure of his company at dinner on Sunday next.

"Hill Street, Tuesday ye 2nd of Decber."

The Bishop's letter is dated Novr. 1, 1760—

"SIRE,

"Amidst the Congratulations that surround the Throne, permit me to lay before your Majesty the Sentiments of a Heart, which tho' oppressed with Age and Infirmity, is no Stranger to the Joys of my Country. When the melancholy news of the Late King's Demise reached us, it Naturally Led us to Consider the Loss we had sustained, and upon what our Hopes of futurity Depended: the first Part excited grief and put all the tender Passions into motion, but the Second Brought Life and Spirit with it, and wiped away the tear from every face.

"O how graciously Did the Providence of God provide a Successor able to bear the weight of government in that unexpected Event.

"You, Sir, are the Person whom the people ardently Desire, which Affection of theirs is happily returned by your Majesty's Declared Concern for their prosperity; and Let Nothing Disturb this Mutual Consent. Let there never be but one Contest between them, whether the King Loves the people best, or the people him, and may it be a Long, very Long, Contest between them, may it never be decided, but Let it remain doubtful, and may the paternal affection on one side, and the filial Obedience on the other, be had in perpetual Remembrance. As this will probably be the Last time I shall ever trouble your Majesty, I beg leave to express my warmest wishes and prayers on your behalf: may the God of heaven and earth have you always under his protection, and Direct you to Seek his honour and Glory in all you Do, and may you reap the Benefit by an increase of Happiness in this world and in the next."

Lord Bath's answer was—

"MADAM,

"I suppose you intended that I should return you the Bishop's letter, which I promise you nobody has taken a copy of, nor have I done it myself, and I have shown it but to two persons.

"What a charming thing it is to be able to write with such vivacity and spirit, at past four score; and oppress'd as he says with age and infirmitys. But strange as that may be, I know a more extraordinary thing, and that is of a Person near the same age (but without infirmitys indeed) that is at this Instant over head and ears in Love. How does he wish he could write with as much Spirit and Love to his Mistress, as the Bishop does with Loyalty to his Master, with this difference only, the one wishes this contention of Love may never be decided, the other hopes it may be brought to an issue as soon as possible, by the only proper means of Determination, and let the Posterity arising from thence be a proof to future Generations of the ardency of the Affection of her

"Most passionate Adorer.

"Wednesday, 10 a clock, Decr., 1760."

To this Mrs. Montagu replies—

"MY LORD,

"I have sent your Lordship back the Bishop of London's letters, which cannot be more honourably placed than in your Cabinet. From an apprehension that this letter may be degraded by appearing in a magazine or Chronicle I was desirous to communicate it to my friends, under such restraints as would secure me from blame in case of accident. As I do not expect a billet-doux every morning, I was unluckily asleep (observe that I do not say not dreaming of Lord Bath) when your letter arrived. I cannot express how much I admire your Lordship's parody of a Bishop's pastoral letter. As I have got but halfway towards the ardours of four score, your Lordship will not expect I should immediately comply with your proposal; but if you will be content with a sentimental love till I arrive at the tender age of eighty, a person and a passion so ripened by time must be very yielding. And according to the latest reckoning of the learned and ingenious Mr. Whiston, the Millenium will then commence, so that we may have a proper period in which to prove our constancy and love; and at a moderate computation, may produce a thousand of those proofs of it which your Lordship seems to think the best testimony.

"I am now very much, but at the commencement of the next century hope to be entirely,

"Yours.

"I hope your Lordship will not forget your engagement on Sunday, for I have been interrupted in my letter by a visit from a very pretty man of five and twenty, whose conversation is so far from the spirit of your Lordship's letter that I cannot but be tired of the insipidity of these young people."

Writing to her husband on December 2, Mrs. Montagu says—

"I dined with Lord Bath on Sunday; he was in high spirits. At his table I heard an admirable *bon mot* of Lord Chesterfield's; he said the King was in doubt whether he should burn Scotch coal, Pitt coal, or Newcastle coal! . . . Our young King had a fall from his horse this morning, but no mischief, except a little bruise on his shoulder. His attendants seemed much frightened, at which he smiled and told them they forgot he had four brothers."

Mr. Montagu writes on December 7 from Newcastle to say that he is going to the Election at Durham to vote for Sir Thomas Clavering. He says, "I shall set off with Sir Thomas' cavalcade to-morrow, and to dine and lye at Newton, where Mr. Liddell has invited me to take a bed during the whole time of the Poll." On December 12 he writes to say the Poll was not over and cost each candidate £1000 a day.

Lord Bath writes to Mrs. Montagu in return for her last letter—

"MADAM,

"I have sent you some game, which I hope to partake with you to-morrow. Indeed, Madam, you are too cruel to desire to postpone my happiness till the beginning of the next century. I can die for the lady I love any day she pleases to command me, but to live 40 years for her is more than I can promise; besides, Madam, I would have you consider that in all the conquests Love makes, there is on the male side, constantly a little pride and vanity; do you think that I have not something of that kind, in the pleasure I propose to myself of making Mr. Montagu jealous, and of triumphing and insulting over Dr. Monsey; and can you yourself promise me either of these forty years hence? In conscience therefore reduce the horrid period of forty years to twenty at most, and tell me in your next, come twenty years hence and be happy. But all you promise in your letter is, that the beginning of next century, perhaps, you may begin to listen. This cold proceeding, with an impetuous Lover of fourscore, who is impatient to convince you how much he loves you and how passionately he is yours for the remainder of the millenium, whenever it begins,

"BATH."

From St. James's on December 14, Dr. Monsey writes a folio letter to Mrs. Montagu, beginning—

"SERENISSIMA PRINCIPESSA!

"There are no bounds to Pride, because an Earl is fallen in love with you, you must kiss a King, and just as he is on the brink of matrimony. How dare you do so audacious a thing, whilst your Hubby is alive too? Had he broke his neck down a coal pit the matter had been nothing, but to inflame the heart of a young monarch when he can reap no benefit from it without breaking the laws of his Kingdom, or your breaking the Laws of God. Let me tell you, Madam (if I now may presume to tell you anything), it is a very imprudent step. Emin has miscarried in Persia, and so now you will let yourself down to the deluding hopes of being Queen of England. Can you sleep this night while Majesty lies tumbling and tossing, and starts at Montagu peeping thro' his curtains;—My Kingdom for this Woman, or this Woman for my Kingdom. Have you chosen your ladies of the bedchamber, pitched upon your coronation, and made me your chief Physician. . . ."

After a long rhodomontade, he falls into doggerel verse, a frequent habit of his in his letters. As I have not hitherto recorded any verses of his in this work, I will give this specimen—

"What power can withstand Gt. Britain's King,
Where for a Queen he has so fair a thing?
Nations fight Nations, and one fool beats t'other,
And Frederick * pommels his dear Polish brother.
He burns a town and then knocks down a Church,
Then Daun comes thundering with a rod of birch.
He scampers, then he rallies, whip goes Daun,
Old boy, I'll meet you on a Torgau † lawn.
They meet, they fight, and then more bloody noses,
And then great victories, as our news supposes.
They both are Victors, yet both beaten well,
And who's best man the Devil himself can't tell.
Things are by both into confusion hurled,
Montagu speaks, and she subdues the world."

Lord Bath had been most anxious about his son, Lord Pulteney, who had been appointed to the secret

* Frederick "the Great."

† The battle of Torgau, fought on November 3, 1760.

expedition which Mr. Pitt designed to send to France. This scheme was given up, and Mrs. Montagu wrote to congratulate Lord Bath upon this.

In a letter to Mr. Montagu his wife informs him that "Lord Bute has given Mr. R. Berenger * a place of £300 per annum, with a house in the Meuse: it came *à propos*, for a few weeks ago he was in danger of a perpetual lodging at the Fleet."

It will be remembered Berenger was nephew to Mr. Gilbert West, his mother being a Temple.

Lady Forbes, mother of Mrs. Gregory, wrote on December 20 to Mr. Montagu to ask his influence in procuring for Doctor Gregory the Professorship of Botany at the University of Edinburgh.

In a letter dated 1760, presumably in February, Lord Bath writes to Mrs. Montagu—

"MADAM,

"There is more easy natural witt in any two of your most careless lines than there is in all Colman's Play,† and as for his dedication you may be sure the Rogue meant to abuse me for pretending to chide him for his neglect of Lord Cooke; ‡ however, I have this day, to amend his manners, constituted him a Judge in Shropshire, on condition that he never makes another Rhime, unless it be an Epithalamium twenty years hence, when the Millenium begins.

"I return you many thanks for the kind present you sent me, and will keep them till you do me the honour to dine with me, which I hope will be Wednesday or

* Master of the Horse; author of "The History and Art of Horsemanship."

† George Colman the elder, born 1732, died 1794; dramatist, etc. His first acknowledged comedy, "The Jealous Wife," first acted at Drury Lane on the 12th of February, 1761, and dedicated to the Earl of Bath as a "lover of the belles lettres."

‡ Means Lord Coke, in his work upon Lyttelton. In 1775, Colman had been entered by Lord Bath at Lincoln's Inn and called to the bar.

Thursday, as you chuse, but on Tuesday evening I cannot be sure of being free, since Sir Phil Boteler, Miss Desbouveries, and some other company are to dine with me, and stay the evening at cards."

George Colman was nephew, by marriage, to Lord Bath, his mother being a Miss Gumley, sister of Lady Bath.

CHAPTER V.

1761—DEATH OF ADMIRAL BOSCAWEN—CORRESPONDENCE WITH LORD BATH—CORONATION OF GEORGE III.—IN LONDON, AT SANDLEFORD, AND AT TUNBRIDGE WELLS.

MATTHEW ROBINSON, Mrs. Montagu's eldest brother, who had been member for the borough of Canterbury, did not propose to offer himself for re-election to the new parliament, but presented the Canterbury address to the new king at Court. He was clad in such a peculiar and uncourtierlike garb that his sister writes to her husband at Newcastle—

"I am glad he is gone into the country, but he has made a most astonishing appearance at court with the Canterbury address. Morris says he hears of nothing else. I wish the Beefeaters had not let him pass the door. Lord Harry Beauclerc on the buzz his appearance occasioned, desired the people to be quiet, for that he had never seen the gentleman so well dressed before."

Mr. Montagu, having attended the Durham election in favour of Sir Thomas Clavering, was preparing to go to Huntingdon for his own re-election. In Mrs. Montagu's next letter she says—

"I told you in my last that Admiral Boscawen was ill of a fever, I hope he is out of danger. The noble admiral does not fight so well with a fever as he does with the French; he will not lye in bed, where he would soonest subdue it. Poor Mrs. Boscawen is very anxious and unhappy about the Admiral, and indeed the loss to her and her children would be as great as possible."

In this letter she remarks upon having heard from Mrs. William Robinson, her sister-in-law, from Lisbon dated November 12: "they are all well, and going on to Madrid." "They" were the Rev. William Robinson, his wife, and her brother, Mr. Richardson, who, being in bad health, was ordered abroad, and was going to Italy. On December 20, Admiral Boscawen is reported as out of danger, but on the 27th Mrs. Montagu writes—

"His fever still hangs upon him, his strength is quite subdued; any sudden attack, any degree more of fever, and my dear Friend loses a good husband, her children a fond father, their situation in life will suffer a grievous alteration, and the publick will be deprived of a man who serves it with zeal and ability and is always more tender of the honour of his country than of his own person."

The admiral had a relapse, and Mrs. Montagu, with her husband's permission, flew to see her friend, but, to avoid alarming the admiral, slept at Mr. Botham's at Albury. She, however, returned to London, as the admiral could not bear his wife out of his sight, and begrudged any friend taking her away from him for an instant. In this same letter she mentions that old Mr. Wortley Montagu was very ill.

Dr. Monsey, who himself was very unwell, wrote on January 9 to tell Mrs. Montagu he was sure the admiral would not recover; he begs her to remember it is God's will, and "to try and guard Mrs. Boscawen's mind and let money and the world be thrown into the Coal Hole."

The admiral expired on January 10 at 7 a.m. He died of a putrid fever, and before death sent for his sister, Mrs. Frederick, to desire her to take his wife and children to London the moment he was dead. Mrs. Montagu went at once to her friend to endeavour to comfort her. Mr. Montagu, with his characteristic kindness, begged Mrs. Boscawen to go to Hill Street, but she remained at the Admiralty. Mrs. Montagu writes of her on January 17—

"I thank God her mind is very calm and settled, she endeavours all she can to bring herself to submit to this dire misfortune; I know time must be her best comforter, so that I oppose her lamentations rarely and gently, but when they continue long, set before her the merit of her five children, the want they will have of her, and the comfort she may derive from them. . . . Mr. Boscawen has left all his fortune, except a purchase he made in Cornwall, to Mrs. Boscawen at her entire disposition, the land in Cornwall he has left her only for life, and then to his eldest son. This estate cost but £10,000, and so is a small part of his fortune, so that the children are entirely dependent on her. I hear old Mr. Wortley can last but a very short time. It is supposed Lady Mary will come to England."

Writing to her husband, still at Newcastle, at the end of January, Mrs. Montagu says—

"I believe it will be agreeable to you to hear that Lord Sandwich called on me this morning to desire me to write you word that he hopes that the second week in February you will be ready for Huntingdon; his Lordship says he will give you only two days' trouble, one to canvass, another to be elected. . . . Mr. Wortley

Montagu dyed last night, the disposition of his effects not known as yet, by next post you shall hear."

In her next letter she says—

"I have had a full account of Mr. Wortley's will, it runs thus:—'To his son £1000 per annum rentcharge, with an order it should not be liable to his debts, which by-the-bye is nonsense. The Leicestershire estate, we know to our sorrow is his. If the present wife * dyes and he has legitimate issue, that issue is to have the Wortley estate. In case he has not such issue, then the whole of his personal and real estate is to go to Lady Bute's second son, he taking the noble name of Wortley. Two thousand pounds apiece indeed to each of Lady Bute's younger children! The old gentleman's wealth is reckoned immense."

In another letter his estate is stated to be £800,000 in money, and £17,000 per annum in land, mines, etc.!

Mr. Montagu writes in reply to this—

"I am extremely sorry that Mr. Wortley has made such a will as you mention. I think he has been unworthy of being a Father. I cannot pretend to say but his son gave him too good reason to take care he should not waste and consume his estate, it was mine and the opinion of others that, as the phrase is, he would have tyed him up, but if he had done it in the literal sense he would have been less cruel to him; this poor man was not without very good parts, he was greatly altered; if he had done kindly by him, it was not impossible that he might have been reclaimed and have yet made some figure in life. What is now to become of him I don't know. I suppose he is not to come into Parliament again, and if so I cannot see what he can do but leave his native country, and live in perpetual

* Caroline Feroe, *née* Dormer.

banishment abroad. I cannot but greatly commiserate this poor man, and reflect with horror on his cruel unrelenting parent."

On February 15 Mr. Montagu writes from Hinching-brooke, as he spells it—

"MY DEAREST,

"We got here on Friday night. Our canvassing the town is put off to Tuesday. Lord Hinching* is here, who is much grown and every way improved. My Lord has made considerable alterations to the house, and by the addition of two or three rooms is very convenient, and he says without much expense. . . . Calling at Barnet j heard poor Wortley's stock upon his farme was the day before sold by auction, and fetched a thousand pounds, which j fear will be devour'd by the creditors."

Soon after this Mr. Montagu joined his wife in Hill Street. A folio letter from James Stuart† (Athenian Stuart) ends the month of February. In it he represents himself as an English horse—a hunter dragging Greek treasures to Mrs. Montagu, whom he addresses in verse as—

"Fairest and best! hail Montagu Minerva!
Smile on my labours. Say that my rich freightage
Amply deserved the Price and Pains it cost.
So that the Muses thy companions dear,
The Graces and the Virtues all approve
My bold Emprise:
And end at once and recompense my toil."

Lord Bath writes March 4, 1761—

* Viscount Hinchinbrook, afterwards 5th Earl of Sandwich; born 1742-3, died 1814.

† James Stuart, born 1713, died 1788; author of "Antiquities of Athens."

"MADAM,

"I am sorry that I cannot wait on you this evening, being engaged to go to Lady Strafford's,* and afterwards to Lady Darlington's† to play at cards; but on Saturday I will have the honour to call on you and stay the evening with you, if you are not otherwise engaged, and your feverish disorder will allow you to come down stairs. I have sent for your amusement Voltaire's Tancred, which has many fine lines in it, but the speeches are too long, as they generally are in French Plays. When I have the honour of waiting on you I will bring with me Emin's letter.

"I am, Mad^{me},

"Yours most truly,

"B."

To this Mrs. Montagu replies—

"MY LORD,

"I return the Tragedy with many thanks. The character your Lordship gave of it kept up my hopes and my spirits through the long tedious speeches with which it opens, and upon the whole it appears to me to be one of the best of Voltaire's Tragedies, as it is, what few of his are, interesting. Pompous declamation season'd with Moral reflections is surely far from the perfection of dramatick writing, tho' in a nation too much polish'd and refin'd, it is prefer'd to the natural sallies of passion in our Shakespear, as fops love essences better than the flowers from whence they are extracted. I find in this Tragedy many petty larcenies from Corneille. The character of Aménaide is in part an imitation of the Sister of Horatius, but the Roman name supports the *fierté* of her character, born in any other city I should call her a termagant, there I consider her as a She Roman, the female of the Lion.

* Lady Strafford, Anne, second daughter of the 2nd Duke of Argyll.

† Lady Darlington was a cousin of Lord Bath's; her mother was a Pulteney.

The fair Amenaide is too much an *esprit fort* in regard to her duties to please me. She does not follow Virtue as by law establish'd, but despises forms and follows sentiment, a dangerous guide. Design'd by Nature to act but a second part, it is a woman's duty to obey rules, she is not to make or redress them. I must confess that Aménaide is noble and heroick, and a proper mistress for a Knight Errant, whose motto is 'l'amour et l'honneur.' I have seen many poems form'd on the manners of Chivalry, but I never saw them before in Drama. They admit of the bombast in honour and love, which the French and Spanish Theater affect, and will furnish those brilliant sentiments they so much admire, but which indeed come better from any Muse but the pathetick Melpomène.

"I shall be very glad of the honour of your Lordship's company on Saturday evening. I was to have gone to the play that night, but if my fever should have left me by that time, I have a cough which would be louder than Mrs. Prichard.* I have taken the liberty to enclose Mr. Macpherson's proposals, and if your Lordship designs to subscribe to the work, and have not already done so, I should be very glad to have the honour of your name on my list. I have read the first canto,† which far exceeded my expectation. The various incidents recited take off that sameness of character which appeared in the detached pieces, and which were their greatest fault. The original Ersh is to be seen at Mr. Millar's. I have also enclosed a letter from Edinburgh which gives an account of these poems. By this long letter I have taken some revenge upon your Lordship for not coming here last night, and now I am in perfect charity, mix'd with some compassion for the trouble I have given you.

"My Lord,

"Your Lordship's
Most obliged and obedient H[ble] Ser[vt],

"E.M."

* Celebrated actress.

† This must be "Fingal."

At this period Mrs. Montagu and Mrs. Carter went to stay with Lord Bath at Ives Place.* Dr. Monsey was to have accompanied them, but he was suffering with acute pain in his back, for which Dr. Gataker gave him a plaister, which he said would pull his head to his back.

Lord Bath writes to Mrs. Montagu the following:—

"MADAM,

"I am going to entrust you with a most prodigious secret; and in order to engage you the better to keep it, must desire you to be a joynt agent with me in conducting it, and carrying it on, and yet it is not every woman neither that can keep that very important *secret of joynt agency*, but you, I am very sure, will be true to me when I tell you what it is. You must know, Madam, that I have a great desire of making a small present to Mrs. Carter, to make her fine, when she comes to Tunbridge, and I must beg of you to take the trouble of buying the silk or Damask, or what you please, and in order to engage her to have no difficulty or scruples in accepting it, I will send with it the following letter:—

"'*To Mrs. Carter.*

"'MADAM,

"'I have sent you a trifling present which I desire you will accept, and that you may have no difficulty in doing it I will tell you the plain truth. The first thing is this—I have found in my Library some books, which tho' they may be very good ones, can be of no use to me, as they are in Greek,† and possibly they may be of service to you. The next thing is that I have two pounds of very bad tea, which I cannot so much as take myself, nor offer to anybody else, unless it

* His country house near Maidenhead.

† This is an affectation, as he constantly uses Greek phrases in Greek character in his later letters.

be to you: the last thing is this: I found in the drawer of an old India Cabinet a piece of silk with this wrote in a paper upon it: *Enough for a Mantua and petty coat.* Now, Madam, as I neither wear a mantua nor pettycoats, I do not know what to do with it, unless you will accept of it, which you may very readily do, since you may perceive that it lays you under no manner of obligation to your, etc.

"'BATH.'

"But after all I have said, if you think, Madam, giving you the two enclosed Bank bills of 20 pounds each to send privately to her without letting her know or guess from whom they come, may be of more real use and service to her, you may do it as you think fit, and I can venture to say of the Bank Bills just what I have done of the Greek books, that they are of little use to me, and possibly may be of great service to her, and more in that I hope than any other.

"I am, Madam,
"Your most obedient and very
humble servant,
"BATH.

"Piccadilly, April 2, 1761.

"P.S.—I am afraid you will be puzzled at first to know what all this nonsensical stuff can mean, but you may remember that when you were at Ives Place, I mentioned something of this kind to you."

Mrs. Montagu and Mrs. Carter proposed a visit to Dr. Young at Welwyn, and on April 9 he writes as follows—

"DEAR MADAM,
"Your letter, etc., lay me under great obligations, but the greatest lies in the kind promise you make me that I shall kiss the hands of two fair Pilgrims at Wellwyn. I hope they are too much Protestants to

think there is anything sacred in the shrine you speak of. I have too many sins beside, to pretend that I am a Saint. Was I a Saint and could work miracles I would reduce you two ladys to the common level of your sex being jealous for the credit of my own; which has hitherto presum'd to boast an usurp'd superiority in the realms of genius and the letter'd world. For you, Madam, I shall say nothing, for who can say enough? Miss Carter has my high esteem for showing us in so masterly a manner that Christianity has a foil in one of the brightest jewels of Pagan Wisdom, a jewel which you will allow she has set in gold. Might not such an honour from a fair hand, make even an Epictetus proud without being blamed for it? Nor let Miss Carter's amiable modesty become blameable, by taking offence at the truth, but stand the shock of applause, which she has brought upon herself; for tho' it pains her, it does credit to the publick, and she should support it patiently, as her Stoical Hero did his broken leg. I rejoice that you are recovered; I too, Madam, have been very ill of late, and stand in no small need of a cordial: hasten therefore your favour, which the sooner it is, will be the kinder to, dear Madam,

"Your most obedient
and obliged, humble servant,
"E. Young."

On April 28 Lord Bath writes to Mrs. Montagu—

"Madam,

"I would sooner have answer'd your letter, and sent you back the enclosed Dialogue, but that I went out to take the air in my chaize. You may depend upon my secrecy, but should it ever be published, it will be known to be yours, because nobody can write like it. I will endeavour to wait on you when you return from Dr. Young's, unless I go to Ives Place for a day or two.

"I am, with the greatest regard and truth,
"Your most humble and obedient servant,
"Bath."

This is the dialogue which I believe has not yet been published:—

"BERENICE AND CLEOPATRA."

Berenice. The similitudes and dissimilitudes of our fortune have long made me wish to converse with you, if the charming, the victorious Cleopatra by her lover prefer'd to glory, to empire, to life, will deign to hold converse with the forsaken, the abandon'd, the discarded Berenice.

Cleopatra. The scorns of Octavius, the bite of the aspic, the waters of Lethe have so subdued my female vanity, that I will own to you I greatly suspect my greater success with my lover did not arise so much from my charms as in my skill of management of them.

Berenice. I can scarce understand you. Beauty and love I thought to be the greatest attractions. In the first you must have excell'd me, but in the second you certainly could not: I had beauty, youth, regal dignity, and an elevated mind. I was distinguished by many qualities and accomplishments which were so dedicated to my Lover, that of all I had been and all I could be, I was, I would be, only *l'amante* of Titus. I thought the next person in merit and dignity to Titus himself was the woman who ador'd him, and I was more proud of the homage I paid him, than of all I had receiv'd from lovers or subjects. But you, Cleopatra, had loved Cesar before Anthony, and other passions besides the gentle one of love seemed still to have your heart. Yet for you Anthony despised the dangers of war, the competition of a rival in Empire, the motives of military glory, and the resentment of a Senate and people not yet taught to submit to or flatter the passions of a master. Over these you triumph'd; but I was sacrificed to the low murmurs of the people, and the cautious counsels of gray-headed Statesmen. Was it that Minerva desired to triumph over Venus in the noblest and gentlest heart that ever was contain'd in the breast of mortal? Tell me, Cleopatra, for 1700 years have not made me forget my love and my grief?

Cleopatra. I have often with attention listen'd to your story; and your looks, on which still remain the sadness of a lover's farewell, move my compassion. I wish I could have assisted you with my counsels when Titus was meditating your departure. I would have taught you those arts by which I enslaved the Soul of Anthony, and brought Ambition and the Roman Eagles to lye at my feet.

Berenice. Your arts would have been of little service to me, I had no occasion to counterfeit love. From Titus's perfection one learn'd to love in reality beyond whatever fiction pretended; no feigned complaisance could imitate my sympathy; if he sigh'd I wept, if he was grave I grew melancholy, if he sicken'd I dyed. My heart echoed his praises, it beat for his glory, it rejoiced in his fortunes, it trembled at his dangers.

Cleopatra. Indeed, Berenice, you talk more like a Shepherdess than a great Queen. You might perhaps in the simplicity of pastoral life have engaged some humble Swain, but there was too much of nature and too little of art in your conduct, to captivate a man used to flattery, to pleasures, to variety. I find you was but the mirror of Titus, you gave him back his own image, while I presented every hour a new Cleopatra to Anthony. I was gay, voluptuous, haughty, gracious, fond and indifferent by turns; if he frown'd on me, I smiled on Dollabella; if he grew thoughtful, I turn'd the Banquet to a Riot. I dash'd the soberness of counsels by the vivacity of mirth, and gilded over his disgrace by show and magnificence; if his reason began to return, I subdued it by fondness, or disturb'd it by jealousy. Thus did I preserve my conquest, establish my fame, and put Anthony first in the list of

"all the mighty names by love undone."

Had I only wept when honour and Octavia call'd him home I might have been the burthen of a love ballad, or subject of a tender Elegy, who now am the glory of our sex, and the great instance of beauty's power. Do not you wish you had used the same managements?

Berenice. I might have used them had I loved the same man: Cleopatra, the coquette was a proper mistress for the Reveller Anthony; but the god-like Titus, the delight as well as Master of Mankind, left no part of the heart unengaged and at liberty to dissemble. What had not yielded to his wisdom, submitted to his witt, was subdued by his magnanimity, or won by his gentleness; when affection does not vary, behaviour cannot change; and methinks Anthony should have quitted you from distrust of your love, and Titus have retain'd me from confidence in mine. After what you have told me, I am more than ever surprised at your fate and my own.

Cleopatra. If you want this explain'd ask Eneas, Theseus, Jason, and the infinite multitude of faithless lovers, but if my authority will pass, believe me Anthony was preserved by his doubt of my love, and Titus was lost by his confidence in yours. Do not look so concern'd. From the era of your disaster to this very day you will find every faithful and fond Berenice discarded, while the gay, vain, and capricious fair one is to her Anthony a Cleopatra and the "world well lost."

From the following letter of Dr. Young's to Mrs. Montagu it would appear that she had sent this dialogue for him to read.

"DEAR MADAM,

"I hope you will allow that a curiosity is better than a good thing. I send you a paper which may be called a curiosity, as it is printed, but not for the publick, only for your ease in perusing it.

"I much thank you for the bright specimen of genius you was so kind as to send me. I admire it as much as you I hope you are recover'd of the Indysposition you mention'd in your Last, and that you, the cloud remov'd, will continue to shine on,

"Dear Madam,
"Your most obedient
and Humble Serv[t],
"E. YOUNG."

"May 26, 1761."

Emin, from "Standgate Creek, on board of the ship *Northumberland*," writes on May 5 to Mrs. Montagu, addressing her thus—

"To the wisdom of Europe, sister to the great King of Prussia, excellent Mrs. Montagu."

Not only did he think Mrs. Montagu equal in cleverness to Frederick the Great, but he considered her forehead and eyes like his, to the great indignation of Lord Bath and Dr. Monsey, who pronounced it impossible she should resemble so bloodthirsty a character.

Mrs. Carter took leave of Mrs. Montagu on May 18, and that very evening Mrs. Montagu writes to her—

"You left London only this morning, and I am writing to you to-night; does it not seem unreasonable? I hope not, as you must know there are habits which it is hard to break, and alas! I was in the habit of conversing with you every day. I feel like a traveller, who by the chearfull light of the Sun has pleasantly pursued his day's journey, but seeing it below the horizon, enjoys and would fain prolong the twilight, which tho' it has not the warmth and lustre of the noon-day, yet is a kind interposition between it and the gloom of the night."

She dates her letter from Ealing, where she had gone to the Botham's for the night, "imagining I should hear your tones better from the nightingale than in the din and chatter of London." So much did Mrs. Carter value Mrs. Montagu's letters that she always noted the day and year of their reception of them, which is a great help to an editor in compiling, as many of Mrs. Montagu's letters are undated. In the end of this letter she mentions that she is returning to London next day to spend the evening with Mrs. Boscawen, who was to leave the Admiralty that day for her new house.

"She will be too apt to reflect on the change of her condition upon such an occasion, and the less time she has to dwell on the subject the better. Alas, how few people are there so happily situated that they can intrepidly look on their condition! Mr. Melmoth * made me a visit this evening. I exhorted him to give his leisure hours to the publick, and hope he will do it, as his health is now much improved."

A most curious anonymous letter to Lord Bath concerning his house in Piccadilly, dated June 5, 1761, is next in order. The handwriting is large and bold.

"MY LORD,

"A zeal for the glory of the Nation and of the town, also of your Lordship, induces me to recommend to you to modernize your house in Piccadilly, at least externally, by facing it with stone or Stucco, as brick has an ignoble appearance, and is considered by foreigners only fit for a *Maison bourgeoise*; a Portico with a *Rampe*,† as at the Hotels of Prince Eugene and Swartzenburg at Vienna, unites Conveniency, Elegance, and Grandeur, as chairs and coaches can go up the *Rampe* and under the Portico, whereas a *Perron* ‡ or

* William Melmoth, born 1710, died 1799. English scholar; translated the "Letters of Pliny," etc., etc.

† Means a rising gradient.

‡ A flight of steps.

open steps are always inconvenient, and often dangerous in snowy, wet, and frosty weather. I hope that your Lordship will give a Proof and monument of your Taste, Spirit, and Generosity in architecture, contributing thereby to the embellishment of the Metropolis. A House of Distinction sho'd be always *insulated* without any Building contiguous thereto, which insulation has many advantages.

"I have the Honour to be, with Respect,

"ETC.

"June 5, 1761."

The British Museum, containing the library and collection of Sir Hans Sloane, the Cottonian and Harleian MSS., etc., had been established in Montagu House, bought of the Earl of Halifax, and opened in 1759. The following letter from Mr. Charles Morton, the curator, will show the conditions under which the Museum was then shown. The Earl of Halifax, who had owned Montagu House, was a cousin of Mr. Montagu's.

"*To Mrs. Montagu.*

"MADAM,

"I am extremely sorry not to have received the Honour of your Message before eleven o'clock last night, being detained abroad by Business till that Time. I flatter myself, however, that the affair you mention will not have suffered by my absence; for on fridays and mondays the Museum is open in the afternoon only, at the Hours of four and six, calculated to accommodate for a few months persons of a different class, and on Saturdays the Museum is shut up. I have therefore secured places for Mrs. Montagu and her company for Tuesday sennight, at one o'clock, and promise myself the Pleasure to send the Tickets on Wednesday next, unless the Time I have engaged should be inconvenient to you; in which latter case, I beg the Honour of a note to-morrow some time before noon.

"Madam, I remain, with great respect,

"Your most obedient
and most humble Servant,
"CHAS. MORTON.

"Montagu House, June 7, 1761."

From Sandleford, on June 23, Mrs. Montagu writes to Mrs. Carter—

"DEAR MADAM,

"I told you in my last that I was going to take a flight into Berkshire; and here I have been ever since Friday evening, leading a Pastoral life in the finest weather I ever saw. Tho' the most sage Horace says we change our climate without changing our disposition, I must be of another opinion, for by only the difference of latitude and longitude between Hill Street and Sandleford I am become one of the most reasonable, quiet, good, kind of country gentlewoman that ever was. In the days when misses employ'd their crimping and wimpling irons upon cheese-cakes and tarts, not on flounces and furbelows, and matrons used no rouge, but a little cochineal to give a fine colour to a dried neat's-foot tongue, they could not be further from the temper and qualities and conditions of a fine lady than your humble servant at this present writing. My health is much improved by the country air; I saunter all day, and when Phœbus sets in the material world, he rises in the Intellectual; then I sit down to read what he has inspired, and I find the amusements of the day here prepare me well for my evening's lecture. . . .

"The mention of poetry puts me in mind to tell you I am very well satisfied with the share of praise you give to Cowley.* He had a rich vein of thought, but being too ostentatious of it, we are disgusted at the

* Abraham Cowley, born 1618, died 1667; poet

proud display of his treasures, as at the pomp of a rich man, when it goes beyond the bounds modesty and a sound judgment should set to it. I agree with you that his love verses are insufferable. I think you and I who have never been in love, could describe it better were we ask'd, *what is it like?* I think some of his verses, like Anacreon, very pretty, and the verses by the god of love in honour of Anacreon are very pretty tho' a little too long. I think you was too temperate in your commendation of 'La Mort D'Abel.'* I was infinitely delighted with it as a work of genius. On your recommendation I lent it to my Lord Lyttelton, who sent it back with great approbation. But to be sincere in spite of you both, some silly prejudices against the Author and the language the poem was originally written in, a little damped my expectations, and the beginning, in which he imitates Milton, with all the faintness of reflected beams, make me advance very soberly. But what a feast is the Patriarchal dinner! How sweetly innocent their manners! Eve's horror at the first storm, her surprize at Adam's fastening up the mouth of the cave, concern at the first sight of death, which is finely supposed to seize a dove, because in that animal only could the grief of a surviving friend be shown, with ten thousand other circumstances in hers and Adam's narration, all so natural and yet so new that I must call Mr. Gesner a Poet. A Poet should create, but he should not make monsters. I think our Author has not the sublime, but his genius suits his subject. What a noble piety! what a purity of heart in Abel! and how finely is his character contrasted with Cain's. Abel's are virtues of disposition and temper in a great degree, and so are Cain's vices, which rightly imagined in a state of life where example and discipline could not have so much influence as in a larger society and more mix'd life. Milton's and Mr. Gesner's pastoral scenes are so ennobled and refined by Religion, that the Shepherds and Shepherdesses who

* By Salomon Gesner, born 1730, died 1788. "Tod Abels."

worship the wanton Pan and drunken Silenus, make a mean figure when compared to them. I agree with you in liking Mr. Gesner's Pastorals extreamly, but let him still keep to the more than golden age of the Poets. I would fain propose to him to take the story of Joseph next. He has a fine genius for Drama! The last three books of Abel make a noble tragedy. Did you not drop a tear at the lamentation of Cain's children over Abel's body? *Il ne se reveillera plus! Il ne se reveillera plus!* How simple! how natural! how affecting! What a witchcraft is there in words! repeat, *il est mort*, it is nothing, but the simplicity of children who had not a name for death and the words at once signifying the circumstance is very touching. . . . I have taken a house at Tunbridge from the 3rd of July. I hope my dear friend will be ready to come to me. I shall send the post-chaize to you as soon as I am at Tunbridge.

"I am, my dear Madam,

"With most sincere and tender affection,

"Yours,

"E. MONTAGU."

Writing from Sandleford on June 26 to Mrs. Scott, Mrs. Montagu mentions that she is going to Tunbridge

"for 6 or 7 weeks perhaps, and the rest of the summer I shall pass at Sandleford, except my excursion to Bath Easton. Mrs. Carter is to come to Tunbridge to me as soon as I get thither, and, I hope, stay with me the whole season. I was so fortunate as to enjoy her company much longer in town this year than usual, but that only makes me wish the more to have her again. She was not in the house with me in town, preferring the quiet of a lodging to herself, and indeed it would not be any delight to Mr. Montagu to have her in the house; tho' he says she would be a good sort of woman *if she was not so pious.** My Lord Bath told me he was to

* Mr. Montagu, though a most moral man and a Church attendant, objected to religious conversation.

go to Bath on Wednesday, the day we dined with him. . . .

"I shall have Mrs. Boscawen for my neighbour at Tunbridge; she is to be at Sir Sydney Smythe's, only three miles from the Wells. Lady Frances Williams is in the deepest affliction for Lady Coningsbye.* To show the last respect to her, Lady Frances staid in the house with the dead body in spite of all her friends could do; she did not leave Lady Coningsbye's house till last Saturday; she has been so singularly unfortunate that, had she not the strongest piety and the strongest reason to support her, she must sink under the repeated strokes of affliction. . . . I suppose you have read Dr. Hawkesworth's† 'Oriental Tales,' it is not written with so much spirit as the Oriental tales in 'the Adventurer' which were by him, but there are some fine things in it. . . . I have heard my Lord Bath speak with great regard for you and Lady Bab Montagu. I believe we shall call on him on Monday, on our way to London. We were asked to dine or lye there in our journey down, and at our return. He has recovered his health and spirits and is the most delightfull companion imaginable. I think he has great good qualities, and I do not perceive the least of that covetousness which was attributed to him while his wife lived; he lives nobly, entertains generously, and I know many acts of generosity he has done, and I have known them from the report and acknowledgements of the persons obliged, for by his behaviour to such of them as I have seen at his house you would think he had received favours from them, which nobly enhances the benefit. He seems to have the strongest sense of Religion, and on all occasions to show it without the ostentation of one who wants to be praised for piety, nor does he ever in the gayest of his conversation forget the respect due to every moral duty. It would give one pain to discover any faults in one who has such extraordinary

* Her sister.

† John Hawkesworth, LL D., essayist and novelist, died 1773.

perfections and endowments, and I think his Lordship has outlived the errors which the hustling of a mighty Spirit may in youth have led him: as to his consort, she was, in Milton's phrase, *a cleaving mischief in his way to virtue.*

"I am glad Lord Bath is to be at Tunbridge. Mrs. Carter is a great favourite, and I hope we shall have a good deal of his company."

She winds up her letter with high commendation of Gesner's "Death of Abel" mentioned before.

Dr. Young now writes—

"DEAR MADAM,

"You and I are playing blind man's buff; we both fancy we are catching something, and we are both mistaken. You say you have sent me two somethings, and I have not received so much as one, and you expected one from me, which is not yet come to your hand, which will kiss your hand this week, and if you are at the trouble of reading it over you will find a sufficient excuse for my delay. By what you say in your kind letter, you give me a very keen appetite for both the books which you promise. I have heard nothing yet of the time of my going to Kew: when I am there I shall make it my endeavour to enjoy as much of you as I can. I have been in very great pain with my rheumatism for some time, but now, I bless God, I hope the worst is over. May health and peace keep company with that benevolence and genius which are already with you.

"I am, dear Madam,
"Your much obliged
and most obedient humble Servt.,
"E. YOUNG.

"Mrs. Hallows * sends her best respects.

"Wellwyn, the 2nd July, '61."

* Mrs. Hallows was Dr. Young's lady housekeeper.

Dr. Young's allusion to Kew was the fact that he had recently been appointed Clerk of the Closet to the Princess Dowager of Wales.

On July 7 Mrs. Montagu started for Tunbridge Wells, and on the following Monday sent her post-chaise to fetch Mrs. Carter, and Lord Bath arrived from London on the same day. Mr. Montagu, who was going to Sandleford for a while, mentions in a letter of July 11 to his wife that

"there was a great appearance of the privy council when the King declar'd his intention of demanding the Princess of Mecklenburgh in marriage, a request that can never be denied. The family is ancient, and the blood high, but I suppose the Dukedom not very rich, but this may be helped with subsidies, etc., but this is not much to be grudged if by making our young Monarch happy it contributes to that of the Nation, tho' Princes are under a disadvantage from which their subjects are free, of marrying those whom they have never seen or convers'd with, still I hope there is reason to be believed that this alliance, as it was of the young Monarch's choosing and not of the imposing of a Father, and as money, etc., is out of the case, that care has been taken by those employ'd to give a true information both of the perfections of the mind and body of this Princess, and he will be happy."

Mr. Montagu adds that the pictures at Newbold Verdon were to be sold for Mr. Edward Wortley-Montagu's debts, but that a list of them had been sent to him by Mr. E. Wortley-Montagu, who desired to know which he would accept of as a present. Mr. Montagu had marked his brother's portrait (Mr. James Montagu), and asks his wife to say if there were any she wished for. Very probably the picture by Sir Peter Lely of the first Earl of Sandwich, Mr.

Montagu's grandfather, which I possess, came from there.

Lord Bath conveyed Mrs. Montagu and Mrs. Carter "to Mr. Pratt's * place, call'd Bayham Abbey, which I believe you once saw with Mr. Pitt. The ruins of the Abbey are very noble. Tho' the Gothick buildings have not in their time of utmost perfection the beauty of the Græcian ; time seems to have a greater triumph in the destruction of strength than of grace. . . . I have just now the pleasure of hearing Pondicherry † is taken. I hope this will depress the spirits of the French. . . . Lord Bath and Lord Lyttelton and Mrs. Carter and Doctor Smythe and many others desire their compliments."

On July 20 Dr. Stillingfleet writes from Stanlake, Berks, the seat of his friend, Richard Neville Aldworth, expressing his regret that he cannot accept Mrs. Montagu's kind invitation to Tunbridge Wells, as his friend, Mr. Aldworth, had made him promise to spend a summer with him at Stanlake. "This friend has had his constitution broken so by the gout, that he is become a valetudinarian, and therefore I can the less think of leaving him. He is ordered by his Physician to drink the Sunning Hill Waters, and we are going there as soon as he is able." Mr. Aldworth was an ancestor of Lord Braybrooke's.

Mr. Richardson, the author of "Clarissa Harlowe," etc., died on July 4, to the great grief of Dr. Young, who was a bosom friend of his. Mrs. Montagu bade Dr. Young come to Tunbridge to cheer his spirits. He writes—

* Afterwards Lord Camden.

† Pondicherry in the East Indies was taken on January 15, 1761.

"DEAR MADAM,

"On your very kind invitation I have inquired if it is in my power to accept of it, but I am not yet satisfied in that point. Probabilities will not excuse me if her R. H. should go to Kew. I should be very happy to be with you. I have so much to say to you that at present I shall say nothing. You will hear further of me in a little while. I beg my humble service to Mrs. Carter. May the Waters continue to be as serviceable to you as I would be if it was in my power.

"I am, dear Madam,
"Your obliged
and most obedient humble Servt.,
"E. YOUNG.

"July 21, 1761."

On July 30 Dr. Young writes that he is obliged to refuse Mrs. Montagu's kind invitation "as he had a friend with him he could not leave," and as "her Royal Highness sent me word she would send for me when she wanted me; for these reasons I deny myself the great pleasure of waiting on you. I have ordered some Stanzas to be sent to you; they are of a cooling nature, and may qualify your waters."

In this year (1761) a complete collection of the doctor's works was printed.

On the 8th of July George III. had announced his intention of demanding in marriage the Princess Charlotte of Mecklenburg Strelitz; negotiations were immediately commenced. Mrs. Montagu writes from Tunbridge Wells to her husband thus—

"We are all disappointed here at hearing our new Queen is fair; the first report was that by a lively bloom she would cast a shade over the white complexions of our royal family. The sight of our brilliant Court, the salutations of our navy on her arrival, the opulent appearance of our towns, and the greatness of our capital city will astonish her. I hope her mind is more proportioned to her lot in marriage than such a situation is to her present circumstances. A noble mind will fill a great situation, and enjoy it with pleasure and gratitude, without the swellings of insolence, but such a change is dangerous where there is a mediocrity of sense and virtue. I heartily wish she may be worthy of our young King, be pleasing in the domestick scene, and great in the publick; his good nature will impart to her a share of power and a degree of confidence, and I wish for the publick she may never abuse the one, nor misapply the other. There seems not to be a very good choice of ladies about her, there is not one who is quite fit to teach her even the forms of her publick conduct, none at all equal to advise her private, ignorant as she must be of the behaviour that will be expected of her, she should have had some woman of quality of remarkable discretion, character, and politeness, whom high birth and great situation had approached as nearly as a subject can to the station of a Queen. Lady Bute would have been the properest person, but I suppose she might out of delicacy avoid putting herself about the Queen's person, as thinking it might look like watching her, and indeed so happy as Lady Bute is in her circumstances, the slavery of personal attendance is more than anything but great ambition could pay her for. I think, however, they have chosen the ladies * of the bedchamber; her Majesty must consult Lady Bute upon everything. . . . Lord Bath always inquires after you and sends his compliments. Lord Lyttelton is gone on a party of pleasure with Mr. Selwyn.† This place is pretty full of I know not who. Sir Edward Dering and

* The Duchess of Ancaster and Duchess of Hamilton were sent to escort Queen Charlotte to England.

† George Selwyn, celebrated wit; born 1719, died 1791.

his family and the Lambarts breakfasted at Tunbridge, and go back again.

"I am, my Dearest,
"With the greatest gratitude
and affection, your most faithful wife,
"E. M."

Mrs. Montagu's letter of advice to Mr. Thomas Lyttelton, who had now left Eton and gone to Christ Church, Oxford, though undated, may be placed here.

"Tunbridge, 28 (July ?).

"DEAR SIR,

"I have often check'd my inclination to write to you while you were at Eton for fear of calling you off from your school exercises; but as you are now in a situation, where there is a vacancy of business and pleasure, I do not feel the same scruples, may write you long letters, and expect full answers to them. However, I will be so far reasonable, that if you send me a card, to signify that you are engaged for the week, or month, to Cicero or Livy, it will be a more valid excuse to me than if, on inviting you to dinner, you told me you were engaged to a beauty or a Duchess. My love for you, my hope of you, my wishes for you, and my expectations from you, unite in giving me a respect for your time, and a deep concern for your employment of it. The morning of life, like the morning of the day, should be dedicated to business. On the proper use of that 'sweet hour of prime' will depend the glory of your noon of life, and serenity of the evening. Give it, therefore, dear Mr. Lyttelton, to the strenuous exertion and labour of the mind, before the indolence of the meridian hour, or the unabated fervour of the exhausted day renders you unfit for severe application. I hope you will not (like many young men who have been reckoned good scholars at Eton and Westminster) take leave of it there, and fall into the study of *les belles lettres*, as we call our modern books. I suppose from the same courtesy the weakest part of the rational species is styled the fair sex, though it can boast of few perfect beauties, and perhaps the utmost grace and dignity of the human form is never found in it. As you have got a key to the sacred shades of Parnassus, do not lose your time in sauntering in the homely orchards or diminutive pleasure gardens of the latter times. If the ancient inhabitants of Parnassus were to look down from their immortal bowers on our labyrinths, whose greatest boast is a fanciful intricacy, our narrow paths where genius cannot take his bounding steps, and all the pert ornaments in our parterres of wit, they would call them the modern's folly; a name the wise farmer often gives to some spot from whence the Squire has banished the golden harvest, to trim it up for pleasure with paltry ornaments and quaint conceits. I should be sorry to see you quit Thucydides for Voltaire, Livy for Vertot, Xenophon for the bragging Memoirs of French Marshals, and the universal Tully and deep Tacitus for speculative politicians, modern orators, and the dreamers in Universities or convents. I will own that in Natural Philosophy and some of the lesser branches of learning the Moderns excel; but it would not be right for a person of your situation to strike into any private paths of Science. The study of History will best fit you for active life. From history you will acquire a knowledge of mankind, and a true judgment in politics; in moral, as well as physical enquiries, we should have recourse to experiments. As to the particular study of eloquence, I need hardly exhort you to do it; for eloquence is not only the most beautiful of all the daughters of wisdom, but has also the best dowry; and we may say of her, as Solomon did of her Mother, riches and honours are in her right hand. Elevation of sentiment and dignity of language are necessary to make an orator; modern life and modern language will hardly inspire you with either. I look upon Virtue as the muse of Eloquence, she inspired the phillippics of the Grecian and Roman Orator, her voice awakened Rome, slumbering in the snares of Catiline.

Public spirit will teach the art of public speaking better than the rules of rhetoric, but above all things, the character of the orator gives persuasion, grace, and dignity to the Oration. Integrity of Manners gives the best testimony of sincerity of speech. If you form your conduct upon the sacred book which gives rules far more perfect than human wisdom could contrive, you will be an honour to religion, a support to your country, and a blessing to your family. It may seem strange that I have last mentioned what should be first regarded. The Bible alone will make a good man; human learning without the fear of God, which is the beginning of Wisdom and the knowledge of Him, which is understanding, will produce but a poor inconsistent character; but duties are enlarged and multiplied by the power and circumstances with which God has intrusted us, and in which He has placed us. Your talents and situation will fit you for public trusts; it is a duty in you to qualify yourself for them, to give your virtue every strength, and then to employ it in the service of your country in its most important interests, true religion, and good government. I hope you will excuse my having said so much, that has the air of advice to one who wants it so little, but young people are apt to be prodigal of time because they think they have so many years before them; but if life be long, the season for improvement is short.

"I hope Mrs. Fortescue * liked the Indian paper; it is new and uncommon, and I thought much prettier than any I could get at a moderate price. I beg my respects to her and my dear Miss Lyttelton.† I hear there will be a turnpike road between Oxford and Newbury, and I hope you will frequently make use of it. I shall leave Tunbridge on Monday. I have enjoyed perfect health here, and the society of some of my best friends, so you may believe I have passed the season very happily, but a happy life seems always a short one. Mrs. Carter was so good as to give me her company in my house. My Lord Lyttelton and my

* Mr. Lyttelton's grandmother. † His sister.

Lord Bath were often with us; having had their characters continually before me, you will not wonder I should think great acquirements as well as great talents necessary to make all possible perfection. I am sure you will be pleased to hear that my Lord Bath greatly approves and admires that part of my Lord Lyttelton's history which is already printed. I believe there is not any one living whose approbation would give Lord Lyttelton so much pleasure; talents and virtues and extensive knowledge all in the highest degree join to make him a perfect judge, and his great reputation gives him a decisive authority; your Father is proud of his praise as a critick, and pleased with it on motives of friendship, which touch his heart more nearly than any where vanity has a part, tho' he is an author and a poet. His Lordship's Muse met him in the shades of Penshurst, and with love or flattery prompted two charming pieces, one to Mrs. Carter, and one to my Lord Bath. Mrs. Carter, Dr. Monsey and Mr. Montagu desire their compliments to you.

"I am, dear Sir,
"Your most sincere and affectionate friend
and obedient humble Servant,
"E. MONTAGU."

Dr. Monsey, who had recovered from a severe illness, had joined the party at Tunbridge, and had appeared in a new bloom-coloured coat, to the amusement of the Montagu circle, who chaffed him upon it.

On August 22 Mr. Charles Morton wrote to Mrs. Montagu the following:—

"MADAM,

"As I conceive the following article which I have just received in a letter from Paris, to relate to the Countess of Pomfret,* I thought it might be agreeable to you to acquaint Her Ladyship therewith.

* Lady Pomfret, widow of the 1st Earl Pomfret, had in 1755 presented the University of Oxford with a portion of the Arundel marbles which

DR. EDWARD YOUNG.

[*To face p.* 256, *vol. ii.*

"'Monsr Bejot, who, since the death of the Abbé Sallier, has care of the manuscripts in the King's Library, is a most worthy and obliging gentleman; he has promised me to have copies drawn of the curious Cuts in the beautiful Manuscript of Froissard's Chronicle, for an English lady, a great friend to Oxford.' This letter is dated Paris, August 1st; the writer is the Butler who travels with Mr. Howard, nephew to the Duke of Norfolk. I am much obliged to you for the Highland Poems; and have the honour to remain, Madam,

"Your most obliged and most humble servant,

"CHARLES MORTON.

"Museum, August 22, 1761."

Mrs. Montagu quitted Tunbridge Wells on August 30. On September 2 she wrote to Mrs. Carter—

"I found on my table a poem on 'Resignation' * by Dr. Young; he sent me a copy for you which I will send by the Deal coach. . . . You will be pleased I think with what he says of Voltaire, you know we exhorted him to attack a character whose authority is so pernicious. In vain do Moralists attack the shadowy forms of Vice while the living Temples of it are revered and admired."

Dr. Young writes on September 2—

"DEAR MADAM,

"I was in too much haste and ordered a thing to be sent to you (which I suppose you have received) before I had read it myself. On reading it, I find my distance from the Press has occasioned many errors;

had been purchased by her husband's father. She was the daughter of the second and last Baron Jeffreys, of Wem. She had been Lady of the Bedchamber to Queen Caroline.

* "Resignation" was written with a view of consolation for Mrs. Boscawen on her husband's death.

so that in some parts I have had the impudence to present you with perfect nonsense.

"Page 18, Stanza 2nd, should be thus (viz.)—

"'Earth, a cast Mistress *then* disgusts, etc.'

"Page 34: It should be thus (viz.)—

"'Receive the triple prize, etc.'

"Pray pardon this trouble from, dear Madam,
"Your much obliged and most obedient
"H. Servant,
"E. YOUNG.

"P.S.—I know not how to direct the enclosed, excuse my insolence in desiring you to do it for me."

Lord Bath was having his picture (now in the National Portrait Gallery) painted by Sir Joshua Reynolds for Mrs. Montagu. He left London for Ives Place, and writes—

"I shall be in town again in a few days, but not till after the Queen's arrival, for I have had the opportunity of making my excuses, in the proper place, for not attending the marriage ceremony. You will judge of the likeness of the Picture best, when I am not present, if it could speak, it would tell you, what I can scarce venture to do. How much I love and am, etc."

Mrs. Montagu went to London for the coronation, which took place September 22, leaving Mr. Montagu at Sandleford. She writes to him—

"I have not got any cold or mischief from the coronation, at half an hour after four I got into the coach, went by Fulham to Lambeth, from whence I crossed the water in a boat which landed me at the cofferer's office, where I was to see the Show. I had

Sir J. Reynolds P.R.A. Pinx. Emery Walker Ph. Sc.

William Pulteney, 1st Earl of Bath

a perfect view of the procession to and from Westminster to the Abbey, and I must say it rather exceeded my expectation. The ladies made a glorious appearance; whenever there was any beauty of countenance or shape or air they were all heightened by the dress. Lady Talbot was a fine figure. The Queen, being very little, did not appear to advantage. The King had all the impressions of decent satisfaction and good-natured joy in his face; looked about him with great complacency, and tried to make himself as visible as he could to the mob, but the canopy carried over his Majesty's head and the persons who carried his train made him not so conspicuous. His behaviour at the Abbey pleased much. It was perfectly dark before the Procession returned from the Abbey, so we lost the second view. I got into a barge which I hired for *7s. 6d.*, and got to the coach which waited at Yorke buildings. Mr. Botham and his daughters are just gone. Lord Lyttelton was near fainting away just as the procession set out from the Hall, and was obliged to sit down and take drops till a chair could be got to carry him home. Lady Albemarle fainted presently after. Lord Grantham was ill, but able to go thro' the ceremony.

"The early hour the Peers and Peeresses are forced to rise at and the weight of their robes and all the whole affair is fatiguing, but they make a good figure, for there is something very majestick in the dress.

"I believe my Lord Bath will come down to us about Wednesday or perhaps Tuesday. I shall be at Sandleford on Monday."

In another letter describing the coronation to Mrs. Carter, Mrs. Montagu says—

"It is impossible to say enough of the behaviour of the King. During the procession his countenance expressed a benevolent joy in the vast concourse of people and their loud acclamations, but with not the least air of pride or insolent exultation. In the religious offices his Majesty behaved with the greatest reverence and deepest attention; he pronounced with earnest solemnity his engagements to his people, and when he was to receive the Sacrament he pulled off his crown. How happy that in the day of the greatest worldly pomp and adorned with the ensigns of regal power he should remember his duty to the King of Kings. The Archbishop pleased much in the Coronation Service. I am indeed grieved at the heart for Mrs. Chapone:* all calamities are light in comparison of the loss of what one loves, uniquement; after that dear object is lost the glories of the golden day are for ever overcast, and there is no tranquillity under the silent moon, the soft and quiet pleasures are over, business may employ and diversions amuse the mind, but the *soul's calm sunshine and the heartfelt joy* can never be regained. Mrs. Chapone has great virtues, and if she has the Martyr's sufferings will have the martyr's reward."

The following letter is from Lady Pomfret:—

"Richmond Hill, October 4, 1761.

"DEAR MADAM,

"The reason you give for my being deprived of the pleasure of a visit from you before you left London doubles the mortification. I was in hope Tunbridge had established your Health. The return of my fever (which has left me but a few daies) was the cause that I made no attempt to wait on you, the week you stayed after the Coronation, and when I did found you had been gone the day before; but soon after, Froissart and your letter informed me that your goodness to me subsisted, in all the bustle of magnificence and oppression of sickness, since you found time to read my old Chronicle with my Lord Lyttelton, to whom, and to you,

* *Née* Hester Mulso, a friend of Mr. S. Richardson's, and authoress of "Letters on the Improvement of the Mind"; born 1727, died 1801.

I know not how to express my gratitude enough, but I really feel a great deal.

"Your criticism delights me, as it was always my opinion that such words as you mention ought to be changed for more intelligible ones, and that it might be done, with propriety, without altering the idiom, but I was so charged not to deviate from the old language that, till I had such authorities as you and my Lord Lyttelton, I did not dare to follow my own judgment, but shall now with alacrity go about it, being very happy in your approbation of the rest of the book, which I hope will be finish'd before the meeting of the Parliament, and that I shall have the assistance of such friends for the perfecting of it. Your partiality to me, dear Madam, is very flattering; but let Mrs. Montagu know that if I ever was or am proud of my discerning faculty 'tis because I see her in her true light; of brightness with modesty, Reason without Vanity, and a thorough knowledge of this and the next world as far as is permitted to mortals; this I might have heard, but I glory that I see it. I need not add what must be the consequence; that

"I am, Madam,
"Your sincere admirer: and
"Most faithful Hum[e] serv[t],
"J. POMFRET.

"Lady Sophia Carteret and Mrs. Shelley beg your acceptance of their best respects."

Lady Pomfret died on December 16, 1761, at Marlborough, Wilts.

On October 5 Lord Lyttelton writes to Mrs. Montagu from Hagley a long letter, an extract of which I give—

"Tom proposes to give a ball to some young people of the neighbourhood on this day sennight, which will add to our number and our jollity. He desires me to tell you that if you were within twenty miles of our Ball-room he would invite you to it among the handsome *young* women; which you may notify to the cynic Monsey, when he talks to you next of the *horrid gulph of forty*, and bid him hold his fool's tongue. I believe you fib about your age and make yourself at least ten years older than you are, to be nearer to Lord Bath. I hope you have been, and are still as happy with him at Sandleford as your heart can desire. You will not think it a compliment to either of you when I say, that I would be glad to exchange all the mirth of our ball for the dullest of your evenings; but I will add in great truth, that I would give up the finest day in Hagley Park for a rainy one in your company. I had a letter last post from the Dean,* in which he says, 'Your Lordship must not be surprised if you hear in a post or two of Mr. Secretary Pitt's and Lord Temple's being out of their employments. Unless something extraordinary happens, this event will certainly take place in a few days. I have this intelligence not from common report, but from the best authority. The reason given for their resignation is the opposition made in the Cabinet to Mr. Pitt's proposal of sending a fleet immediately to intercept the Spanish Flota daily expected home, and likewise to attack their men-of-war wherever they are to be found, but your Lordship knows there are other causes of discontent.' If this should be true, I imagine Lord Egremont † will be Secretary of State and Lord Hardwick ‡ Privy Seal. Mr. James Grenville will probably lay down with his brother, which will make a vacancy at the Cofferer's Office, one of the few I might take if there was an inclination to bring me into employment. I wish much to know Lord Bath's opinion of Pitt's advice. To me it seems to be that of a man who (in a political sense) *fears neither God nor man.* It certainly must be founded upon a supposition that a war with

* Charles Lyttelton, Dean of Carlisle.

† Charles, 2nd Earl of Egremont, born 1710, died 1763.

‡ Philip Yorke, 1st Earl of Hardwick, born 1690, died 1764.

Spain is inevitable, which I should hope is not true; and even in that case I think England ought to be very cautious not to appear the aggressor, which this conduct would make her. But I had rather hear his Lordship's judgment upon this question than give my own."

Lord Bath had left Sandleford before this letter arrived there.

On October 8 he writes—

"I can never sufficiently, Madam, acknowledge my great obligations to you and to Mr. Montagu for the honours I received at Sandleford. Six more agreeable days I never passed in my whole Life, but when one has been excessively happy we always pay most severely for the change, when forced to quit it. This made the Doctor's * journey and mine most excessively stupid and melancholy. He was seized with such a soporifick Torpor (as if a deluge of rain was hanging in the clouds), and yet we had not a drop the whole way, and I was so wretchedly miserable, that all I could say to him was, 'Doctor, I passed over this same ground yesterday from coming from Padworth much more cheerfully and happily than I do now, but one comfort is that we are allowed the liberty of hoping for a renewal of the same happiness some other time.' When we got to Reading, where we stopped for 10 or 12 minutes (without getting out of our chaize), our landlady seeing we looked melancholy, endeavoured to comfort us by telling us a piece of good news, that an express was just arrived with an account of a complete victory obtained by the King of Prussia over the Russians. On this we speculated and ruminated for some time, when we met Mr. Cambridge, who assured us it was all a lye, but that another event had occurred which would surprize us extremely, and then told us Mr. Pitt † had quitted the seals; this astonished the Doctor more than it did me,

* Dr. Monsey. † Mr. Pitt resigned the Seals on October 5, 1761.

who had received some hint of it before, but we both agreed it was a very unlucky time for adventuring on such rough measures, so near the Meeting of Parliament, and before anything was fixed for the obtaining of peace, or preparing for a further prosecution of the War; in short, we ended in wishing all Ministers at the Devil, rather than that their disagreements and dissentions amongst one another should bring any difficulties or dishonour on the best man in the world, the master of all of them. . . . I will make this reflection upon all human happiness, that the state and duration of it is extremely uncertain. A minister may be a very great and think himself a very happy man one day, and nothing at all the very next. Just so was I, Madam, happy beyond measure a few days ago, and now forced at a terrible distance to be assuring you that I am, with all possible respect,

"Your Ladyship's most humble
and most obedient Servant,
"BATH."

Lord Lyttelton writes on October 14 to Mrs. Montagu—

"Since my last, Mr. Pitt has brought his bark into a happy port. A Barony for his wife and a pension of £3000 a year for three lives are agreeable circumstances in a retreat, which delivers him from the difficulty of carrying on the War, or making the Peace, and keeps all his laurels green and unfading on his brow. No Minister in this country has ever known so well the times and seasons of going in and coming out with advantage to himself. I hope there will be new gold boxes sent to him by the cities and Boroughs to express their sense of his noble and *disinterested* conduct, and to assure him that their lives and fortunes are all at his service. In effect, I hear that all over this country since first we had the news of his resigning the Seals, the cry of the people in Taverns and Alehouses is, 'No Pitt, no

King.' However, I imagine that as he has condescended to accept of this mark of royal favour, he will be so good as to allow the King to remain on the throne."

On the same day as this last letter Dr. Monsey writes from St. James's to Mrs. Montagu. This paragraph is interesting—

"But here's a Rout about giving a patriot 3*s.* 6*d.* for his past services either for speaking to the purpose, or holding his tongue for a very good one. Why, he might have been Governor-General of all North America with a pension of £5000. This was confidently said at the 'Mount' Coffee House as offered by the King, and was told by Manby as coming from P—, *no joke indeed*, no more than he has advertised seven good horses, '*late Mr. Pitt's*,' to be sold. There's an act of humility for you."

Miss Mary Pitt, Mr. Pitt's sister, writes to Mrs. Montagu—

"DEAR MADAM,

"Tho' I suppose you know all that has happened since last Monday, I cannot forbear talking to you upon what the King has been so very gracious as to do for my family, in granting a pension of three thousand pounds a year to Mr. Pitt for three lives, and as he knows that he feels a repugnancy to having his name upon the Irish pensions, his is upon the American Duties, and the Peerage which his Majesty has also done him the honour to bestow upon his family is given to Lady Hester,* who is made Baroness of Chatham, by which means he is left still at liberty to be an Alderman; as to all the rest, which you may know, I will do *comme si vous ne saviez pas.* My Lord Egremont received the Seals of Secretary of State yesterday, my Lord Temple

* Lady Hester's patent made out on December 4, 1761.

gave up his seals yesterday, and I was informed last night that my Lord Hardwick was to be Privy Seal, which I do not doubt, tho' it is not declared. Mr. George Grenville is not to be Speaker, that he may have the management of the House of Commons. My Lord Temple is very angry with him, and I believe very much disappointed; at the same time I am assured that my Lord Bristol writes in the strongest manner everything that can give satisfaction to the present Ministry with regard to the intentions of the Spanish Court, and those despatches are said to have come Wednesday last. . . . I heard a few days ago from Paris that the Duc de Nivernois * had got a passport for my nephew." This was for Mr. Tom Pitt.

At this period Dr. Gregory lost his wife, and was in great despair; she was a daughter of William, Lord Forbes.

At the end of October Mrs. Montagu set out on a short visit to her sister, Mrs. Scott, and Lady Bab Montagu at Bath Easton. Dr. Monsey was then at Bath, whither later Mrs. Montagu also repaired. Bath society was enthusiastic upon the subject of Mr. Pitt and a political letter he wrote at this period. From a letter written from Bath to Mrs. Carter about a Mrs. Talbot, a reduced lady, who was an applicant for a lady's-maid situation, we learn that £10 per annum were regarded as adequate wages for such an attendant. I subjoin a curious paragraph as to a widow's dress—

"The fashionable dress for a widow is a gown with two broad plaits in the back, a short cuff which comes a little below the elbow, round double ruffles very shallow. The dress weed is made of silk made on purpose, undress crape, a black silk long apron, black handkerchief,

* French ambassador and writer.

black hood, and a plain sort of night-cap. Either a night-gown or sack may be worn with a short train, no flounce or ornament of any sort, and if a sack scanty, and only two broad plaits. Many women of condition who are not young, wear merely a common crape sack, the younger sort wear the dress that denotes their widowhood, and in a country town I should suppose the full form must be observed. I imagine your enquiry is for poor Mrs. Primrose."

On November 17 Mrs. Montagu writes from Hill Street to Mrs. Carter—

"My dear Friend,

"I had this day the pleasure of receiving my dear Friend's most charming ode. I, alas! am like Monsr. Jourdain, I speak nothing but prose, but I believe my heart feels with all the enthusiasm of poetry. . . . My Lord Bath is vastly happy that you are to be in town the 1st of January. My Lord Lyttelton is better, but his fever is not quite gone. . . . I think you should print the verses my Lord Lyttelton addressed to you from Penshurst. Pray write some more odes, and let your seamstresses do your plain work, and the Clerk transcribe your verses."

This year an edition of Mrs. Carter's various works was printed. When Mrs. Carter was in London she lodged with Mrs. Norman in Clarges Street. Mrs. Montagu having ascertained that she could have her lodgings there from the 1st of January, adds—

"You do not deign to mention Fingal, etc., but that I could pardon, for Poet Ossian has been dead full many a day, but there is a head on which laurels now grow, and it bears more than Parnassian bays, even wreaths of sacred Virtue, and this head is apt to ake, and then my heart akes for sympathy. Poor Lady Pomfret by weary stages reached Marlborough, from thence she yesterday morning quitted the weary journey of human life and passed with resignation to a better. I am angry with Dr. James for sending her in so hopeless a state from her quiet home to the noise and inconvenience of Inns. . . . I think Mr. Rivington must be bewitched. I will send the books as you direct. I had a quadrille table last night; and last week the Bard Macpherson and many others of the tuneful train and we had the feast of shells and drank out of a nautilus to the immortal memory of Ossian. The Nautilus, you know, is a perfect sailor as the other is a poet by nature. I am a little mortified that you had not a word to fling at Ossian. Take a modern Poet Laureate and put out his eyes and see whether he will sing as sweetly, tho' he sings darkling."

The *bas-bleus* from this time constantly celebrated, amongst their *intimates*, the feast of shells mentioned in Ossian by drinking out of them on any particular occasion.

Lord Bath's portrait, not satisfying Mrs. Montagu, had been returned to Mr. Reynolds for amendment, and Lord Bath writes—

"MADAM,

"I will sitt to Mr. Reynolds either Wenesday or Saturday next, whichever is most convenient to him, and shall be glad to meet Mr. Tristram Shandy (as you call him) or Mr. Sterne (as I must call him) there, but where it is to be you do not mention. If the alteration can be made in a quarter of an hour, it is scarce worth taking the Picture out of your house, but if it is to be altered at Mr. Reynolds' I will be there on either of the days mentioned. Last night I slept extreamely well and the better since I went from Mrs. Vesey's, happy in seeing you look so charmingly and well. . . .

"3 a clock, Dec. 26th, 1761."

Lord Bath had remarkably penetrating and brilliant eyes, and one of the faults found with the picture was in the representation of this feature.

The next letter from Lord Bath runs—

"How cruel was it, before I got out of bed, to receive a letter forbidding me coming to you this night! but I hope nothing will prevent me from having that happiness to-morrow. On Wenesday about one of the Clock, I will most certainly be at Mr. Reynolds' to mend my sickly looks, and to sitt down in my chair, as I should do; instead of being half standing, which criticism of Mr. Sterne's I think perfectly right; as for my looks, I fear they will not be much mended by any Physick of Mr. Reynolds. He has made an old man look as if he was in pain, which an old man generally is, and so far he is right."

Mrs. Montagu took Mr. Sterne to the sittings so that he might amuse Lord Bath with his *bons mots!* Surely this would form a pretty and historical picture if any artist would paint it.

On the publication of her poems, to which Mrs. Carter looked forward in a nervous frame of mind, Mrs. Montagu says—

"I am sorry for your tremors and trepidations, but they are mere nervous disorders, and the manuscript must be printed, so my dear Urania, away with your lamentations, sit down, revise, correct, augment, print, and publish. I am sure you will have a pleasure in communicating the pious, virtuous sentiments that breathe in all your verses. My inferior Soul will feel a joy in your producing such proofs of genius to the world. . . . The very best of your poetical productions have never been published, they may indeed have been seen by a few in manuscripts, but the finest things on sheets are soon lost—

> 'Foliis tantum ne carmina manda ;
> Ne turbata volent rapidis ludibria Ventis.'

Print them and bind them fast I beg you."

Writing to her brother, William Robinson, then at Rome, at this period, Mrs. Montagu congratulates him on the prospect of a son or daughter—

"I desire to have all the share I can in the little one, shall be happy to be accepted as a godmother, and thank you for being so obliging as to intend it my name if it is a girl; it will not disgrace her if she should be a toast, for I once knew a Miss Betty Robinson that set up for one; if it is not disagreeable to you I should be glad if it was christened Elizabeth Montagu, which will be also a compliment to my husband. I envy you, my dear brother, the pleasure of seeing at your leisure the Queen of Cities, Imperial Rome."

The Rev. Laurence Sterne had been in bad health for some time; he had just completed his fifth and sixth volumes of "Tristram Shandy," and with permission from the Archbishop of York for absence for a year or more, he left Coxwould for the South of France, leaving the following paper with Mrs. Montagu, who, it will be remembered, was his cousin by marriage.

"December 28, 1761.

"Memorandums left with Mrs. Montagu in case I should die abroad.

"L. STERNE.

"My sermons in a trunk at my friend Mr. Hall's, St. John's Street, 2 Vols. to be picked out of them.—N.B There are enough for 3 Vols.—

"My Letters in my bureau at Coxwould and a bundle in a trunk with my sermons.—

"Note. The large piles of letters in the garrets at York, to be sifted over, in search for some either of Wit, or Humour—or what is better than both—of Humanity and good Nature—these will make a couple of Volumes *more*, and as not one of 'em was ever wrote, like Pope's or Voiture's, to be printed, they are more likely to be read —if there wants ought to serve the completion of a 3rd volume—the Political Romance I wrote, which was never publish'd—may be added to the fag end of the volumes. . . . Tho' I have 2 reasons why I wish it may not be wanted—first an undeserved compliment to one, whom I have since found to be a very corrupt man—I knew him weak and ignorant—but thought him honest. The other reason is I have hung up Dr. Topham in the romance in a ridiculous light—which upon my soul I now doubt whether he deserves it—so let the Romance go to sleep not by itself—for 'twil have company.

"My *Conscio ad Clinum* in Latin which I made for Fountayne, to preach before the University to enable him to take his Doctor's Degree—you will find 2 copies of it, with my sermons—

"—He got Honour by it— What got I?— Nothing in my lifetime, then let me not (I charge you Mrs. Sterne) be robbed of it after my death. That long pathetic letter to him of the hard measure I have received—I charge you, to let it be printed— 'Tis equitable you should derive that good from my sufferings at least.

"I have made my will—but I leave all I have to you and my Lydia—you will not Quarrel about it—but I advise you to sell my estate, which will bring 1800 pds. (or more after the year), and what you can raise from my Works—and the sale of the last copyright of the 5th and 6th Vols. of Tristram—and the produce of this last work, all of which I have left (except 50 pds. in my bookseller Becket's hands, and which Mr. Garrick will receive and lay out in stocks for me)—all these I would advise you to collect—together with the sale of my library, &c., &c.—and lay it out in Government Securities— If my Lydia should marry—I charge you,—I charge you over again (that you may remember it the more)— That upon no Delusive prospect, or promise from any one, you leave yourself DEPENDENT; reserve enough for your comfort—or let her wait your Death. I leave this in the hands of our Cosin Mrs. Montagu—not because she is our cosin—but because I am sure she has a good heart.

"We shall meet again.

"—Mem^{dum}. Whenever I die—'tis most probable, I shall have about £200 due to me from my living— If Lydia should dye before you; Leave my Sister something worthy of your self—in case you do not think it meet to purchase an annuity for your greater comfort; if you chuse that—do it in God's name—

"—The pictures of the Mountebank and his Macaroni —is in a Lady's hands, who upon seeing 'em most cavaliery declared she would never part with them—and from an excess of civility—or rather weakness I could not summon up severity to demand them.

"—If I dye, her Name, &c., is inclosed in a billet seal'd up and given with this—and then you must demand them— If refused—you have nothing to do but send a 2d. message importing—'tis not for her Interest to keep them.

"LAURENCE STERNE.

"Memorandums left by Mr. Sterne in Mrs. Montagu's hands before he left England."

Two teardrops are on this paper, which indicate Sterne's emotional temperament.

And now, patient reader, I, the Editress of this literary mosaic of my great-great-aunt's letters and those of her friends, take leave of you. If life and eyesight are vouchsafed to me, I hope to write the

Sir J. Reynolds. pinx. E. Fisher. sc.

Laurence Sterne.

Walker & Cockerell, ph. sc

remainder of her life some day, for she lived till 1800. Each year added to her enormous circle of clever acquaintance, British and foreign. The letters of Garrick and his wife, later ones of Sterne and Dr. Johnson, Mrs. Vesey, Edmund Burke, Hannah More, and a host of other notabilities, belong to a different period. As it is, the compilation of this work has occupied me five years. One whole winter was devoted to arranging the correspondence in chronological order, as very few of the letters are dated.

APPENDICES.

"LONG" SIR THOMAS ROBINSON.

Sir Thomas was the eldest of the seven sons of William Robinson, of Rokeby, Yorkshire, by his wife, *née* Anne Walters. He was born and baptized at Rokeby in 1700. After his school-days he made the grand tour, as was the fashion of the day, and then entered the Army. At the death of his father in 1719, he succeeded to the family estates in Yorkshire. At the General Election of 1727 he became M.P. for Morpeth. On October 25, 1728, he was married at Belfreys, in Yorkshire, to Elizabeth, widow of Nicholas, Lord Lechmere, and daughter of Charles Howard, 3rd Earl of Carlisle. Between the years 1725 and 1730 he rebuilt the house at Rokeby, removed the church which stood behind the house and rebuilt it in another spot, he added a stone wall all round the park, made a bridge over the Greta river, and erected an obelisk to his mother's memory in 1730. All these acts were recorded on two stone piers at the Greta entrance of the park. He planted many trees at Rokeby. He designed the west wing of Castle Howard for his brother-in-law, Lord Carlisle. In 1731 he was made a Baronet of England, with remainder to his brothers. His nickname of "Long" Sir Thomas Robinson was given to him from his great height, and to distinguish him from another Sir Thomas Robinson, a diplomat of note, afterwards created Lord Grantham. These two men were the reverse of each other in appearance, "Long" Sir Thomas being exceptionally tall, and the other very short and fat. One of Lady Townshend's *bon mots* about the two was, "Why one should be preferred to the other I can't imagine, there is but little difference, the one is as broad as the other is long;" and Lord Chesterfield, on being told "Long" Sir Thomas was reported to be "dying by inches," said, then it would be some time before he was dead. On April 10, 1739, his wife, to whom he was tenderly attached, died at Bath, and was taken to Rokeby and buried under the new church he had erected. A monument was erected to her there. In accordance with Sir Thomas's will, though he himself was buried at Merton Abbey, Surrey, a cenotaph was placed in Poets' Corner, Westminster Abbey, to his and his wife's memory, with medallion portraits of her and himself, and bearing the following inscription :—" To perpetuate his grateful sense of the pleasure he had in the conversation of an accomplished woman, a sincere friend, and an agreeable companion." They had no children, so the English baronetcy went to his next brother, William.

Sir Thomas was greatly given to hospitality; too much so for his income. On October 22, 1741, he gave a great ball, as Horace Walpole relates, " to a little girl of the Duke of Richmond's; there are already 200 invited, from miss in a bib and apron to my Lord Chancellor in bib and mace." The ball began at 8 p.m., and ended at 4 a.m. A few days after Horace Walpole writes, " There were a 197 persons at Sir Thomas's, and yet it was so well conducted that nobody felt a crowd. He had taken off all his doors, and so separated the old and the young that neither were inconvenienced by the other. The ball began at 8; each man danced one minuet with his partner, and then began country dances. There were four-and-twenty couple, divided into twelve and twelve; each set danced two dances, and then retired into another room, while the other set took their two, and so alternately. . . . We danced till 4, then had tea and coffee and came home." A month later he writes about a second ball. What with his numerous entertainments and his building at Rokeby and elsewhere, he became impoverished, and accepted the Governorship of Barbadoes in January, 1742, from which he was recalled in 1747. In Barbadoes he married his second wife, a widow named Salmon, *née* Booth. She had a considerable fortune, but on her husband's return to England, she refused to accompany him, preferring Barbadoes. Sir Thomas was intimate with Lord Chesterfield, who made an epigram on him, beginning—

" Unlike my subject will I make my song,
It shall be witty, and it shan't be long."

He must have been a bore, for Sir John Hawkins says of him, " Sir Thomas Robinson was a man of the world, or rather of the town, and a great pest to persons of high rank or in office. He was very troublesome to the Earl of Burlington, and when in his visits to him he was told his lordship had gone out, would desire to be admitted to look at a clock, or play with a monkey that was kept in the hall, in hopes of being sent for to the Earl. This he had so frequently done that all the household were tired of him. At length it was concerted amongst the servants that he should receive a summary answer to his usual questions; and accordingly, at his next coming the porter, as soon as he had opened the gate, and without waiting for what he had to say, dismissed him with these words, 'Sir, his lordship is gone out, the clock stands, and the monkey is dead!'" The Duchess of Portland used to name him to Mrs. Montagu as "your inimitable cousin!"

Appearing in Paris one day at a dinner in his hunting suit of green and gold, and booted and spurred, a French abbé asked who he was, and, on being told his name, and looking at his attire, inquired if he was Robinson Crusoe. His house at Whitehall he sold to Lord Lincoln, and he afterwards lived at Prospect Place, Chelsea. He bought the gardens once belonging to Lord Ranelagh, and, with other shareholders, erected the Rotunda in 1741–42. This place of amusement lasted for quite forty years; the site of it is in the gardens of Chelsea Hospital.

At the Coronation of George III. Sir Thomas, probably from his great height and majestic presence, was chosen to represent the mock Duke of Normandy and Acquitaine, the kings of England still pretending to own those provinces.

In 1769 he sold the estate of Rokeby, Yorks, to John Saurey Morritt, the father of Sir Walter Scott's friend. The Rokeby estate had been in the possession of the Robinsons 160 years. On March 3, 1777, Sir Thomas Robinson died at his house in Prospect Place, Chelsea, at the age of seventy-six.

SANDLEFORD PRIORY, BERKS.

SANDLEFORD PRIORY was founded for Austin Canons by Geoffrey, 4th Count of Perche, and his wife, Matilda of Saxony, grand-daughter of Henry II. of England, and niece of King Richard Cœur de Lion, and King John, before the year 1205. The town and manor of Newbury, in Berkshire, were bestowed on the first Count of Perche, who accompanied the Conqueror to England. The Priory was dedicated to the Virgin Mary and St. John the Baptist. A dispute arising between the Prior and Richard Beauchamp, Bishop of Salisbury and Dean of Windsor about 1480, the religious forsook the house, and King Edward IV. allowed the Priory to be annexed to the Chapel of St. George's, Windsor. In the Ayscough Register, folio 50, will be found an account of irregular and scandalous behaviour of the Prior of that period, which probably was the cause of the disruption. The Priory now formed a parcel of the properties of the Dean and Canons of Windsor, and it is stated by the commissioners of Henry VIII. (*vide* c. 3, Henry VIII.) to be worth £10 annually.

In the reign of James I. Sandleford was declared to be a separate parish from Newbury, and not subject to tithes which had hitherto been paid to the Rector of Newbury. After this a commutation was made that the lessee of the house paid £8 a year to the Rector of Newbury, and for that sum had a pew in perpetuity. It is stated that after this award the chapel of the Priory was allowed to fall into decay. This chapel was separate from the house, and continued to be so till 1781–2, when Mrs. Montagu employed Wyatt to build her an octagonal drawing-room with ante-chambers, which united the house and the chapel. Long previous to this it was used as a bedroom or bedrooms, and in the Montagu manuscripts Hannah More and others are described as sleeping in the chapel bedroom when the rest of the house was occupied. At the beginning of the eighteenth century the lessees of Sandleford were the Pitt Rivers of Strathfield-saye, and they were succeeded by the Montagu family as early as 1730, or perhaps earlier. At any rate, at that date Mr. Edward Montagu was resident there, and as his mother, *neé* Sarah Rogers, lived with him (as is shown by a letter of 1733 which I possess), it is possible Mr. Charles Montagu had been lessee before his son. He died in 1721. At what period the chapel was dismantled I have no record, but it may have been done by order of the Dean and Canons of Windsor before their letting it as a residence. Elias Ashmole, the great antiquarian, who died in 1692, describes the chapel as he saw it, and says, "Upon the first ascent of steps towards the high altar lyes a freestone tomb of a knight in mail, cross-legged, with a deep shield on his left arm, and seeming to draw his sword, his feet resting on a dragon. Written on the west wall is a Latin inscription." In a paper belonging to my uncle, the last Baron Rokeby, it is stated the inscription was "written on the north wall of the chapel, but more anciently on the west wall."

This was the inscription:—

"Lancea, crux, clavi
Spine, mors quam tolleravi,
Demonstrant qua vi
Miserorum Crimmia lavi
In Cruce sum prote qui peccas
Desine pro me desine, do Veniam
Die culpam, Corrige Vitam."

As to the monument, it has been stated to have been that of the founder, Geoffrey, Count of Perche; but as he died in France at the siege of Acre, it is more likely to have been his son Thomas, Earl of Perche, who died at the battle of Lincoln in 1217; or else it is quite possible that it might be one of the Earls Marshal of Pembroke, as at the death of Thomas, Earl de Perche, his uncle William, Bishop of Chalons, seems to have claimed the property and sold it to William, 2nd Earl Marshal. Anyhow, not a trace of this monument is now to be found. And it would be very interesting to ascertain if it was removed to the Temple church, where the other Earls Marshal of Pembroke are buried and a very similar monument exists; but this is only my surmise. Behind the chapel, when Mrs. Montagu made her alterations in house and garden in 1780 to 1782 with the designs of Wyatt and "Capability Browne," a number of skulls and bones were found, and, with the characteristic irreverence of the eighteenth century, were buried in what is now called "Monkey Lane," near Newbury. The present library was originally the refectory. In 1836 Edward, 5th Baron Rokeby, parted with the lease of Sandleford to Mr. William Chatteris, who eventually, in 1875, enfranchised the property from the Dean and Canons of Windsor, and, dying a widower and without issue, he left Sandleford to his second wife's nephew

Mr. Alpin Macgregor. Mrs. Chatteris was the second daughter of Admiral Sir Thomas Hardy, the friend of Nelson. Mrs. Myers, who has a lease of Sandleford now, will not use the chapel as a dining-room. Hannah More, writing in 1784, whilst staying at Sandleford, says, "There is an irregular beauty and greatness in the new buildings, and in the cathedral aisles which open to the great Gothic window (alluding to the east end of the chapel, still all glass), which is exceedingly agreeable to the imagination. It is solemn without being sad, and Gothic without being gloomy."

DENTON HALL, NEAR NEWCASTLE-ON-TYNE, NORTHUMBERLAND.

THE history of Denton Hall dates from the ancient Britons, and a burial-place of theirs, with an urn and bones, was found near the Roman wall within a quarter of a mile from the hall. It subsequently became the site of a Roman camp, which was occupied by a garrison of Hadrian's soldiers, and a wall was built to keep out the Picts and Scots. Of the Roman relics there still exist an altar dedicated to Jupiter, and several carved stones, and in Mrs. Montagu's time many Roman coins and objects were discovered. In No. 7, Vol. 2, of the *Proceedings of Antiquaries of Newcastle-on-Tyne*, 1885, Mr. W. Aubone Hoyle, then living with his brother at the hall, writes, "A little to the south-west stood a chapel, of which a baptismal font remains and a few sculptured stones; adjoining these was a burial-ground, which is now included in the garden. An incised slab, with a memorial cross and sword, was found here some years ago, as well as some large stone coffins; and a cist of ancient British times, containing a funeral urn. The chapel was removed shortly after the Reformation. The earliest record we have of the occupants is of a family of the name of Denton, in the tenth century, who continued to hold lands here and in the neighbourhood, and also at Newcastle."

The Widdringtons seem to have succeeded the Dentons, and Mr. Hoyle continues, "The manor of Denton, saving these rents paid to the Widdringtons, had been, in 1380, granted to the Prior and Convent of Tynemouth, and was used by them as a country residence or grange. Tradition relates that they had an underground passage leading from Denton to their residence at Benwell Tower. The present building was probably erected by them at the beginning of the sixteenth century—1503 being the date of erection. The Roman wall skirting its grounds appears to have supplied the materials, as most of the stones are of the Roman type. The roof was formed of flags fastened with pins made of sheep bones. These have gradually been done away with until only a few courses remain, and the flags have been replaced by tiles. At the Dissolution in 1539, the Widdringtons lost their interest in Denton, and the Erringtons appear."

The Erringtons being Jacobites, Mr. Hoyle continues, "Their loyalty to the Stuarts cost them their estates, which now passed to a family of Rogers, related to the Earl of Sandwich." As has been shown in this book, Mr. Edward Montagu, at the death of his cousin, Mr. Rogers, became owner, to quote his wife's words, "of Denton; Mr. Montagu has half the estate by descent, a share by testamentary disposition, and a part by purchase." At the death of Mrs. Montagu in 1800, the estate passed into the possession of her nephew and adopted son, Matthew Montagu, afterwards 4th Baron Rokeby, who let the hall to Mr. Richard Hoyle, and his descendants occupied the house till 1889. Henry, 6th Baron Rokeby, dying in 1883, left the estate of Denton to his grandson, Lord Henry Paulet, now 16th Marquis of Winchester, who in 1886 sold the whole estate. The hall was bought by Mr. John Henderson, of Allendale, who resold it to Mr. William Andrew I'Anson, the present owner. The Denton ghost, called "Old Silky" by the miners, one of the most authentic on record, is a beneficent spirit, for she is said on various occasions to have warned the miners against coal-damp. A song about her is still sung, I am told, in Newcastle, but hitherto I have failed to obtain it, or to discover who "Silky" was. A further account of her can be read in Ingram's "Haunted Homes," under 'Denton Hall."

INDEX.

The figures in italics refer to the notes only.

C

D

E

F

G

N

O

P

Q

R

S

T

V

W

THE END.

Lightning Source UK Ltd.
Milton Keynes UK
UKOW052151250613

212812UK00001B/60/P